THOUGHT IN TWENTIETH-CENTURY
ENGLISH POETRY

THOUGHT
IN TWENTIETH-CENTURY
ENGLISH POETRY

by

RAYMOND TSCHUMI

OCTAGON BOOKS

A DIVISION OF FARRAR, STRAUS AND GIROUX

New York   1972

First published in 1951 by Routledge & Kegan Paul Limited

Reprinted 1972
by special arrangement with Routledge & Kegan Paul Limited

OCTAGON BOOKS
A Division of Farrar, Straus & Giroux, Inc.
19 Union Square West
New York, N. Y. 10003

Library of Congress Catalog Card Number: 76-154670

ISBN 0-374-98024-1

Printed in U.S.A. by
NOBLE OFFSET PRINTERS, INC.
New York, N.Y. 10003

PREFACE

THE purpose of this study is to interpret the work of some twentieth-century poets who, although they belong to various schools, have a common desire to find a poetical interpretation of the world. In a time when science and philosophy, freed from religious authority, cause a fragmentation of knowledge, these poets have turned to their art for a coherent view which might satisfy their sense of harmony. In other words they have taken over from philosophy the aim of giving our perceptions a coherent meaning. They have often displayed a profundity of thought which is not to be found in philosophical texts. I have tried to interpret their symbols, their myths and their ideas as far as poetry lends itself to this kind of study.

My first incentive has been the impression that in the twentieth century perhaps more than in any other the poets make an effort to think independently and in an original way. The works of Unamuno, Claudel, and Valéry bring thought and poetical emotion together. From my studies in twentieth-century poetry I have drawn the conclusion that this tendency is widely spread in English literature and coincides with a rediscovery of the metaphysical poets of the seventeenth century.

Many recent critical works are devoted to twentieth-century poetry, and it is convenient to mention here two of them which are similar to the present study. C. M. Bowra, in *The Heritage of Symbolism*,[1] analyses the works of five European poets in their relation to French symbolism. It is significant that five poets of five different countries and writing in different languages are so united in their aim of interpreting the world with the help of symbols. While the field of the present study is confined to English poetry, its scope is wider and does not include only the symbolist tradition, but the method is similar.

The most comprehensive book on twentieth-century English

[1] London, Macmillan, 1947.

poetry so far is undoubtedly Geoffrey Bullough's *The Trend of Modern Poetry*.[1] As Mr. Bullough does not consider his subject from any partial or particular point of view, he is able to present a complete survey of the various trends in modern poetry. His book provides the reader with a general idea and an historical grounding, and may serve as a complement to my more fragmentary attempt.

The relation between philosophy and poetry is a vast problem which finds no theoretical solution: I realized that only an analysis of the poems which seemed to be most interesting from my point of view could serve my purpose. The introductory part of the present study is an approach in general terms to the problem, of which particular aspects are shown in the chapters devoted to each author.

Chronological order has been observed whenever the development of a poet serves to elucidate his thought or his philosophical attitude, but my purpose is not to give an historical account of the twentieth-century poetry which follows the tradition of metaphysical poetry. I have rather tried to study a purely speculative problem in a period which is exceptionally rich in poetical thought.

My chief debt of gratitude is due to Professor H. W. Häusermann, without whose advice and encouragement this work would have been impossible. His valuable criticism of some of the earlier drafts of this work has been extremely helpful to me.

My thanks are also due to Mrs. George Yeats for kind permission to publish a few passages from a manuscript of Yeats's letters to Sturge Moore.

I am grateful to Dr. and Mrs. Harrison for their suggestions concerning the chapter on C. Day Lewis.

There remains for me the pleasant duty of expressing my gratitude to Messrs. Herbert Read, Cecil Day Lewis, T. S. Eliot and Edwin Muir for reading a draft of the chapters which concern them and for criticizing my interpretation. I hope, however, that I have not been unduly influenced by them in my study of their work, which I have studied as if they were classical authors. Mr. Herbert Read has been so kind as to give me indications concerning his philosophical background, Mr. Cecil Day Lewis, after some comments on a first draft which showed at places a wrong approach to his poetry, expressed his approval of the revised version, and Mr. Edwin Muir, who admits

[1] Edinburgh, Oliver and Boyd, 1949.

modestly that some passages of my manuscript have helped him to rediscover his own poetry, has explained to me the circumstantial origins of two of his poems, 'The Wayside Station' and 'To J. F. H. (1897–1934)'; I am particularly grateful to these three writers.

R. T.

University of Geneva,
September 1949.

CONTENTS

CONTENTS

Chapter III
THOUGHT IN T. S. ELIOT'S POETRY

Chapter IV
THE PHILOSOPHICAL POETRY OF HERBERT READ

CONTENTS

Chapter V
THE PHILOSOPHICAL ELEMENT IN C. DAY LEWIS'S POETRY

Chapter VI
OTHER POETS

INTRODUCTION

I. PHILOSOPHICAL AND POETICAL THOUGHT

To the purpose of this study which consists in examining the thought of some poets, it may be objected that the study of some philosophical prose works would be more relevant, and that the words 'philosophical poetry' are not far from being a contradiction.

The ideas expressed in the prose works of Yeats, Muir, Eliot, Read, Lewis, Turner and others are studied only as far as they contribute to an explanation of the poems, so that the purpose of this essay is to analyse, as far as this can be done, a certain quality of thought rather than to expound philosophical systems.

It is often argued that philosophical ideas cannot be made explicit in verse, that Lucretius is a poet in spite of Democritus and his atomism, and that wherever ideas are made explicit in a poem, the poem becomes prose.

This does not mean, however, that thought must be excluded from poetry: there can be as much thought in a poem as in any prose work, thought can be even more concentrated in a poem than in any prose work, but the quality of thought differs according to the medium in which thought is expressed and to the author's purpose.

In his 'Introduction' to St. John Perse's *Anabasis*,[1] T. S. Eliot tells how he had to read the poem four or five times before it made any sense. The music attracted him first and that music did not yield much meaning, but he thought it was enough for a poem to be beautiful and that it would be silly to translate a symphony into explicit statements. After five readings he realized that the poem made sense, had a theme (human migrations) and a thought in it. That thought, which cannot be separated from the music of the words and without which the poem would not be beautiful, is expressed in images, and

[1] London, Faber and Faber, 1930.

13

images are facts, they are not theoretical: when thought has verse for its medium, it is implicit.

According to Boileau, who accepts Horatius's two mottoes: *placere et docere*, an author may choose between two purposes: to please or to instruct; Lucretius, for instance, is an author who consciously aims at instructing, unconsciously at pleasing. The difference between philosophical and poetical thought consists precisely in this difference of purpose, whether ideas are used to create a poetical state of mind, or to expound a philosophy.

Ideas can be introduced into a poem, provided that they do not become didactic and explicit. It is perhaps convenient to go further and to say that ideas must be introduced into a poem. This is Valéry's opinion, who finds an answer to the whole problem of poetical thought.[1] A summary of his view will serve the purpose of this study. There is an echo to Valéry's ideas on this subject in *The Dublin Magazine*,[2] in a review of an essay by Patrice de la Tour du Pin, another French poet who 'is concerned with those who would keep apart poetry and the discovery of spiritual truth'. The most original part of Valéry's essay is his criticism of what we call inspiration. According to Valéry, it is impossible for an author to produce a beautiful poem without correcting, expunging, and ordering; in other words thinking consciously. Eliot also maintains that the greater part of a poet's labour is critical work. Valéry goes as far as saying that inspiration is 'une attribution gracieuse que le lecteur fait à son poète'.[3] A poet is not only a first-rate critic, a man who knows himself and chooses what he can best express, but also a thinker, a man who uses his reason and deals with abstract thought.

If a poet is a critic and a thinker, his work is critical and philosophical, although it is not called so. Valéry attacks the current idea of metaphysics as violently as he attacks the current idea of inspiration. If a poetic state of mind is not enough to create a poem, and if a poet must have a philosophy, it does not mean that the poet should be able to express his ideas in abstract concepts; philosophical systems, according to Valéry, are interchangeable, whereas the act of thinking itself and the way of thinking are individual and unique, and as such take part in the composition of a poem.

[1] *Variété*, *V*, Paris, Gallimard, 1945, pp. 127–62.
[2] October-December 1948, *The Poet's Virginity*, by Y. L.
[3] *Variété V*, p. 138.

Abstract thought is not necessarily static, it may be a source of emotion and a creative function. Herbert Read writes: 'In Poetry the words are born or re-born in the act of thinking,'[1] and this act of thinking implies the blending of emotion and of thought attributed by Eliot to the metaphysicals, as well as the symmetry between form and content, music and meaning, word and spirit.

The problem of belief in poetry is one of the touchstones of literary criticism. An acceptable solution to that problem is offered by I. A. Richards in his critical work. In *Practical Criticism* Richards expounds the view that a doctrine can be introduced into a poem, provided that the ideas which are expressed are essential. A doctrine concerned with the fundamental and ultimate problems of life is not dangerous to poetry, and this is due to the fact that such ideas are charged with emotions and present no obstacle to poetic expression. Certain ideas stir the imagination and the feelings, others are neutral. Richards distinguishes between intellectual and emotional belief, the one pertaining to philosophy, the other to poetry. When an intellectual belief is expressed in a poem, Donne's *Holy Sonnets* for instance, the doctrine is an obstacle to the reader who does not share the emotion of the poet. Although some ideas find no place in poetry, while other ideas are not philosophical, the difference between philosophical and poetical thought is a difference of quality rather than of medium. Instead of distinguishing between intellectual and emotional belief, the psycho-analysts would distinguish between conscious and unconscious belief, and admit that there are ideas in our subconscious which can be expressed only in symbols. I. A. Richards is inclined to think that the basis of our knowledge is inscrutable and can be revealed only through the myths of our subconscious: 'We have become used, since psycho-analysis, to conceive consciousness as a somewhat erratic product of conscious processes, and are uncomfortably aware that our conscious aims and beliefs may be a distorted reflection of our deeper needs and wishes.'[2]

If the difference between poetical thought and philosophical thought is easy to understand, the difference between purely lyrical poetry and philosophical poetry is more subtle. There is a great variety of poems which cannot be called lyrical, descriptive, satirical, epic or dramatic. Lucretius' *de rerum natura* is perhaps the best

---

[1] *English Prose Style*, London, Bell, 1934, p. x.
[2] *Coleridge and Imagination* (1934), p. 139.

15

example of a poem where the doctrine stands out clearly and mars the feeling. Robert Bridges' *Testament of Beauty*[1] is also mainly a didactic poem, where myths are replaced by speculations, metaphors by definitions. Here is a typical passage:

> *What is Beauty? saith my sufferings then.*—I answer
> the lover and poet in my loose alexandrines:
> Beauty is the highest of all these occult influences,
> the quality of appearances that thru' the sense
> wakeneth spiritual emotion in the mind of man:
> and Art, as it createth new forms of beauty,
> awakeneth new ideas that advance the spirit
> in the life of Reason to the wisdom of God.
> But highest Art must be rare as nativ faculty is . . .[2]

The vocabulary in this passage is the same, and is used in the same way, as philosophical vocabulary. The author states and prescribes, he does not suggest and convince: instead of using a simile he says: 'Beauty is . . .', and instead of making his judgment emotionally felt he says: 'Art must be . . .'. His method is essentially speculative and didactic, and his prosody is but an elegant cover for a philosophical text.

Virgil's *Georgics* are also didactic, but the poet does not deal with ideas and he chooses poetical themes.

Both Dante and Milton introduce ideas into their poems, and these ideas are religious myths which appeal to the feelings and, being emotionally felt, can be introduced into a poem.

The works of the twentieth-century poets in which a poetical thought can be found do not belong to the tradition of the great didactic and religious poems, and the doctrines which can be extracted from these works cannot be regarded as specifically religious, ethical, speculative, social or practical. There seems to be no universal or generally accepted doctrine. Each author has to build up his own system of thought, as if knowledge had fallen apart and could not be re-united. What characterizes the poetical thought of the twentieth century is its originality, its defiance of all prevailing standards and doctrines, its blending of emotion and of thought and its attempt to reduce all problems to one fundamental problem. This interpenetration of thought and emotion, of science and lyricism,

[1] Oxford, Clarendon Press, 1929.   [2] Ibid., p. 73.

places the twentieth-century poets in the tradition of the metaphysicals more than in any other. It would be futile to discuss again all
the interpretations of the terms 'metaphysical poetry', and it is
enough to remember the definition proposed by Herbert Read: 'felt
thought'.[1] This definition would perhaps apply as well to the poets
chosen for this study, for if each of them has a doctrine, it is a personal doctrine which is individually experienced and, in the poems,
emotionally expressed.

Cecil Day Lewis is an exception among these poets because he is
essentially a lyrical poet who becomes didactic and prosaic as soon
as he struggles with ideas. His career as a poet might be regarded as
a gradual disentangling of his poetry from abstract ideas, and illustrates the fundamental difference between philosophical and poetical
thought. The other poets have expressed their most profound thought
in their poems, whereas their prose works are more explicit. Their
essential ideas, however, can hardly be defined through philosophical terminology. A good example of this non-prosaic quality of
their ideas is Herbert Read's idea of order, which finds its best
definition in a tale (*The Green Child*).

The system of W. B. Yeats is exclusively personal and his thought
is metaphorical. The only purpose of his doctrine, besides an explanation of psychology and of history, is to translate experience into an
ideal vision of beauty, in other words to provide material for poetry.

Edwin Muir's thought can also be termed poetical because it is not
fixed and cannot be grasped in immutable logical concepts which
have also immutable objects. If the objects of thought shift in the
course of a logical deduction, the result is a contradiction: Muir's
thought is contradictory in this sense, and oscillates between two
themes, time and eternity. His poetry arises from the tension or the
solution of this conflict.

T. S. Eliot is the only one who identifies his thought with a well-
known doctrine. But the poems which are clearly connected with this
doctrine, the *Four Quartets*, are related to circumstances of the poet's
life and are inspired by personal experience. The impersonality of the
poet is necessary in order to communicate with the reader, but the

---

[1] 'In Donne we do as a matter of fact find the first consciousness of felt
thought . . .' (Herbert Read, *Reason and Romanticism*, Faber and Gwyer, 1921,
p. 41.) cf. also 'a recreation of thought into feeling.' (T. S. Eliot, *Selected Essays*,
p. 286.)

approach to the ideas of a poem must be emotional, then perhaps intellectual: the substance of poetical thought eludes all conscious efforts at reducing it to abstract terms.

If the preceding considerations are acceptable, we may conclude that there is such a thing as poetical thought, that is, a thought which finds its medium in poetry. Indeed, the first philosophers expressed themselves in verse, the first thinkers were magicians, and the distinction between thought and the words which express thought was introduced at a later stage of development. According to Vico, the first languages were made of emblems and gestures, then men expressed themselves in hieroglyphics, or languages made of symbols and metaphors, and only in the present stage are poetry and prose dissociated.

Poetical thought is neither an unnecessary ornament of philosophy nor an impure element of poetry, but a balance between thought and image, meaning and symbol, impression and expression.

With reference to its etymological sense, the word 'abstract', meaning fragmentary, taken from something concrete, is perhaps misused in this connection. According to Valéry, abstract thought is what is different from any object and not what is chosen from a concrete object and common to others, and the poetic state of mind evokes a superior reality which has nothing in common with known realities. Poetical thought escapes conventional classifications and creates an ideal beauty which finds no place in most philosophical systems, least of all in positivism and materialism, so far as these doctrines consider the object without the subject, the result without the effort, and abstract ideas as derived from matter through the senses.

More or less coherent philosophies, which are very different from one another, could be extracted from the prose works of Yeats, Muir, Eliot, Read and Turner, and the thought in these works is justified by didactic, pragmatic, not aesthetic, purposes, whereas the thought expressed in their poems cannot be translated into, and destroyed by, the things it means, and is not independent from its form, although it can be analysed separately.

II. EMPIRICISM AND IDEALISM

The attitudes of the poet and of the philosopher may be opposed to each other by saying that the philosopher tends to examine his object without taking account of his subjective reactions, whereas the poet tends to give an entirely subjective view of his theme, in other words to transform what, for the philosopher, is independent from the mind or from the senses, into forms and images which exist only in the mind. This comparison, however, is too clear-cut to be true. One might object, first, that the attitude of the philosopher described above is too much like the attitude of the scientist: the scientist is content merely to record facts and to found his knowledge upon 'sense data', whereas the philosopher examines his ideas and draws purely logical conclusions. It is more and more difficult, however, to draw a line between science and philosophy. Bacon's *Advancement of Learning* (1605) and *Novum Organum* (1620) inaugurated an important tradition in English philosophy, in which philosophy appears as a prolongation of science: the philosopher draws general conclusions from the particular certitudes acquired by the scientist. This conception has never been accepted by all the philosophers; although it has triumphed in the eighteenth and nineteenth centuries, it has found strong opponents in the seventeenth and twentieth centuries. This brings us to a second objection to our comparison, which considers only the philosophers who follow the development of empirical science. If objectivity is undoubtedly a fundamental virtue for the scientist, there are philosophers who admit qualitative and subjective perceptions as a basis for their doctrine. This was true in Donne's time, when scholasticism was the strongest opponent to empirical science, and this is also true in the twentieth century, which has witnessed the rise of neo-idealism.

It is not surprising that the poets should turn to the opponents of empirical science and philosophy for support of their poetical thought. A survey of the philosophical atmosphere at the beginning of the present century may serve as an introduction to the study of poetical thought. If the two trends of idealism and empiricism are conflicting with each other in poetry, and sometimes mixed, they are sharply separated in philosophy, and especially with the philosophers of the early twentieth century. The alternation of the two different conceptions is constant throughout the history of English philosophy. W. R. Sorley, in *A History of English Philosophy*, discards Kuno Fischer's description of English philosophy as a whole 'as a stage in the development of realism or empiricism'.[1] Bradley's *Appearance and*

---

[1] Cambridge University Press, 1920, p. 300.

Reality (1893), perhaps the most influential book in recent English philosophy, develops an idealist trend. Bradley's philosophy is founded upon the idea of an absolute. Metaphysics, according to him, have a double task, which is, first, to conceive reality as the opposite to mere appearance, and secondly to think of the universe as a whole instead of dealing with fragmentary notions. Bradley is regarded as the leader of the school of absolute idealists. Rudolf Metz[1] distinguishes three main trends in contemporary English philosophy: idealism, realism, and religious thought. The most important group is that of the idealists, who try to extend and to renew Hegel's thought. Among them are outstanding names, such as Bernard Bosanquet (1848–1923), John Ellis M'cTaggart (1866–1925), and the psychologist James Ward (1843–1925).[2]

Among the religious thinkers the outstanding figure is Von Hügel, who is taken as the symbol of Christianity by Yeats in 'A Dialogue of Self and Soul'.

Although he is classified by Metz among the realists, A. N. Whitehead is mainly a mathematician, and Yeats was not reluctant to share his views, since he saw in Whitehead's philosophy a mixture of the subjective and the objective. Other well-known realists are George Edward Moore, Bertrand Russell, Samuel Alexander, and Cyril E. M. Joad.

'Idealism' and 'realism' are rough distinctions, and a close study of the philosophers would show how precise and complex are the differences between them. The thought of Bertrand Russell, for example, has almost nothing in common with that of Whitehead. The various schools are more and more differentiated and many philosophers become specialists who study only limited aspects of certain problems. With their desire to grasp reality as a whole, however, the idealists are perhaps an exception in this respect, and the most influential foreign philosophers, Bergson and Gentile, whose conceptions have a universal appeal, are nearer to the idealists than to any other school: it is not surprising that their tendency should prevail among the poets, who are interested in philosophy only as far as ideas can affect or alter their personality or their whole conception of the world. The poets are far more interested in general problems

---

[1] *Die Philosophischen Strömungen der Gegenwart in Grossbritannien*, Leipzig, 1935.

[2] Henry Jones (1852–1922) might also be mentioned here; he recognized a perfect expression of idealism in the poetry of Robert Browning.

than in special fields of speculation which may have no emotional significance.

A theory is valuable to the arts if the ideas may be interpreted emotionally and if they show some sort of order which may be transformed into a rhythmical, musical or poetical order.

The result of the development of empirical science has been a dissection of knowledge: the living link is more and more missing. There is only one remedy for this danger of abstraction and specialization: a recourse to the qualitative and an acknowledgment of interior values. The philosophy of Bergson tends towards that goal; Bergson maintained the opinion that reality is more fully perceived in a work of art than in a work of philosophy. If a poet assumes that ideas are more or less real, and does not confine truth or beauty to sense-perceptions, his thought has good chances of becoming poetical without much danger of dryness, abstraction, and didacticism.

There are two main reasons why the thought of an idealist is not a danger to poetry: first because this thought comes from interior conviction, not from external evidence, and must be *expressed*, secondly because it implies a belief in the harmony of the world and helps to conceive the world as a unity which resembles the rhythmical unity of a symphony. Thus the disintegration of culture, which threatened European civilization in the sixteenth century and seems to be an even greater danger in the present century, finds a solution in poetry. Yeats, Muir, Eliot, Lewis, Read and others have all attempted to find their own solution and to express their sense of harmony.

We have seen that, although the poets and the philosophers tend, as a rule, towards opposite directions, there is an important tradition in philosophy which accepts artistic creation as a reliable source of information and enjoyment. We may go further and say that the development of idealist philosophy is analogous to, and sometimes coincides with, the development of philosophical verse.

The seventeenth and twentieth centuries, which are marked by a rapid development of empirical science, are also characterized by a growth of idealist thought in poetry, and to this poetical thought corresponds a revival of old philosophical traditions in which the human soul, rather than the external world, is the theme of philosophical considerations. The metaphysical poets of the seventeenth century opposed to the scientific explanation of the world a poetical philosophy inspired by their religious feelings. The conflict between

science and poetry was acutely felt by John Donne, who was aware
of the discrepancy between experimental science and the Aristotelian
categories.[1] With their feeling of uneasiness and their tendency to
experiment with poetic imagery, the metaphysical poets are nearer
to the twentieth-century poets than Tennyson, whose philosophical
poetry is the sign of another conflict: that between science and religion. In the seventeenth century established values and ideas are
endangered by the new conception of the world proposed by Kepler
and Galileo; scholasticism struggles to survive, but appears as a
bundle of preconceptions:

> The new philosophy calls all in doubt,
> The element of fire is quite put out;
> The sun is lost and the earth, and no man's wit
> Can well direct him where to look for it.
> And freely men confess that this world's spent,
> When in the planets and the firmament
> They seek so many new; they see that this
> Is crumbled out again to his atomies.[2]

The same feeling of the disintegration and collapse of a civilization is expressed in *The Waste Land*. Both Eliot and Donne are in
search for a certitude which is not provided by the science of their
day. Behind the historical circumstances, however, an important
point is at stake: the new science of the seventeenth century favours
an empirical conception of the world and a growth of materialism.
If the world is made exclusively of matter, there is no place for
poetry. The study of science and philosophy is unable to satisfy a
poet, and when Donne plays boldly with ideas, he expresses not so
much ideas as the emotions aroused by these ideas: 'The thought in
(Donne's) poetry is not his primary concern but the feeling. No
scheme of thought, no interpretation of life became for him a complete and illuminating experience. The central theme of his poetry is
ever his own intense personal moods, as a lover, a friend, an analyst
of his own experiences worldly and religious.'[3]

[1] cf. Ralph B. Crum: *Scientific Thought in Poetry*, New York, Columbia University Press, 1931, p. 43.

[2] *The Poems of John Donne*, edited by Herbert J. C. Grierson, Oxford University
Press, 1929, 'The First Anniversary'.

[3] *Metaphysical Lyrics and Poems of the Seventeenth Century*, selected and edited by
H. J. C. Grierson, Oxford, Clarendon Press, 1928, 'Introduction', p. xxviii.

EMPIRICISM AND IDEALISM

The desire to face reality, which is characteristic of twentieth-century poets and which coincides with a materialistic view of nature, is not entirely new. Herbert J. C. Grierson detects in Donne 'the vein of sheer ugliness which runs through his work, presenting details that seem merely and wantonly repulsive'.[1] The mixture of the horrible with the sublime is not less apparent in the work of T. S. Eliot, and in this both Donne and Eliot react aesthetically, not philosophically, against the new thought. Their anxiety finds a relief in their irony and their religious feelings are linked with their aesthetical conceptions. Donne's scepticism may vanish suddenly before a vision of beauty: 'A spirit of scepticism and paradox plays through and disturbs almost everything he wrote, except at moments when an intense mood of feeling, whether love or devotion, begets faith, and silences the sceptical and destructive wit by the power of vision rather than of intellectual conviction.'[2] The intellectual doubts and unrest of John Donne, which may be explained historically,[3] are undermined by a firm conviction that there is a poetic truth. A similar conviction is to be found in a twentieth-century poet: the belief in the harmony and order of nature is often expressed in the work of Herbert Read. These are poetic convictions, although they are shared by some English followers of Hegel. In the seventeenth century as well as in the twentieth century a few poets have felt the need for a principle of unity and for a harmony which might give a coherent form to our disconnected knowledge, lest the world present itself in the form of 'broken images'. As a result of this fragmentation of European culture witticisms, elaborate similes, and abrupt transitions appear in poetry. It would be an exaggeration to say that all the 'metaphysical' poets were conscious of a deep historical change; Richard Crashawe's wit, for example, is at times superficial and even futile:

> Was Car then Crashawe; or Was Crashawe Car,[4]
> Since both within one name combined are?
> Yes, Car's Crashawe, he Car. . . .

[1] *The Poems of John Donne*, edited by Herbert J. C. Grierson, Oxford University Press, 1929, 'Introduction', p. xx.

[2] ibid., p. x.

[3] ibid., p. v.: 'For the historian it is a matter of positive interest to connect Donne's wit with the general disintegration of medieval thought.'

[4] *Steps to the Temple, Delights of the Muses and Other Poems*, Cambridge University Press, 1904, 'Crashawe, the Anagramme, He was Car.', p. 187.

George Herbert also allows himself to play with words, but always
with a high purpose in mind:

$$\text{An-}\begin{Bmatrix} \text{Mary} \\ \text{Army} \end{Bmatrix}\text{gram.}$$

How well her name an army doth present,
In whom the Lord of Hosts did pitch His tent![1]

Donne, however, seems to be the only poet among the 'metaphysicals' who was deeply preoccupied with the new development of
secular thought. To the subtleties of Donne, the scepticism and
cynicism of the Cavalier poets and the fervour of the religious poets,
the seventeenth century adds the atheistic tendency of Cowley, a
friend of Hobbes, an admirer of Bacon and one of the founders of the
Royal Society.

The tradition of philosophical poetry in England goes on without
interruption from Donne to the twentieth century. There are echoes
of Donne's interest in astronomy in Milton's *Paradise Lost*, and the
whole work of Blake gives the example of a poetical thought. The
conflict between idealism and empiricism in poetry rises again in the
nineteenth century with Browning, Tennyson, and Matthew Arnold.
For Browning, the supreme goal of life is knowledge enlightened
by love.[2] According to him, philosophical thought should not
be excluded from poetry, unless this thought consists in dry
statements:

Stop playing, poet! May a brother speak?
'Tis you speak, that's your error. Song's your art:
Whereas you please to speak these naked thoughts
Instead of draping them in sights and sounds.[3]

Whereas Arnold expresses his regret for vanished faith, Tennyson,
who, like Donne, finds a refuge in mysticism, believes in a revealed
truth, although he feels that knowledge is more and more encroach-
ing upon faith:

[1] *The Works of George Herbert in Prose and Verse*, London, Warne, the 'Chandos
Classics' (without date), p. 127.
[2] cf. *La Jeunesse de Browning et le poème de Sordello*, by Henri Brocher (thèse,
Genève, 1936), p. 51 sqq.
[3] *The Poetical Works of Robert Browning*, London, Smith, 1898, 'Transcendental-
ism: a Poem in Twelve Books', p. 508.

EMPIRICISM AND IDEALISM

> We have but faith: we cannot know,
> For knowledge is of things we see;
> And yet we trust it comes from thee,
> A beam in darkness: let it grow.[1]

The catholic poets, Coventry Patmore, Alice Meynell, Francis Thompson, who recalls Crashawe, and Gerard Manley Hopkins, whose influential work was published in 1918, are free from the influence of scientific materialism. Thomas Hardy's mood of bitter resignation is in contrast to Robert Bridges' idealism. Bridges' *Testament of Beauty*, though published in 1929, is a Victorian poem. It is a didactic work where Reason and Nature are spelt with capital letters. This work is characterized by its religious bent:

> . . . yet for man's ignorance
> and frailty the only saving consolation is faith,[2]

and by its idealism:

> Ideas and influences spiritually discern'd
> are of their essence pure.[3]

The main symbol of the work is that of the 'charioteer' and the two horses: the charioteer is Reason and the two horses are Selfhood, or the natural state, and Breed, or the civilized state of mankind. Bridges' idealism is summed up in this stanza from another poem:

> Thy work with beauty crown, thy life with love;
> Thy mind with truth uplift to God above:
> For whom all is, from whom was all begun,
> In whom all Beauty, Truth, and Love are one.[4]

The tradition of idealist thought in poetry enters its most significant phase in the twentieth century with W. J. Turner, W. B. Yeats, and George William Russell (A.E.). The work of A.E. is exceptional: there is no reason to suppose that he was influenced by the scientific development of his time. He stands apart from all the philosophical movements of his time except the revival of theosophy;

---

[1] *In Memoriam.*
[2] *The Testament of Beauty*, Oxford, 1929, line 566.
[3] ibid., 11, line 928.
[4] 'A Hymn of Nature,' *Poetical Works*, Oxford University Press, 1913.

his interest in socialist methods was exclusively a practical one. Both Yeats and Turner had a scientific grounding, but they revolted against the conclusions reached by the scientists: they knew enough to be able to reject science:

> ·In that Great Mythic System
> *Science—*
>
> .   .   .   .
>
> Science—
> A collection of Tin Faces,
> The New Mythology![1]

When Yeats studied philosophy, after he had worked out the principles of his system and no longer needed the help of the spirits, he manifested a violent opposition to the 'realism' of Bertrand Russell and George Edward Moore: their 'common sense' is for the Plain Man. On the contrary Whitehead and Berkeley appealed to Yeats because he found in them, instead of the affirmation of a 'Physical substratum', the belief in a spaceless and timeless reality, 'a transcendental ego'.[2] In spite of his irritation against the materialists, Yeats had some doubts concerning the reality of the spirit, and these doubts increased his eagerness to think. From the symbolists he had inherited a disgust for science, and this attitude was deeply rooted in him, for the scientific mind was too narrow to admit the validity of the dreams in which he lived.

Neither science nor philosophy can satisfy a poet; if Lucretius accepts the atomic theory, it is because it implies a religious attitude, for while rejecting what he calls superstition Lucretius invokes Venus and devotes a shrine to the gods in his theory of the void. It is characteristic also that among the Left-Wing poets Auden finally turned to mysticism, and Lewis abandoned the philosophical implications of his first volumes. Upon the other hand Eliot realized that a purely satirical attitude was negative, and assented to a doctrine which is far from being experimental.

Perhaps the main reason why materialism is not in favour among the poets is that it is not creative and does not exalt artistic creation. The development of psychology in the twentieth century has again withdrawn the attention from the external world and paid a tribute

[1] *The Seven Days of The Sun*, p. 12.
[2] cf. Yeats's unpublished *Letters to Sturge Moore*, Nos. 11 and 12.

26

to the irrational faculties of the human conscience. This development runs concurrently with the influence of idealist philosophy, especially with Hegel's idealism, which is a synthesis of scientific knowledge and spiritualism. In spite of its rigorous logic, Hegel's system, taken as a whole, has something irrational and poetic about it. It is not surprising that the philosophies derived from his system should have influenced the poets.

Ideas for Hegel have a real value: it is as if he could feel them. Whatever may be their meaning, they are real and creative. The difference between philosophical and poetical thought is entirely a difference in the quality of thought, not a divergence of ideas, and depends on whether the ideas are treated as objects detached from the author or as subjective states of mind. When an idea is chosen as the theme of a poem, this idea must be felt as if it were an emotion, and accepted as a fact is accepted. Whether a poet is a realist (in the medieval sense of the word) or not, that is, whether he believes in ideal values or not, is therefore extremely important. A poet, like Yeats or A.E., for whom symbols have a real value, can have but contempt for the philosophers who are certain only of what is given by the senses; in other words he hates positivism or empiricism, for these doctrines imply a negation of artistic creation. In order to understand a poem one must believe, at least for a moment of creation or reading, that the poem is real, apart from the objects it represents or refers to. It is not the task of a poet to believe in a doctrine and to dismiss other doctrines, but it is important for him to know whether reality may be created in the form of ideas, images and poems, or whether the senses are the passive witnesses of a physical, material reality which makes mere illusions of the creations of his imagination.

A bird's-eye view of this chapter reveals that two tendencies are easily recognizable in philosophy as well as in the poetic tradition, and may serve as the starting point of our study of twentieth-century poetry: first, the 'scientific' tendency of the poets who accept what I. A. Richards has called 'the Neutralization of Nature', and secondly a reaction, sustained by a belief in the spirit, against this process of disenchanting the world. Most of the philosophical verse written in the present century belongs to this second category, and is analogous in this respect to the metaphysical poetry of the seventeenth century. When Thomas Carew handles imagery in this way:

Give me more Love, or more Disdain:
  The Torrid, or the Frozen Zone
Bring equal ease unto my paine;
  The Temperate affords me none:
Either extreme, of Love, or Hate,
Is sweeter than a calm estate[1]

he achieves a synthesis of the physical and the spiritual, and thus overcomes the dualism which mars Victorian poetry.[2] Most of Edwin Muir's poems are attempts to solve the opposition of time to eternity and of the physical to the spiritual. Like Carew's, Edwin Muir's poetry unstrings secretly the web of Penelope which science casts over nature separated from the spirit. The poets who indulge in scientific theories and doctrines harvest a growing sense of solitude, and it is significant that 'in the work of Tennyson, Browning (even), Swinburne, Arnold, Meredith, we can trace the fear that nature might be unfriendly';[3] it is significant also that Lewis in *The Magnetic Mountain* interpreted the doctrine of dialectical materialism as a means to come to a future, ideal communion of man with man and man with nature.

The fears and the doubts of the materialists are overcome by an act of belief and by artistic creation. In the seventeenth and twentieth centuries there have been poets to show that if scientific discoveries, and especially astronomical researches, have widened the physical universe, this extension is not necessarily achieved at the expense of the spiritual universe.

[1] First stanza of 'Mediocrity in love rejected', H. J. C. Grierson: *Metaphysical Poetry*, p. 33.
[2] cf. Geoffrey Bullough: *The Trend of Modern Poetry*, Edinburgh, Oliver and Boyd, 1949, p. 1.
[3] ibid.

CHAPTER I

YEATS'S PHILOSOPHICAL POETRY

I. INTRODUCTION TO THE SYSTEM

AMONG the numerous poems written by Yeats throughout his career a whole cycle, written after 1914, can be regarded as philosophical poetry. Most of these poems are unintelligible without reference to *A Vision*,[1] where Yeats's thought is elaborated in a system. The purpose of this study is to give a brief explanation of the philosophy contained in *A Vision* and to try to elucidate those poems which are connected with and influenced by the system.

The problem of the origins of *A Vision* is difficult to solve, probably because the work is at times incoherent and hidden behind a curtain of fakes and hoaxes, especially in the first version. The fact that the principles of the system were partly dictated by 'spirits' to the author through the mediumship of his wife is not important, and its readers need no initiation to a secret doctrine in order to interpret the main symbol of Yeats's philosophy, the Great Wheel. When Yeats started writing *A Vision*, his 'instructors' forbade him to read any philosophy, but his early interest in theosophy, astrology, magic, Swedenborg and Boehme accounts for a great part of his work. Besides, he eagerly studied Berkeley, Vico, Whitehead, Gentile and others before *A Vision* was finished.[2] The comparisons he made between his system and other philosophies prove that he was dubious about the philosophical value of *A Vision* and about the authority of his 'instructors'. More important than the philosophical value of the system, however, is its relation to Yeats's poetry, for his 'instructors' announced that they were to give metaphors for his poetry.

[1] London, Macmillan, 1937. (First Verson 1925.)
[2] These philosophers are mentioned in the 1937 edition of *A Vision* (p. 261). The 1925 edition mentions only Joseph Strzygowski (p. 174).

29

A change came over Yeats's personality and his poetry around 1914 and even before, when he realized that 'Romantic Ireland is gone', and that he had to divest his poetry from its 'coat of images' and 'to walk naked', that is, to face reality. This shifting from mythology to philosophy and from the dreams of the Celtic twilight to an understanding of the events in Ireland involves no contradiction. His deliberate purpose during the 'period of aestheticism', in which he was much influenced by the French symbolists, was to endow Ireland with symbols and myths and to make them real; similarly, in a period where poems like 'September 1913' express his disenchantment, he felt the urge to include in a vast system the events he was witnessing. Moreover, his lifelong, unrewarded, platonic love for Maud Gonne found a compensation when he married Miss Hyde-Lees in 1917 (he was fifty-two) and a sublimation in his philosophy.

Yeats's unpublished letters to Sturge Moore and to Mrs. Shakespeare show that he should not be taken too seriously as a philosopher. His deterministic system is based on the interpretation of geometrical figures and symbols which give an inadequate explanation of both the human mind and history. These figures are helpful to the imagination, but they should not be regarded as *a priori* principles; they belong to the cabbalistic tradition, to the esoteric tradition of neoplatonism and its revival in the Middle Ages with Paracelsus and Boehme. Yeats pretends that the book containing the Great Wheel, entitled *Speculum Angelorum et Hominum*, written by 'a certain Giraldus' and printed at Cracow in 1594, had miraculously been brought to Michael Robartes (a product of Yeats's imagination) by an Arab tribesman. Like many *Specula* of the Middle Ages, Giraldus's book might be derived from an ancient knowledge whose sources and interpretation have been lost. It is quite probable, however, that these books contain a profound truth, and it is better to grasp the principles of the system than to study the abstract signs, which are but dead intuitions.

What is most striking in Yeats's system is that the world or whatever exists is conceived as a series, or rather a cycle, of recurring states of mind. The body, or matter, or fate, are mere projections of the mind. When Yeats applies his system to concrete examples, he finds his evidence in the works of artists, writers and philosophers, so that the system is connected with a clever interpretation of many works of the past. The system includes mostly human states of mind, except two,[1] complete subjectivity and complete objectivity, which cannot be reached on this earth. The whole cycle of the states of mind, conceived as the complete evolution of the 'four faculties', is called 'the Great Memory'.

According to its position on the Great Wheel, the mind tends to be either creative ('lunar' or 'antithetical') or embodied in nature ('solar' or 'primary'). Even when it is creative, the mind is involved in a fatal evolution (although Yeats speaks of a 'thirteenth sphere', which allows for individual freedom). The system is therefore both idealist and determinist. When reading Gentile, Yeats did not realize that Gentile's idealism was quite different from his system, for Gentile's idealism is essentially dynamic, whereas Yeats's system is essentially static, like all rational systems or like those which can be represented by geometrical figures. The movement of the Great Wheel is only apparent, for the Wheel and the faculties remain the same while their positions and their relations to one another differ. Yeats conceives the world as an eternal solar system consisting of a spiritual substance. 'Fixed' would be a better word than 'eternal', for Yeats made no distinction between an objective movement, which can be analysed and artificially stopped (like the movement of the Great Wheel, in which eternity, or the complete cycle, is but an artificial fixity) and a subjective or relative change, and he understood neither Valéry (cf. A Vision, pp. 219 and 220) nor Whitehead, about whom he writes: 'To Whitehead as to Berkeley, there is no "physical substratum", no "permanent possibility of sensation" behind the "sense data".'[2]

Yeats's idealism is linked with his interest in esoteric science and above all with his belief in symbols;[3] his punishment for trusting too much in magical shapes, geometrical figures and mechanical explanations is a static system; the third important characteristic of his

[1] 'The belief that all is experience does not mean that there is no truth unknown to us, for there are unknown minds, but it does not mean that there is no truth where there is no mind to know it.' (Unpublished Letters to Sturge Moore, No. 8.)

[2] Unpublished Letters to Sturge Moore (No. 11, March 31). From a copy by H. W. Häusermann of a transcription by J. Hone.

[3] cf. Ibidem, No. 18, September 21: 'As you know, all my art theories depend just upon this—rooting of mythology in the earth.' Cf. also The Celtic Twilight (London, Bullen, 1902, p. 1): 'I have desired, like every artist, to create a little world out of the beautiful, pleasant, and significant things of this marred and clumsy world, and to show in a vision something of the face of Ireland to any of my own people who would look where I bid them.'

philosophy is intimately linked with his personality, and especially
with the contradictions of his personality. His biographies, by Hone[1]
and by Jeffares,[2] show a solitary man lacking self-confidence and
struggling against his instability; the result of this struggle was a
double personality, a man who could assume a mask and look different from what he was. George William Russell (A.E.) disliked this
double nature; he writes in a letter to George Moore: 'Your account
of Yeats is very amusing, quite in the *Ave Vale* mood, but I don't
think you have dealt yet seriously with the psychology of Yeats.
He began about the time of *The Wind among the Reeds* to do two things
consciously, one to create a "style" in literature, the second to create
or rather to re-create W. B. Yeats in a style which would harmonize
with the literary style. People call this posing. It is really putting on
a mask, like his actors, Greek or Japanese, a mask over life. The
actor must talk to the emotion of the mask, which is a fixed emotion. (. . .) The error in his psychology is, that life creates the form,
but he seems to think that the form creates life. If you have a style,
he argued once with me, you will have something to say.'[3] Yeats's
preoccupation with his mask, and his theory of the anti-self made their
first appearance in his Diary in 1909[4] and were transferred to his
system in the form of the theory of the opposites: Will and Mask (or
desire and the thing desired) and the two other struggling faculties,
Creative Mind and Body of Fate (or thought and its object). A
theory of that kind is valuable only if it is supported by convincing
examples: Yeats applied it successfully, and used to judge men
according to their mixtures of the subjective and objective.[5] He was
himself predominantly subjective, that is, antithetical, exactly a man
of phase 17, whose solitary mind (in some poems he insists upon the
loneliness of God) is at war with his gregarious instinct. He describes
himself in his *Autobiographies* as 'a gregarious man, going hither and
thither looking for conversation, and ready to deny from fear or
favour (his) dearest conviction'; this is the Self (*Hic* in 'Ego Dominus
Tuus'); the anti-Self exalts 'proud and lonely things'. More than on
esoteric doctrines, Yeats's theory of the opposites is based upon his

---

[1] *W. B. Yeats, 1865–1939*, London, Macmillan, 1942.
[2] *W. B. Yeats, Man and Poet*, London, Routledge, 1949.
[3] John Eglington: *A Memoir of A.E.*, London, Macmillan, 1937, p. 33.
[4] Jeffares, op. cit., pp. 159–163.
[5] cf. H. W. Häusermann: *W. B. Yeats's Criticism of Ezra Pound (English Studies)*.

personal experience and is the most reliable and original element of his doctrine.

The system is divided into three parts, for the symbols can be applied to three different categories of facts: psychology, history and life after death. The four faculties are human faculties, but they are related to a divinity which each man bears within himself. Each man is influenced by his Daimon, an invisible power which Yeats identified with Freud's subconscious. The man's Will is the Daimon's Mask, in other words the man's primary nature is the Daimon's antithetical nature. The struggle between man and Daimon ends at death, and after that man goes through certain cycles in which he is freed from pleasure and pain, and then from good and evil. Yeats's account of life after death is very complicated and resembles the various stages of beatitude described by the *Yogas*.[1] This part of the system is also important because the Byzantium poems and 'All Souls' Night' could not be understood without it; the details of the after-death cycles are interesting only so far as they provide an explanation of the poems.

Idealist, static, tragic and religious conceptions of the world are mixed in Yeats's system, but the predominant idea is fatalism. There is a purification from evil after death, but there is no end to evil in life; there is a free will at work in the Great Wheel, but within a deterministic system. Perhaps Yeats did not realize how static and, in spite of its complications, how narrow his system was, but he knew that the symbols would be helpful to his poetry. The system enabled him to create moods which he could recognize as belonging to the system and, paradoxically, to play freely with his settled personality and to extract a great richness from his interior conflicts. His philosophy filled him with enthusiasm, an enthusiasm which could manifest itself in the midst of despair, for nothing is simple (that is, without opposite), and the whole world is inspired by a tragic joy.

Most of Yeats's poems are conceived outside the system, and among those which are directly influenced by the Great Wheel many transform and enrich the symbols. It is necessary, however, to keep in mind a general idea of the Great Wheel, and as technical explanations would be very long, it is better to replace them by a chart of the Great Wheel, which is conceived as a moon with twenty-eight

[1] cf. *Mandookya Upanishad* and *Initiation upon a Mountain* (*The Criterion*, July 1935 and July 1934.)

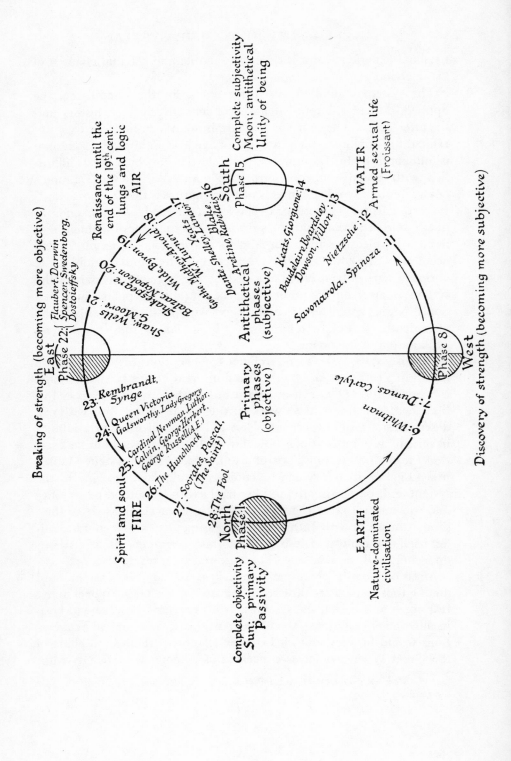

phases, phase 1 being the dark moon, or the phase of passivity with-out antithetical 'tincture', phase 15 being the full moon without primary 'tincture'.

This diagram may help to understand the most important char-acteristics of the system, which could be represented by two gyres in the form of two cones revolving from A (phase 1) to B (phase 15), then again from B to A (phase 28). The antithetical cone or gyre has its summit in A and, from phase 1 to phase 15, develops itself at the expense of the primary gyre.

Will and Mask (the lunar or antithetical faculties) reach in A their lowest stage of development, whereas Creative Mind and Body of Fate (the solar or primary faculties) reach their complete develop-ment. The Will of one gyre is the Mask of the other, and the Creative Mind of the one the Body of Fate of the other, and the gyres revolve in such a way that a man of phase 17, for example, has a Mask from phase 3, a Creative Mind from phase 13 and a Body of Fate from phase 27. The phases are determined according to the position of the Will, and 'when the Will is passing through phases 16, 17 and 18 the Creative Mind is passing through the phases 14, 13 and 12'.[1] This complicated movement of the gyres seems to account for the com-plexities of the human character, and to understand it we need either a book of explanations or a mechanical toy. This mechanism, how-ever, provides the explanation for the poem entitled 'The Double Vision of Michael Robartes',[2] where the symbols of a Buddha and of a Sphinx are used: 'When Will upon the other hand is passing through the phases 12, 13 and 14 the Creative Mind is passing through the phases 18, 17 and 16, or from the sign Pisces to the sign Aquarius, it is, as it were, under the conjunction of Jupiter and

[1] *A Vision*, p. 207.   [2] *Collected Poems*, p. 192.

Saturn. These two conjunctions which express so many things are certainly, upon occasion, the outward-looking mind, love and its lure, contrasted with introspective knowledge of the mind's self-begotten unity, an intellectual excitement. They stand, so to speak, like heraldic supporters guarding the mystery of the fifteenth phase. In certain lines written years ago in the first excitement of discovery I compared one to the Sphinx and one to Buddha. I should have put Christ instead of Buddha, for according to my instructors Buddha was a Jupiter-Saturn influence.'

The first stanza of 'The Double Vision of Michael Robartes' is an example of Yeats's evocation of the Great Wheel, and can be easily understood with the help of our first diagram. The poet's purpose is to evoke the spirits of phase 15, for this phase, as well as the last and first phases, not being human, fascinate him:

> On the grey rock of Cashel the mind's eye
> Has called up the cold spirits that are born
> When the old moon is vanished from the sky
> And the new still hides her horn.

In the same poem, Michael Robartes proceeds to describe the after-life and to evoke a Sphinx and a Buddha. These two symbols are far from the technical details of the system, for the imagination of the poet loads them with a great richness of signification. The system is but the first sparkle of Yeats's poetry, and if the mechanical scheme of *A Vision* can be dismissed as an elementary and unsound philosophy, or as an incongruous mixture of materials, its value as an incentive to poetry and as a suggestive piece of work cannot be questioned.

A Vision does not contain all the philosophical thought of Yeats, but is the result of an attempt at original thinking and of a flight from the philosophical tradition of Bacon, Locke, Spencer, Darwin and Bertrand Russell. Yeats hated science and abstraction. The following passage of his unpublished *Letters to Sturge Moore* is characteristic; Yeats is writing about the postulate that 'nothing exists that is not in the mind as an element of experience'. 'This seems to me the simplest and to liberate us from all manner of abstraction and create at once a joyous artistic life. However, when one admits, if one does, the mind which creates all is limited from the start by certain possibilities one admits Platonic ideas, and so a prenatal division of the "unconscious" into two forms of mind. This is a Vedantic thought. However, I try always to keep my philosophy within such classifications of thought as will keep it to such experience as seems a natural life. I prefer to include in my definition of water, a little duckweed or a few fish. I have never met the poor naked creature H_2O.'[1]

For Yeats, science and abstraction were menacing art, and he was so anxious to believe in the independence of art from external things that he created a system in which nature is essentially symbolical and dismissed any theory which says that art is an imitation: 'In the last letter, but one, you spoke of all art as imitation, meaning I conclude, imitation of something in the outer world. To me it seems that it often uses the outer world as a symbolism to express subjective moods. The greater the subjectivity, the less the imitation. Though perhaps, there is always some imitation. You say that music suggests now the roar of the sea, now the song of the bird, and yet it seems to me that the song of the bird itself is perhaps subjective, an expression of feeling alone. The element of pattern in every art is, I think, the part that is not imitative, for in the last analysis, there will always be somewhere an intensity of pattern that we have never seen with our eyes. In fact, imitation seems to me to create a language in which we say things which are not imitation.'[2]

The preceding passage throws light on the relations between Yeats's system and his poetry. He needed a philosophy which would motivate his symbols and confer an invincible authority upon his poetry. This explains his dislike of British common sense and his being influenced by Eastern philosophy: 'To-morrow I write a story to be added to the Michael Robartes series (a prelude to *A Vision* which I am now revising in proof). It is almost an exact transcript from fact. I have for years been creating a group of strange disorderly people on whom Michael Robartes confers the wisdom of the East.'[3]

Yeats did not, however, write his poems systematically according to his system, and he went on writing autobiographical poems and creating fictitious characters: 'I had a moment's jealousy, I had

[1] No. 1, December 8 (1926?).

[2] *J. B. Yeats, Letters to his Son*, ed. by Joseph Hone, London, Faber and Faber, 1944. Letter of 5 March 1916, p. 233.

[3] *Letters on Poetry from W. B. Yeats to Dorothy Wellesley*, Oxford University Press, 1940. Letter of 26 July 1936, p. 91.

thought of expending my last years on philosophic verse but knew now that I was too old.'[1] Yeats often changed the meaning of his symbols, published two consecutive versions of *A Vision* which show many discrepancies and transformed his system according to his own experiments or in order to fulfil the requirements of his poetry. The system is therefore a skeleton or a mere scaffold and should be understood metaphorically, as in this passage: 'Michael Robartes called the universe a great egg that turns inside-out perpetually without breaking its shell.'[2]

Whatever the philosophy underlying the symbols may be, the symbols must be taken seriously if they have a real significance; Yeats believed that the creations of the mind—symbols, images— were real and independent of the creator's imagination. By the aid of these symbols, man, whose mind has shifting borders, can communicate with the mind of nature, the *Anima Mundi* or the Great Memory.

II. POEMS RELATED TO THE FIRST PART OF 'A VISION'

The first part of *A Vision*, an explanation of the 28 phases, contains Yeats's psychology. One of his autobiographical poems, 'Ego Dominus Tuus',[3] is particularly connected with this aspect of his philosophy. The poem is conceived as a dialogue between *Hic*, the self, and *Ille*, the anti-self. This duality or, as Yeats would term it, this conflict, has been experienced by many creative writers, among whom the poet chooses Dante and Keats for his examples. Both had the power to call their own opposite; Keats's self was a poor 'schoolboy', whereas his anti-self expresses himself in 'luxuriant song'. Art is not an expression of the artist's personality: it is a role to be acted and a means to purify the artist's soul, for 'this struggle between the self and the anti-self is ended in death only, or in the work of art'.[4] This thought is already developed in *Per Amica Silentia Lunae*, which was published before *A Vision*: 'Some years ago I began to believe that our culture with its doctrine of sincerity and self-realization made us gentle and passive, and that the Middle Ages and the

[1] ibid., 8 September 1935.
[2] *A Vision*, p. 33.
[3] *Collected Poems*, p. 180. Composed on 5 December 1915.
[4] H. W. Häusermann: *W. B. Yeats's Criticism of Ezra Pound*, (English Studies).

Renaissance were right to found theirs upon the Imitation of Christ or some classic hero.'[1]

Yeats's interpretation of the *Mandookya Upanishad*, written nineteen years after 'Ego Dominus Tuus', shows his preoccupation with the same problem: 'The Eastern poet saw the Moon as the Sun's bride, now in solitude, now offering to her Bridegroom a self-abandonment unknown to our poetry. A European would think perhaps of the moonlit and moonless nights alone, consider the crescent man's personality, as it fills into the round and becomes perfect, overthrowing the black night of nature.[2] Am I not justified in discovering there the conflict between subjectivity and objectivity, between self and not self, between waking life and dreamless sleep?'[3]

An interpretation of 'Ego Dominus Tuus' which has not yet been proposed by Yeats's critics is that the conflict between Hic and Ille is the contrast between the man of action and the artist, and especially between the Renaissance artist and the man of to-day, who aims at self-expression and is consequently unable to create, for

> We have lit upon the gentle, sensitive mind
> And lost the old nonchalance of the hand;

The poet alludes to the nonchalance of the actor who plays the part of his double and masters the 'hysterica passio'. Ille refutes the assertion that art is spontaneous:

> No, not sing,
> For those that love the world serve it in action,
> Grow rich, popular and full of influence,
> And should they paint or write, still it is action:
> The struggle of the fly in the marmalade.

The whole argument of Ille is against self-expression, and could be applied to Yeats's autobiographical poems, which are a perpetual creation of an imaginary character. These lines spoken by Hic:

> A style is found by sedentary toil
> And by the imitation of great masters

---

[1] *Essays*, p. 496.

[2] This is the idea developed by W. J. Turner in 'The Signs of the Zodiac' and in 'Nature and Mind' (*Fossils of a Future Time*) O.U.P., 1946.

[3] *Initiation upon a Mountain* (*The Criterion*, July 1934, p. 554).

are not heard by Ille, who is in search of the unheard-of and who, by the help of magical shapes, evokes his invisible double:

> By the help of an image
> I call to my own opposite, summon all
> That I have handled least, least looked upon.

It has been suggested that Yeats as a man, or Willie, is Hic, whereas Yeats as an actor or a character is Ille; this interpretation deprives the poem of its profound meaning, for Ille is not considered by Yeats as a fictitious character: Ille is a reality, or a real image of the immortal Yeats, the 'dominus' created by Yeats as a mortal. The duality of Yeats's character explains his correspondence with Sturge Moore, where the poet is anxious to find a philosophical proof that creatures of the imagination and spiritual beings are real.

Whereas the anti-self has the last word in 'Ego Dominus Tuus', the self is stronger in 'A Dialogue of Self and Soul'.[1] He is summoned by his soul to the tower of wisdom, and by self to the folly of love and war. The tower is the emblem of night and contemplation, but the poet removes this image from his mind, for he has no regret over his past follies and does not want to change his life, in which everything was well done:

> We must laugh and we must sing,
> We are blest by everything,
> Everything we look upon is blest.

Another autobiographical poem, 'Vacillation',[2] shows a new aspect of the same conflict. The poet rejects the exhortation of his soul:

> *The Soul.*   Seek out reality, leave things that seem.
> *The Heart.*   What, be a singer born and lack a theme?

The theme of 'Vacillation' is in apparent contradiction to the one of 'Ego Dominus Tuus', for the poet no longer yearns for an unknown beauty, but

> Homer is my example and his unchristened heart.

Although he grows old and should think of death, he is resolved to deal once more with original sin, for sanctity is but one extreme of

---

[1] *Collected Poems*, p. 265 (1927).   [2] ibid., p. 282.

life, more exactly a characteristic of phase 27, and a man of phase 15, like Yeats, cannot choose to be somebody else. The idea of metempsychosis through the recurrence of the gyres appears in this poem. Von Hügel and Saint Teresa, symbols of sanctity, are the opposites to Pharaoh, with whom they are identified in eternity:

> Those self-same hands perchance
> Eternalized the body of a modern saint that once
> Had scooped out Pharaoh's mummy. . . .

In *Last Poems and Plays*[1] the conflicting calls for wisdom and for sensuous poetry give birth to a wide diversity of themes. 'The Spur'[2] is a good example of Yeats's escape from wisdom, or 'the simplicity of fire':

> You think it horrible that lust and rage
> Should dance attention upon my old age;
> They were not such a plague when I was young;
> What else have I to spur me into song?

But lust and rage are acted rather than lived, they are as it were a creation of the imagination and leave the mind unimpassioned. The other side of Yeats's personality manifests itself in 'An Acre of Grass',[3] in which he feels that he does not share the interests of his contemporaries. He has done his duty to the world, to which he cannot give anything more than his poetry, and he has no ambition to discover anything new. But what he cannot obtain through flashes of light and hard work he will obtain through intensity of feeling and profundity of thought. Intensity of feeling, or passion, frenzy, belongs to the propagandist and gregarious man of phase 17, who dreams of converting the world and of remaking himself:

> Grant me an old man's frenzy,
> Myself I must remake
> Till I am Timon and Lear
> Or that William Blake
> Who beat upon the wall
> Till truth obeyed his call;

Profundity of thought refers to the solitary man of phase 17, and to his ability to include every single fact in a whole (for a great poet of

---

[1] London, Macmillan, 1940.   [2] ibid, p. 37.   [3] ibid., p. 17.

this phase, Dante, achieves *unity of being*), and his ability to make the past live again in the living whole, in the all-embracing look of the poet:

> A mind Michael Angelo knew
> That can pierce the clouds,
> Or inspired by frenzy
> Shake the dead in their shrouds;
> Forgotten else by mankind,
> An old man's eagle mind.

Other poems express Yeats's conviction that the past is living in the present:

> Our shadows rove the garden gravel still,
> The living seem more shadowy than they.[1]

or that the opposites coexist:

> Nor know that what disturbs our blood
> Is but its longing for the tomb.[2]

The most famous of the autobiographical poems, 'The Tower',[3] show a Yeats who is not vacillating, but full of self-confidence: it is the man who told Dorothy Wellesley that only in his old age could he guess what he might have done. In his last years his creative powers were far from waning and, as he was too old to devote himself entirely to philosophical verse, it is natural that he should 'rage against old age'.

There are some poems, among those inspired by the first part of *A Vision*, which are an evocation of the extreme phases of the Great Wheel, around phase 1 or phase 15. The whole sequence is presented in a didactic manner in 'The Phases of the Moon',[4] a poetical summary of Yeats's 'psychology', written in the form of a dialogue. Aherne laughs at Yeats in his tower and Robartes explains the system; the poet studies in vain and tries in vain to achieve wisdom, for he does not understand the perpetual struggle between objectivity and subjectivity. The fool and the wise man are but two extremes and only those who know that they act and free themselves from a predestined part are wise. Robartes appears as the supernatural teacher who reveals what Yeats could not have learnt by himself: the dark

---

[1] 'The New Faces,' *Collected Poems*, p. 238. [2] ibid., p. 237. [3] ibid., p. 218.
[4] ibid., p. 183.

moon and the full moon, the twenty-eight phases and the correspondence between the physical and the spiritual:

> All dreams of the soul
> End in a beautiful man's or woman's body.

The migration of the soul throughout the Wheel is summarized in
these lines:

> Before the full
> It sought itself and afterwards the world.

The description of the extreme phases is also clear and concise. Here
is phase 15 (complete subjectivity):

> When the moon's full those creatures of the full
> Are met on the waste hills by country men
> Who shudder and hurry by: body and soul
> Estranged amid the strangeness of themselves,
> Caught up in contemplation, the mind's eye
> Fixed upon images that once were thought;
> For separate, perfect, and immovable
> Images can break the solitude
> Of lovely, satisfied, indifferent eyes.

Here is phase 28:

> Because all dark, like those that are all light,
> They are cast beyond the verge, and in a cloud,
> Crying to one another like the bats;
> And having no desire they cannot tell
> What's good or bad, or what it is to triumph
> At the perfection of one's own obedience;
> And yet they speak what's blown into the mind;
> Deformed beyond deformity, unformed,
> Insipid as the dough before it is baked,
> They change their bodies at a word.

The contrast between antithetical men, for whom everything appears as images of their own minds, and primary men, who abandon
themselves to the powers of nature, suggests the diversity of inspiration which may be prompted by the system. Yeats was particularly
interested in the extreme phases, and the three last ones inspired a
series of poems which are directly connected with the system; these

phases are successively called the Hunchback, the Saint and the Fool, and are characterized in 'The Phases of the Moon':

> Hunchback and saint and fool are the last crescents.
> The burning bow that once could shoot an arrow
> Out of the up and down, the wagon-wheel
> Of beauty's cruelty and wisdom's chatter—
> Out of that raving tide—is drawn betwixt
> Deformity of body and of mind.

Whereas the antithetical phases are the phases of beauty and wisdom—of the self—the three last phases are the phases of deformity, authority, and mirth, or of light; the wagon-wheel is used as a symbol of nature, compared in *A Vision* to a cook who kneads the self and destroys beauty and wisdom. The Hunchback 'stands in the presence of a terrible blinding light, and would, were that possible, be born as worm or mole'. The Saint manifests 'an extreme desire for spiritual authority' and 'his joy is to be nothing, to do nothing, to think nothing; but to permit the total life, expressed in its humanity, to flow in upon him and to express itself through his acts and thoughts'. The Fool is 'but a straw blown by the wind'; his thoughts and acts are aimless, 'and it is in this aimlessness that he finds his joy'.[1] These quotations help to interpret 'The Saint and the Hunchback'.[2] The Hunchback complains that he is not powerful and adds that

> A Roman Caesar is held down
> Under this hump.

The complaint is urged by the Hunchback's malice, 'because, finding no impulse but in his own ambition, he is made jealous by the impulse of others'. His deformity is 'symbolized in the hump that thwarts what seems the ambition of a Caesar or of an Achilles'. The Saint, on the contrary, has no antithetical impulse, no malignity; he accepts his suffering and he is glad that, by sacrificing himself, he holds down the tyrant who is in his flesh:

> That great rogue Alcibiades.

But the Hunchback praises Alcibiades, who dazzles him. It is not profitable to look in *A Vision* for the interpretation of 'Two Songs of a Fool', for the speckled cat, the tame hare and the brown hare men-

[1] *A Vision*, pp. 176, 180 and 182.   [2] *Collected Poems*, p. 189.

tioned in this poem symbolize three women; a passage, however, alludes to Yeats's philosophy:

> And what can I
> That am a wandering-witted fool
> But pray to God that He ease
> My great responsibilities?

It may seem surprising that Yeats, a man of phase 17, should identify himself with a fool. But the man of phase 17, like the Fool, has no Will and his Body of Fate is derived from a phase of renunciation. Yeats's prayer is his 'hope that the *Body of Fate* may die away'.

'The Double Vision of Michael Robartes'[1] is the evocation of a phase which is still more outside the range of Yeats's own experience. In this allusion to phase 1 Yeats has found the basis for his interpretation of history, for if in phase 1 the old moon has gone and the new has not yet shown its first crescent, there is an analogy between this phase and the time when the poem was written, a time from which Yeats inferred that an era was dying and a new era about to begin.

In the first section of the poem Michael Robartes appears as the man who has universal knowledge, that is, who is aware of the revolving wheel of the faculties. The first stanza is easily understood:

> On the grey rock of Cashel the mind's eye
> Has called up the cold spirits that are born
> When the old moon is vanished from the sky
> And the new still hides her horn.

The mind has not yet started to think consciously and nature has not yet produced a self-willed man, so that life begins before the will awakens:

> Under blank eyes and fingers never still
> The particular is pounded till it is man.
> When had I my own will?
> O not since life began.

As they are unconscious and overwhelmed by objects, the creatures of that phase are innocent:

> Constrained, arraigned, baffled, bent and unbent
> By these wire-jointed jaws and limbs of wood,
> Themselves obedient,
> Knowing not evil and good;

[1] ibid., p. 192.

45

They are completely absorbed in nature and without substance, and yet they manifest themselves in our desire for obedience:

> Obedient to some magical breath.
> They do not even feel, so abstract are they,
> So dead beyond our death,
> Triumph that we obey.

   The poet, however, is not satisfied with these glimpses, and creates three symbols: a Sphinx, a Buddha, and, between them, a dancing girl, which are emblems of the opposite phases (this explains why Robartes' vision is double). The Sphinx is 'introspective knowledge, of the mind's self-begotten unity, an intellectual excitement':

> One lashed her tail; her eyes lit by the moon
> Gazed upon all things known, all things unknown,
> In triumph of intellect
> With motionless head erect.

The Buddha, on the contrary, is 'the outward-looking mind, love and its lure':[1]

> That other's moonlit eyeballs never moved,
> Being fixed on all things loved, all things unloved,
> Yet little peace he had,
> For those that love are sad.

Both emblems, it should be remembered, result from the conjunction of Jupiter and Saturn. The dancing girl is another emblem of phase 15, a phase of complete beauty. As there is no mixture in that phase, but complete subjectivity, there is no life, and yet the Wheel is turning:

> In contemplation had those three so wrought
> Upon a moment, and so stretched it out
> That they, time overthrown,
> Were dead yet flesh and bone.

   In the third section the poet rejoices because he has found at last the symbol of perfect beauty:

> I knew that I had seen, had seen at last
> That girl my unremembering nights hold fast
> Or else my dreams that fly
> If I should rub an eye,

----

[1] cf. p. 36 of the present essay.

46

POEMS RELATED TO THE FIRST PART OF 'A VISION'

The historical signification of the first section (evoking phase 1) is developed in 'The Second Coming'.[1] Other poems also connected with the extreme phases, 'Michael Robartes and the Dancer', 'Solomon and the Witch', 'An Image from a Past Life', 'Under Saturn', and 'Demon and Beast', are personal rather than philosophical, that is, they are connected with Yeats's life rather than with his system. The same could be said about 'The Tower', but this poem requires a special interpretation.

Yeats's complaint about old age in the first section of 'The Tower'[2] is made all the more vivid because he desires his opposite:

> Never had I more
> Excited, passionate, fantastical
> Imagination, nor an ear and eye
> That more expected the impossible—

In the second section Yeats tells the story of those who dwelt in the tower of Thoor Ballylee before him: all of them seem to have felt a longing for what is lost. There was among them a blind poet who praised the beauty of a country girl and inspired violent action in his listeners for the sake of her:

> the tragedy began
> With Homer that was a blind man,
> And Helen has all living hearts betrayed.
> O may the moon and sunlight seem
> One inextricable beam,
> For if I triumph I must make men mad.

With his predecessors in the tower, Yeats calls the memory of a character of his earlier books, Hanrahan, probably because Hanrahan, frustrated like Yeats, is 'fire blown by the wind', or 'the simplicity of an imagination too changeable to gather permanent possessions, or the adoration of the shepherds', whereas the Michael Robartes of the earlier books is 'the pride of the imagination brooding over the greatness of its possessions, or the adoration of the Magi',[3] and could not have been associated with the setting of the tower. Hanrahan also expected the impossible—for Yeats believes

---

[1] *Collected Poems*, p. 210.   [2] ibid., p. 217.
[3] cf. *The Wind among the Reeds*.

that Hanrahan is a real character—and must have made many
discoveries in the grave:

> For it is certain that you have
> Reckoned up every unforeknown, unseeing
> Plunge, lured by a softening eye,
> Or by a touch or a sigh,
> Into the labyrinth of another's being;

What was lost, however, will be found again, and those who are
not dazzled by the sun, the proud, antithetical men, may expect
confidently what they are looking for in vain. In the third section
the poet makes his will, and thinks of those who will be free like him:

> It is time that I wrote my will;
> I choose upstanding men
> That climb the streams until
> The fountain leap, and at dawn
> Drop their cast at the side
> Of dripping stone; I declare
> They shall inherit my pride,
> The pride of people that were
> Bound neither to Cause nor to State,

If these people are proud, it is because they are not overwhelmed
by nature or by their environment: they create their own world:

> Death and life were not
> Till man made up the whole,
> Made lock, stock and barrel
> Out of his bitter soul,
> Aye, sun and moon and star, all,
> And further add to that
> That, being dead, we rise,
> Dream and so create
> Translunar Paradise.

In the concluding passage the poet expresses his wish to live a
secluded life in search of wisdom. The imagery is entirely derived
from his antithetical or lunar character, associated with darkness and
mystery:

48

Now shall I make my soul,
Compelling it to study
In a learned school
Till the wreck of body,
Slow decay of blood,
Testy delirium
Or dull decrepitude,
Or what worse evil come—
The death of friends, or death
Of every brilliant eye
That made a catch in the breath—
Seem but the clouds of the sky
When the horizon fades;
Or a bird's sleepy cry
Among the deepening shades.

Yeats realized later, however, that instead of spending his last years preparing for death he had to be preoccupied solely with life, and that his old desire to conquer bodily inclinations and to be lonely was but one side of his character. His wish was only half fulfilled, for there is in his last work an alternation of sensuous and intellectual poems. His idea of creation in 'The Tower' is definitely and only antithetical, and indicates that he dismisses the conception of a world which is independent from the human mind and that he thinks of nature as of a projection of the mind.

The other side of his character is best expressed in the last poems. Many of them have no special meaning, at least no metaphysical implications, but the system is lurking behind them. Some are beautiful descriptions, like 'Sweet Dancer',[1] 'Beautiful Lofty Things',[2] 'A Crazed Girl',[3] 'A Drunken Man's Praise of Sobriety',[4] 'The Pilgrim',[5] 'In Tara's Halls',[6] 'News for the Delphic Oracle',[7] 'Why should not old Men be Mad?',[8] 'The Statesman's Holiday',[9] and 'Crazy Jane on the Mountain'.[10] All these poems are of a transparent beauty and full of mysterious sensuality, often verging on madness, which expresses passion in its most naked, spontaneous, and uninhibited form. These extreme outbursts, written in a conversational manner imitating the ballad style, and containing perfect unity of effect and severity of form (the stanzas are often closed by a burden),

[1] to [10] *Last Poems and Plays*, pp. 7, 19, 20, 38, 56, 59, 76, 77 and 79.

are a sign of the poet's control over his irrational themes: madness, beauty, and passion. It is rare that a poet attains to the perfect expression of passion in his old age, yet, apart from a medical explanation, there is an answer. Madness, beauty, and passion are such as Yeats creates them; it does not mean at all that they are an expression of his own feelings: they may be pure creation from which he is detached. They are certainly an aspect of his mind, or a necessary complement to his mind, and we know that his system allows for a split of the personality. As Poe contends in *The Philosophy of Composition*, passion is best expressed when it is created in an unimpassioned, voluntary, and lucid way: this is probably what happened with the creation of some of Yeats's last poems. It does not mean that they left Yeats cold: if so, the reader would not be deeply moved, and any reader who does not know anything about Yeats's doctrine is moved by his poems because, although strange, their beauty is so direct, so genuine, and so naked that it is impossible not to react strongly to it. When brought to its extreme limits, passion becomes universal, for it is isolated from circumstantial details and at the same time integrated in the whole which comprises and destroys it. The logic of Yeats's system is the necessity of his poetry, and perhaps the dialectics underlying all kinds of poetry.

The alternation of intellectual and sensual poetry is another aspect of the conflict between the subjective, antithetical man and the objective, primary man symbolized by fire, but does not correspond exactly to the terminology of *A Vision*. This aspect of the conflict is adequately explained in a letter to Dorothy Wellesley:[1] 'We have all something within ourselves to batter down and get our power from this fighting. I have never 'produced' a play in verse without showing the actors that the passion of the verse comes from the fact that the speakers are holding down violence or madness—'down Hysterica passio'. All depends on the completeness of the holding down, on the stirring of the beast underneath. Even my poem 'To D. W.' should give this impression. The moon, the moonless night, the sensual silence, the silent room and the violent bright Furies. Without this conflict we have no passion, only sentiment and thought. . . . About the conflict in 'To D. W.', I did not plan it deliberately. That conflict is deep in my subconsciousness, perhaps in everybody's. I dream of clear water, perhaps two or three times (the moon of the

[1] 5 August 1936, p. 94.

poem), then come erotic dreams. Then for weeks perhaps I write poetry with sex for theme. Then comes the reversal—it came when I was young with some dream or some vision between waking or sleep with a flame in it. Then for weeks I get a symbolism like that in my Byzantium poem with flame for theme. . . . The water is sensation, peace, night, silence, indolence; the fire is passion, tension, day, music, energy!

It is not necessary to insist on the similitude between these symbols and those used in *A Vision*. The water is antithetical and, associated with darkness and mystery, it is a source of intellectual poetry, whereas the fire is primary and expresses the 'gregarious' man in Yeats who delights in erotic poetry.

III. YEATS'S HISTORICAL VISION

Yeats's system is valid for the explanation of both individual men and historical periods, since life is conceived as an emanation from the *Anima Mundi*. His philosophy of history, however, is not as systematic as his psychology; it originates in his romantic patriotism and is based upon his conviction that a new era is about to come.

The historical books of *A Vision* are confused, conjectural, and tend towards a mythology—rather than a philosophy—of history. The historical gyres are similar to the psychological ones: there is a perpetual alternation of primary and antithetical eras, each one lasting about two thousand years and determined mainly by the forms of their civilizations. The antithetical era of the ancients includes the two millennia preceding the birth of Christ and the present era is just about to complete its cycle and to give way to another antithetical era.

The essential idea of the system concerning history is the negation of progress and the belief in the return of similar periods. Yeats's view of history in this respect resembles Vico's, and Yeats found in Spengler's *Decline of the West* 'a correspondence too great for coincidence between most of his essential dates and those I had received before the publication of his first German edition'.[1]

Vico's history, however, is not a mere mechanical alternation of conflicting trends; divine Providence is struggling against evil and

[1] *A Vision*, p. 261.

is necessarily victorious; what is bad serves a good cause and Providence elevates man from the animal state of after the Fall to humanity. Man is essentially religious and history implies progress. There are, however, some striking analogies between Yeats's system and Vico's philosophy. For example, Yeats's four faculties are analogous to Vico's three faculties (knowledge, will, and might), and the following, essential, points of Vico's philosophy are only apparently different from Yeats's tenets: all things draw their being from God, all come back to God through a circular movement, all have their essence in God in whom they remain, and all outside God are but darkness and error. Vico's sources are analogous to Yeats's; both interpret works of art; for example, a great part of Vico's theory is founded upon an interpretation of Homer, and his philological method is more reliable and scientific than Yeats's abstract, *a priori* generalizations. Yeats's historical cycles are based upon a belief in metempsychosis and in Platonic ideas:

> I, proclaiming that there is
> Among birds or beasts or men
> One that is perfect or at peace,
> Danced on Cruachan's windy plain,
> Upon Cro-Patrick sang aloud;
> All that could run or leap or swim
> Whether in wood, water or cloud,
> Acclaiming, proclaiming, declaiming Him.[1]

and:

> I have been a king,
> I have been a slave,
> Nor is there anything,
> Fool, rascal, knave,
> That I have not been,
> And yet upon my breast
> A myriad heads have lain.[2]

Although Yeats believes in a purification from evil, his system is static: there is no escape, nor any improvement; his conflicts are conflicts between subjectivity and objectivity, whereas Vico's conflict is between good and evil, solitude and love, animality and civilization.

[1] 'The Dancer at Cruachan and Cro-Patrick,' *Collected Poems*, p. 304
[2] 'Mohini Chatterjee,' ibid., p. 279.

Yeats's distinction between the primary man and the antithetical man, however, is similar to Vico's theory that men believe in God, then in heroes, then in men, but the comparison cannot be further extended. Vico's philosophy is more coherent than Yeats's; to the development from belief in God to belief in heroes, then in men, corresponds the developments from animal state to the grouping in families, then in nations, and from 'mute languages' to hieroglyphics or symbolical languages made of metaphors, and finally to articulate, abstract languages. Vico adds to these parallel developments the progression from barbarous customs to severe laws, then to successively refined, dissolute, corrupted, and barbarous customs. Instead of emphasizing the invisible work of divine Providence and the progression of humanity, Yeats emphasizes the conflicts and the alternation of primary and antithetical civilizations in the following manner: 'After an age of necessity, truth, goodness, mechanism, science, democracy, abstraction, peace, comes an age of freedom, fiction, evil, kindred, art, aristocracy, particularity, war.'[1] Yeats does not believe that one era is better than the other; they are simply opposed to each other. His system enables him to relate all events, and among them the most frightful, to his eternal vision: 'We came from no immaturity, but out of our own perfection like ships that "all their swelling canvas wear".' Yeats's system is all the more static and determinist because it is associated with geography and astrology: 'South and East are human form and intellectual authority, whereas North and West are superhuman form and emotional freedom,'[2] which amounts to saying that South and East are antithetical, North and West primary. The symbol of the East is 'that of a central altar and sixteen roads radiating outward', whereas the symbol of the West is the Cavern.

Yeats's poems dealing with history might be arbitrarily divided into two parts: those concerned with the present time and more particularly with contemporary events in Ireland and those concerned with the past. A special category of poems deals with history in general without mentioning any particular period.

'The Gyres'[3] belongs to this category. The gyres turn in such a way that what appears in one era disappears in the next and reappears later; things melt into one another, and although everything dies,

---

[1] *A Vision*, p. 52.   [2] ibid., p. 258.
[3] *Last Poems and Plays*, p. 5.

everything is permanent as a whole and inspires a great joy in the poet, whatever may happen:

> We that look on but laugh in tragic joy.

There is a passage in prose explaining Yeats's fatalism: 'I murmured, as I have countless times, I have been part of it always and there is may be no escape, forgetting and returning life after life like an insect in the grass. But murmured it without terror, in exultation almost.' The first stanza of 'The Gyres' is inspired by the exultation of the poet who sees all things relative and fatal, and rejoices that each civilization reaches its own stage of perfection:

> The gyres! the gyres! Old Rocky Face, look forth;
> Things thought too long can no longer be thought,
> For beauty dies of beauty, worth of worth,
> And ancient lineaments are blotted out.
> Irrational streams of blood are staining earth;
> Empedocles has thrown things about;
> Hector is dead and there's a light in Troy;
> We that look on but laugh in tragic joy.

'Old Rocky Face' is Shelley's Jew. Jeffares[1] mentions that in Shelley's *Hellas*, where the Jew is described after the entrance of Hassan, the theme of a chorus:

> Worlds on worlds are rolling ever
> From creation to decay

and speeches of Mahmud and Ahasuerus on the future are not dissimilar to Yeats's basic ideas. The idea of the second stanza is that we should neither regret the past nor be afraid of the future:

> What matter though numb nightmare ride on top,
> And blood and mire the sensitive body stain?
> What matter? Heave no sigh, let no tear drop,
> A greater, a more gracious time has gone;
> For painted forms or boxes of make-up
> In ancient tombs I sighed, but not again;
> What matter? Out of cavern comes a voice,
> And all it knows is that one word 'Rejoice!'

---

[1] *W. B. Yeats, Man and Poet*, note 50, p. 337.

YEATS'S HISTORICAL VISION

The cavern is rather an allusion to Shelley's Jew who lived in a cavern amid the 'Demonen',[1] but it may refer also to the symbol of the West. In the third stanza Yeats predicts a new, antithetical civilization:

> Conduct and work grow coarse, and coarse the soul,
> What matter? Those that Rocky Face holds dear,
> Lovers of horses and of women, shall,
> From marble of a broken sepulchre,
> Or dark betwixt the polecat and the owl,
> Or any rich, dark, nothing disinter
> The workman, noble and saint, and all things run
> On that fashionable gyre again.

The whole poem shows Yeats's reaction to the bloody events which marked the struggle for the independence of Ireland. As an antithetical man, he disliked the present primary civilization (democracy, science) and longed for a new, aristocratic one. Yeats's ideas on the future are defined in two passages of *A Vision*: the next civilization will be antithetical, but we cannot predict exactly what it will be, for 'the particulars are the work of the *thirteenth sphere* or cycle which is in every man and called his freedom'.[2] And: 'My instructors certainly expect neither "a primitive state" nor a return to barbarism as primitivism and barbarism are ordinarily understood; *antithetical* revelation is an intellectual influx neither from beyond mankind nor born of a virgin, but begotten from our spirit and history.'[3] In other words, an antithetical revelation is subjective, and not imposed from outside. Yeats's antithetical character manifests itself in his exaltation of pride and aristocracy and his dislike for coarseness and democracy.

These feelings are expressed in 'Nineteen Hundred and Nineteen',[4] where the poet does not hope that things will improve in Ireland:

> We, who seven years ago
> Talked of honour and of truth,
> Shriek with pleasure if we show
> The weasel's twist, the weasel's tooth.

[1] cf. *Queen Mab*, note on Ahasuerus. [2] *A Vision*, p. 302.
[3] *A Vision*, p. 262. [4] *Collected Poems*, p. 232.

All that is precious is disappearing:

> Many ingenious lovely things are gone

and:

> Man is in love and loves what vanishes,

The most interesting passage of the poem from a philosophical point of view is the one introducing the symbol of the swan. The swan represents the antithetical revelation and announces the Greek or classical era as well as the coming one:

> The swan has leaped into the desolate heaven:
> That image can bring wildness, bring a rage
> To end all things, to end
> What my laborious life imagined, even
> The half-imagined, the half-written page;

The same symbol is used in 'Coole and Ballylee, 1931',[1] and in 'Leda and the Swan'.[2]

Although 'Nineteen Hundred and Nineteen' begins with an allusion to Greece, the poem is concerned with the present time, whereas 'Leda and the Swan' contains no allusion to the present and only a faint evocation of Greece, for the poem is inspired by Michael Angelo's sculpture now in Florence (Museo Nazionale):

> A shudder in the loins engenders there
> The broken wall, the burning roof and tower
> And Agamemnon dead.

Among the poems concerned with the present, the one which is most closely related to Yeats's system is 'The Second Coming'.[3] The beginning of the poem:

> Turning and turning in the widening gyre
> The falcon cannot hear the falconer;

expresses Yeats's idea that the present era is dying, that man (the falcon) has forgotten Christ (the falconer). The image of the falcon, according to Jeffares,[4] is borrowed from Dante. Yeats had seen a picture by Doré representing a dragon in the form of a gyre. The rest of the first section of 'The Second Coming' is a curious allusion to

---

[1] ibid., p. 275.   [2] ibid., p. 241.   [3] ibid., p. 210.
[4] *W. B. Yeats, Man and Poet*, p. 202.

events in Ireland in which the poet uses the terminology of *A Vision*:

> Things fall apart; the centre cannot hold;
> Mere anarchy is loosed upon the world,
> The blood-dimmed tide is loosed, and everywhere
> The ceremony of innocence is drowned;
> The best lack all conviction, while the worst
> Are full of passionate intensity.

The primary era is disintegrating and shows its worst aspect—vulgarity, to which Yeats's aristocratic mind is opposed. The French Revolution is interpreted by Yeats as the first sign of disintegration and the rise of abstraction, science, and democracy. The second section of the poem contains a prediction of the next two millennia, in which solitude and a 'rough beast' symbolize the antithetical era and are opposed to the gentle, primary Bethlehem:

> Surely some revelation is at hand;
> Surely the Second Coming is at hand.
> The Second Coming! Hardly are those words out
> When a vast image out of *Spiritus Mundi*
> Troubles my sight: somewhere in sands of the desert
> A shape with lion body and the head of a man,
> A gaze blank and pitiless as the sun,
> Is moving its slow thighs, while all about it
> Reel shadows of the indignant desert birds.
> The darkness drops again; but now I know
> That twenty centuries of stony sleep
> Were vexed to nightmare by a rocking cradle,
> And what rough beast, its hour come at last,
> Slouches towards Bethlehem to be born?

Yeats's aversion to coarseness, vulgarity, his romantic regret for the past and his desire for an aristocratic civilization inspire many poems. His aristocratic ideal is defined in 'A Prayer for my Daughter':[1]

> And may her bridegroom bring her to a house
> Where all's accustomed, ceremonious;
> For arrogance and hatred are the wares
> Peddled in the thoroughfares.

[1] *Collected Poems*, p. 211.

57

His romantic belief in Ireland is expressed in patriotic songs like 'The O'Rahilly',[1] 'Come, Gather round me, Parnellites',[2] 'The Great Day',[3] 'Parnell',[4] 'The Municipal Gallery Revisited',[5] 'Three Songs to the one Burden',[6] 'Three Marching songs',[7] 'Hound Voice',[8] 'Cuchulain Comforted',[9] and 'Under Ben Bulben.[10] These poems are characterized by Yeats's belief that the Celtic race is opposed to the present civilization:

> We Irish, born into that ancient sect
> But thrown upon this filthy modern tide
> And by its formless spawning fury wrecked,
> Climb to our own proper dark, that we may trace
> The lineaments of a plummet-measured face.[11]

Yeats's admiration of the past is equalled by his contempt for the present time:

> The Muse is mute when public men
> Applaud a modern throne:[12]

This attitude results in his ignoring the present platitudes:

> I sing what was lost and dread what was won,[13]

and in his praising a statesman who forgets his official duties:

> Am I a great Lord Chancellor
> That slept upon the Sack?
> Commanding officer that tore
> The khaki from his back?
> Or am I de Valéra
> Or the king of Greece,
> Or the man that made the motors?
> Ach, call me what you please!
> Here's a Montenegrin lute
> And its old sole string
> Makes a sweet music
> And I delight to sing:
> *Tall dames go walking in grass-green Avalon.*[14]

[8] to [10] *Last Poems and Plays*, pp. 27, 29, 34, 35, 48, 52, 59, 72, 85 and 89.

[11] ibid., p. 57. In the preceding stanza Yeats gives as an example of primary civilization, where 'nature' overwhelms 'spirit' ('knowledge increases unreality'), 'a fat dreamer of the Middle Ages'.

[12] *Last Poems and Plays*, 'A Model for the Laureate,' p. 44.

[13] ibid., 'What was Lost,' p. 36.

[14] ibid., 'The Statesman's Holiday,' p. 77.

The burden is an allusion to Irish tradition. Avallon (or Avalon) was a legendary island inhabited by beautiful women; in an article about that island, Th. M. Th. Chotzen[1] writes that the monks of Glastonbury, then Giraldus in his *Speculum Ecclesiae*, had proposed the cult of Avallon as an explanation for the name of Avallon. We might wonder if the Giraldus mentioned above, author of the *Speculum Ecclesiae*, is not Yeats's Giraldus, author of the *Speculum Angelorum et Hominum*. After describing the book as printed at Cracow in 1594, Yeats writes: 'I had made a fruitless attempt to identify my Giraldus with Giraldus of Bologna. . . . The day after, an old Arab walked unannounced into my room. He said that he had been sent, stood where the *Speculum* lay open at the wheel marked with the phases of the moon, described it as the doctrine of his tribe. . . .'[2]

Yeats's ideas on the present time find their last and most perfect expression in 'Under Ben Bulben'.[3] The present appears to Yeats as contemptible and submerged by eternity:

> Many times man lives and dies
> Between his two eternities,
> That of race and that of soul,
> And ancient Ireland knew it all.

This double eternity is not a simplification of what Yeats says about the after-life in *A Vision*: it is a new idea which preoccupied him during his last year, and strengthened his belief in metempsychosis, or the return of the same phases:

> Though grave-diggers' toil is long,
> Sharp their spades, their muscles strong,
> They but thrust their buried men
> Back in the human mind again.

There are some moments when men, through the intermediacy of their *daimons*, may communicate with the Great Memory:

> Something drops from eyes long blind,
> He completes his partial mind,
> For an instant stands at ease,
> Laughs aloud, his heart at peace.

and:

> Bring the soul of man to God,

[1] *Études Celtiques*, vol. 4, fasc. 2, 1948.   [2] *A Vision*, pp. 38 and 40.
[3] *Last Poems and Plays*, p. 89.

Works of art, according to Yeats, have the perfection of eternity
and the power to bring men into communication with God, or with
the eternal spirit which animates the movements of the gyres.
Egyptian architecture, Greek sculpture, and Renaissance paintings are

> Proof that there is a purpose set
> Before the secret working mind:
> Profane perfection of mankind.

Art purifies the soul, for it brings us to the states of mind described
in the *Mandookya Upanishad* and in *A Vision*:

> Quattrocento put in paint
> On backgrounds for a God or Saint
> Gardens where a soul's at ease;
> Where everything that meets the eye,
> Flowers and grass and cloudless sky,
> Resemble forms that are or seem
> When sleepers wake and yet still dream,
> And when it's vanished still declare,
> With only bed and bedstead there,
> That heavens had opened.

The same conviction, that works of art are eternal, is to be found
in 'Lapis Lazuli'.[1] 'Under Ben Bulben' contains a summary of
Yeats's history, or history of art. Since Michael Angelo the decline of
art has been gradual, and our epoch is unworthy of art:

> Gyres run on;
> When that greater dream had gone
> Calvert and Wilson, Blake and Claude,
> Prepared a rest for the people of God,
> Palmer's phrase, but after that
> Confusion fell upon our thought.

Considering the indignity of our time, Yeats turns to Irish poets
and advises them to look back to the past, when life was worth living:

> Irish poets, learn your trade,
> Sing whatever is well made,

[1] ibid., p. 4.

Scorn the sort now growing up
All out of shape from toe to top,
Their unremembering hearts and heads
Base-born products of base beds.
Sing the peasantry, and then
Hard-riding country-gentlemen,
The holiness of monks, and after
Porter-drinkers' randy laughter;
Sing the lords and ladies gay
That were beaten into the clay
Through seven heroic centuries;
Cast your minds on other days
That we in coming days may be
Still the indomitable Irishry.

Democracy, in Yeats's system, means confusion, and the best order is that of a state with its One, its Few and its Many. In the last section of the poem Yeats expresses his utter indifference towards the present time. The same feeling inspires 'The Old Stone Cross':[1]

> Because this age and the next age
> Engender in the ditch

The contrast and the coexistence of the present and eternity, of the light of day and the mystery of night, of human activity and of still water (a lunar, antithetical symbol) are the themes of 'The Long-legged Fly'. A fly walking upon a stream, touching the surface but not sinking, is the symbol of man emerging from silence, mystery and death. Caesar or power, feminine grace or beauty and Michael Angelo or art are successively compared to the fly, and the three stanzas are united by the burden:

> *Like a long-legged fly upon the stream*
> *His mind moves upon silence.*

which suggests the vain and incessant activities of life as opposed to the evenness and fixity of the system. As Yeats used to go fishing every day during certain periods, the image of the burden refers precisely to a small, calm stream, in a silent place. Each of the three stanzas exalts what the poet praises in 'Under Ben Bulben': profane

[1] ibid., p. 45.

perfection of mankind; the first symbolizes human power and is partly explained by Yeats's saying that 'a civilization is a struggle to keep self-control':[1]

> That civilization may not sink,
> Its great battle lost,
> Quiet the dog, tether the pony
> To a distant post;
> Our master Caesar is in the tent
> Where the maps are spread,
> His eyes fixed upon nothing,
> A hand under his head.

The theme of the second stanza is Helen's perfect beauty, for the sake of which Troy was burnt:

> That the topless towers be burnt
> And men recall that face,
> Move gently if move you must
> In this lonely place.
> She thinks, part woman, three parts a child,
> That nobody looks; her feet
> Practise a tinker shuffle
> Picked up on a street.

The contrast or 'conflict' between war and Caesar's fixity in the first stanza, between destruction and beauty in the second stanza show the influence of the system. Another form of human perfection is Michael Angelo's art. The contrast between the luxuriant paintings and the silence of the working hand is an effect inspired by the system: 'The eighth gyre, which corresponds to phases 16, 17, and 18 and completes itself say between 1550 and 1650, begins with Raphael, Michael Angelo and Titian, and the forms, as in Titian, awaken sexual desire—we had not desired to touch the forms of Botticelli or even Da Vinci—or they threaten us like those of Michael Angelo, and the painter himself handles his brush with a conscious facility or exultation. The subject-matter may arise out of some propaganda as when Raphael in the Camera della Segnatura, and Michael Angelo in the Sistine Chapel, put, by direction of the Pope, Greek Sages and Doctors of the Church, Roman Sibyls and Hebrew Prophets opposite

[1] *A Vision*, p. 268.

one another in apparent equality.'[1] After the Renaissance, art becomes more and more primary, the painters are overwhelmed by
nature and paint what they do not desire at all. These considerations
are in the background of the third stanza, although the images are
beautiful when stripped of their meaning:

> That girls at puberty may find
> The first Adam in their thought,
> Shut the door of the Pope's chapel,
> Keep those children out.
> There on that scaffolding reclines
> Michael Angelo.
> With no more sound than the mice make
> His hand moves to and fro.

The contrast between the mysterious silence of eternity and human
activities is carried further in 'What Then?'[2] The poem seems puzz-
ling at first sight, but the meaning is simple and easy to find. The
answer to 'What Then?' is that nothing comes to an end on the earth,
that everything turns and comes back, so that what we achieve is indecisive, necessarily unfinished and has its solution in death or in
another life, or in several other lives. Yeats chooses, very appropri-
ately, the type of the successful man for his subject, that is, the man
who is likely to boast of having arrived at something. It is a man who
is successful at school, in love, and a successful writer who did
exactly what he had projected to do:

> Let the fools rage, I swerved in nought,
> Something to perfection brought;
> But louder sang that ghost, 'What then?'

Man does not complete his destiny in this life only, and history is
not a succession of periods which end definitively and never appear
later. The past is also the future, and any prediction must be founded
upon a sure knowledge of the past: this is why, in 'News for the
Delphic Oracle', the poet, in order to look at the future, remembers
the past, and especially the classical era and the heroic age of the
Celts. Niamh and Oisin are associated with Pythagoras.

Yeats's indifference towards the present, which is disguised in
'News for the Delphic Oracle', becomes indifference towards life

---

[1] *A Vision*, p. 293. [2] *Last Poems and Plays*, p. 18.

in 'The Man and the Echo',[1] where Yeats shows his concern for the influence of his works and for the evil times:

> And all seems evil until I
> Sleepless would lie down and die.

But the Echo answers:

> Lie down and die.

Instead of lamenting the disappearance of all that men loved, we should rejoice, for a new era is coming. The works of art participate in eternity, and therefore are not influenced by the sadness of the times: this is the theme of 'Lapis Lazuli'.[2] It is a mistake to think that works of art should be useful: they cannot change or improve the world, but they can transfigure it and show the eternal aspect of all changing, dreadful things: 'poets are always gay.' This is an opportunity for Yeats to develop his ideas on tragedy, which are similar to those of Euripides, who said that only joy can engender a tragedy, the joy, according to Yeats, of performing a part of the divine scheme:

> They know that Hamlet and Lear are gay;
> Gaiety transfiguring all that dread.
> All men have aimed at, found and lost;
> Black out; Heaven blazing into the head:
> Tragedy wrought to its uttermost.

Civilizations and works of art are destroyed, but only for a time:

> All things fall and are built again,
> And those that build them again are gay.

A Chinese carving on lapis lazuli admired by the poet suggests that, although the scene is tragic, the characters are gay:

> Their eyes mid many wrinkles, their eyes,
> Their ancient, glittering eyes, are gay.

The gaiety of these Chinese eyes as well as the gaiety of Hamlet and Lear is immortal: the works of art stand beyond history, although they manifest themselves in time. Yeats's immortal souls, which are independent from changing appearances, correspond to the Platonic ideas. The soul is wrapped in a cloth of changing thoughts and

[1] ibid., p. 83.   [2] ibid., p. 4.

desires and is immovable, whatever the 'conflicts' and changes may be. This explains an image of the gyres which appears frequently:

> Wound in mind's wandering
> As mummies in the mummy-cloth are wound.

The soul's independence from time and its purification in a solitary life is the subject of 'All Souls' Night, Epilogue to "A Vision" '.[1] The poet calls before him the ghosts, that is, the eternal shape, of some of his dead friends. The distinction between a thing and its idea or its essence is applied even to physical things, for a ghost can drink the essence of wine:

> A ghost may come;
> For it is a ghost's right,
> His element is so fine
> Being sharpened by his death,
> To drink from the wine-breath
> While our gross palates drink from the whole wine.

Then the poet announces that he has to tell a mummy-truth, that is, a truth which is not concerned with time, but with eternity. Among the friends he calls to his memory is Florence Emery, or the actress Florence Farr who left her country for Ceylon, where she taught at the Ramanathan College and was initiated in Buddhism:

> Before that end much had she ravelled out
> From a discourse in figurative speech
> By some learned Indian
> On the soul's journey. How it is whirled about,
> Wherever the orbit of the moon can reach,
> Until it plunge into the sun;
> And there, free and yet fast,
> Being both Chance and Choice,
> Forget its broken toys
> And sinks into its own delight at last.

Yeats had written *The Land of Heart's Desire* for Florence Farr and both belonged to a secret society (called the O.G.D.) for the study of occultism.[2] The third friend 'called up from the grave', MacGregor,

---

[1] *Collected Poems*, p. 256.
[2] cf. *Florence Farr, B. Shaw and W. B. Yeats, Letters*, London, Home & Van Thal, 1946.

is the type of man whose thoughts estrange him from other men
and whose life is half-terrestrial, half-celestial:

> He had much industry at setting out,
> Much boisterous courage, before loneliness
> Had driven him crazed;
> For meditations upon unknown thought
> Make human intercourse grow less and less;
> They are neither paid nor praised.
> But he'd object to the host,
> The glass because my glass;
> A ghost-lover he was
> And may have grown more arrogant being a ghost.

Yeats had met MacGregor at the British Museum and had been
introduced by him to a society of Christian cabalists, 'The Hermetic
Students'. This meeting kindled Yeats's interest in symbolic systems
and did not pass unnoticed in the *Autobiographies*.[1] Some points in
Mathers' doctrine influenced Yeats's system; for example, his interpretation of solar as meaning elaborate, rich, and resembling the
work of goldsmiths (this interpretation, already mentioned in 1896,
does not correspond exactly to what is meant by 'primary tincture',
which inspires the Byzantium poems), and of lunar as meaning all
that is simple, traditional, and emotional.[2]

The concluding section of 'All Souls' Night' is concerned with the
states of mind described in *The Soul in Judgment*[3] and *Initiation upon a
Mountain*,[4] evoking the circles of Hell and Paradise which are for
Yeats a symbol of eternity:

> Such thought—such thought have I that hold it tight
> Till meditation master all its parts,
> Nothing can stay my glance
> Until that glance run in the world's despite
> To where the damned have howled away their hearts,
> And where the blessed dance;
> Such thought, that in it bound
> I need no other thing,
> Wound in mind's wandering
> As mummies in the mummy-cloth are wound.

[1] p. 230.   [2] cf. Jeffares, *Yeats*, p. 105.   [3] *A Vision*, pp. 219 to 240.
[4] *The Criterion*, July 1934.

Although closely connected with the system, this description is made in general terms and reminds us of the familiar images of Hell, Purgatory, and Paradise, so that the reader does not need the help of esoteric science.

Yeats's desire for eternity and for the eternal symbols of history is expressed in the two Byzantium poems. The first one, 'Sailing to Byzantium',[1] is built upon the contrast between the present primary civilization and the antithetical civilization of Byzantium, for we are now approaching the dark moon, whereas Byzantine civilization corresponded to the full moon: 'If I were left to myself I would make Phase 15 coincide with Justinian's reign, that great age of building in which one may conclude Byzantine art was perfected.'[2] Byzantine civilization is described as 'elaborate, rich, and resembling the work of goldsmiths', but it is typically lunar and represents the perfection of the spirit as opposed to nature. This contrast, which summarizes Yeats's system, is clearly defined in the following passage: 'There is a continual conflict—I too have my dialectic—the perfection of Nature is the decline of Spirit, the perfection of Spirit is the decline of Nature.'[3] The sensual imagery of 'Leda and the Swan', representing the birth of both the classical era and the next one, is shown, in 'Sailing to Byzantium', in contrast to the intellectual beauty of Byzantium, and the voyage to Byzantium is the symbol of the poet's desire to leave his own time, a time of revolution where nature overwhelms the spirit, and where works of art, of the immortal spirit, are destroyed.

The essential ideas of the Byzantium poems are expressed in prose in *A Vision*, and, to elucidate the meaning of the poems, a long passage should be transcribed: 'With a desire for simplicity of statement I would have preferred to find in the middle, not at the end, of the fifth century, Phase 12, for that was, so far as the known evidence carries us, the moment when Byzantium became Byzantium and substituted for formal Roman magnificence, with its glorification of physical power, an architecture that suggests the Sacred City in the Apocalypse of St. John. I think if I could be given a month of Antiquity and leave to spend it where I chose, I would spend it in Byzantium a little before Justinian opened St. Sophia and closed the Academy of Plato. I think I could find in some little wine-shop some

[1] *Collected Poems*, p. 217.   [2] *A Vision*, p. 281.
[3] *Initiation upon a Mountain* (*The Criterion*, p. 552).

philosophical worker in mosaic who could answer all my questions, the supernatural descending nearer to him than to Plotinus even, for the pride of his delicate skill would make what was an instrument of power to princes and clerics, a murderous madness in the mob, show as a lovely flexible presence like that of a perfect human body.

'I think that in early Byzantium, maybe never before or since in recorded history, religious, aesthetic, and practical life were one, that architect and artificers—though not, it may be, poets, for language had been the instrument of controversy and must have grown abstract—spoke to the multitude and the few alike. The painter, the mosaic worker, the worker in gold and silver, the illuminator of sacred books, were almost impersonal, almost perhaps without the consciousness of individual design, absorbed in their subject-matter and that the vision of a whole people.'[1]

In the first stanza of 'Sailing to Byzantium' the poet explains why he leaves the present time. An old man like Yeats, with a vigorous, creative mind, should escape from a time of dissolution, confusion, physical power, and sensuality. The images evoking this ordeal are similar to those used in 'News for the Delphic Oracle'. Here is the first stanza:

> That is no country for old men. The young
> In one another's arms, birds in the trees,
> —Those dying generations—at their song,
> The salmon-falls, the mackerel-crowded seas,
> Fish, flesh or fowl, commend all summer long
> Whatever is begotten, born, and dies.
> Caught in that sensual music all neglect
> Monuments of unageing intellect.

When Yeats says that a Byzantine artist is nearer to the supernatural than anyone else, he does not mean that the artist receives his inspiration from outside: 'antithetical revelation is an intellectual influx neither from beyond mankind nor born of a virgin, but begotten from our own spirit and history.'[2] 'Does not every civilization as it approaches or recedes from its full moon seem as it were to shiver into the premonition of some perfection born out of itself, perhaps

---

[1] *A Vision*, pp. 279 and 280.   [2] ibid., p. 262.

even of some return to its first Source?'[1] This idea is expressed in two lines:

> Nor is there any singing school but studying
> Monuments of its own magnificence;

This idea is dramatized in the third stanza, where the poet calls for the eternal spirit in the form of the sages represented in Byzantine mosaics, to come and inspire him:

> O sages standing in God's holy fire
> As in the gold mosaic of a wall,
> Come from the holy fire, perne in a gyre,
> And be the singing-masters of my soul.
> Consume my heart away; sick with desire.
> And fastened to a dying animal
> It knows not what it is; and gather me
> Into the artifice of eternity.

The fourth and last stanza is a clear description of the forms of art influenced by the antithetical inflow (coming from 'fire' and opposed to nature), and corresponds exactly to the long prose passage quoted above:

> Once out of nature I shall never take
> My bodily form from any natural thing,
> But such a form as Grecian goldsmiths make
> Of hammered gold and gold enamelling
> To keep a drowsy Emperor awake;
> Or set upon a golden bough to sing
> To lords and ladies of Byzantium
> Of what is past, or passing, or to come.

There is no allusion to purification in 'Sailing to Byzantium': the poet imagines that he can grasp eternity immediately, artificially. 'Byzantium'[2] is different in that respect, for the second poem is not built upon a violent contrast, but involves a transition and contains the images of dolphins and of flames which symbolize the transit or purification of the soul. The idea of these emblems is not taken from *A Vision*, but from *Apotheosis and After-Life*, by Mrs. Strong. The contrast between the confusion of our time, where all activities are

---

[1] *Initiation upon a Mountain* (*The Criterion*, p. 556).
[2] *Collected Poems*, p. 280.

specialized, and the perfect order and 'unity of being' achieved by Byzantine civilization is also suggested in 'Byzantium', but it implies a progressive transition instead of a sudden change, a spiritual expiation instead of a voyage by sea. The difference between the two poems is summed up at the end of Norman Jeffares's excellent interpretation:[1] 'Yeats had been near death in the fiery heat of Maltese fever; and he makes the birds (in the draft of the poem) offer their backs to the wailing dead that they may carry them to Paradise. Both poems are an attempt to praise eternity as a means of forgetting regrets for youth and vigour; but the later poem has been written out of an experience further from life and nearer to death.' The result of Yeats's preoccupation with the life after death is an extension of his system in which he describes the several stages and gyres of conscious or unconscious life undergone until final beatitude is reached. The whole of this complicated and hardly imaginable account, however, has very little influence on the poems, but the following passage should not pass unnoticed: 'I think of those phantoms in ancient costumes seen by some peasant seers exercising such authority. "We have no power," said an inhabitant of the state, "except to purify our intention," and when I asked of what, replied: "Of complexity." But that *Purification* may require the completion of some syntheses left unfinished in its past life. Because only the living create, it may seek the assistance of those living men into whose "unconsciousness" or incarnate *Daimon*, some affinity of aim, or the command of the *Thirteenth Cone*, permits it to enter. Those who taught me this system did so, not for my sake, but their own. . . . I connect them in my imagination with an early conviction of mine, that the creative power of the lyric poet depends upon his accepting some one of a few traditional attitudes, lover, sage, hero, scorner of life. They bring us back to the spiritual norm. They may, however, if permitted by the *Thirteenth Cone*, so act upon the events of our lives as to compel us to attend to that perfection which, though it seems theirs, is the work of our own Daimon.'[2] The images of perfection evoked in 'Byzantium' must therefore be understood as the work of Yeats's Daimon. Perfection as opposed to complexity, purification to death, is symbolized in the first stanza by the white dome emerging from the night:

[1] *W. B. Yeats, Man and Poet*, pp. 261 and 262.
[2] *A Vision*, pp. 233 and 234.

The unpurged images of day recede;
The Emperor's drunken soldiery are abed;
Night resonance recedes, night-walkers' song
After great cathedral gong;
A starlit or a moonlit dome disdains
All that man is,
All mere complexities,
The fury and the mire of human veins.

The second stanza alludes to the stages and gyres of expiation and purification, and to the bonds which characterize these stages: 'So closely do all the bonds resemble each other that in the most ascetic schools of India the novice tortured by his passion will pray to the God to come to him as a woman and have with him sexual intercourse.'[1] Here is the second stanza:

Before me floats an image, man or shade,
Shade more than man, more image than a shade;
For Hades' bobbin bound in mummy-cloth
May unwind the winding path;
A mouth that has no moisture and no breath
Breathless mouths may summon;
I hail the superhuman;
I call it death-in-life and life-in-death.

In the third stanza the theme is the same as in the first one, and to the image of the dome corresponds the image of an eternal bird on a golden bough:

Miracle, bird or golden handiwork,
More miracle than bird or handiwork,
Planted on the star-lit golden bough,
Can like the cocks of Hades crow,
Or, by the moon embittered, scorn aloud
In glory of changeless metal
Common bird or petal
And all complexities of mire or blood.

Although the theme of expiation is already introduced in the second stanza, the symbols of purification appear only in the fourth

[1] ibid., p. 239.

and fifth. The word 'fire', as it is used in 'Byzantium', does not refer to antithetical phases, but to purgation, for the gyres of the after-life involve again primary as well as antithetical phases: '*antithetical* cruelty and deceit must be expiated in *primary* suffering and submission, or the old tragedy will be repeated.'[1] 'Byzantium' is not built, like 'Sailing to Byzantium', upon the contrast between primary and antithetical civilizations. According to Jeffares,[2] Yeats had read *The Age of Justinian and Theodora*, by W. G. Holmes, and marked the passage describing the Forum of Constantine, known as 'The Pavement'; this explains part of the imagery of the fourth stanza:

> At midnight on the Emperor's pavement flit
> Flames that no faggot feeds, nor steel has lit,
> Nor storms disturbs, flames begotten of flame,
> And all complexities of fury leave,
> Dying into a dance,
> An agony of trance,
> An agony of flame that cannot singe a sleeve.

The passage from 'blood' to 'fire', from complexity to 'unity of being', and the symbolic dolphins transfigured by Byzantine artists are described in the last stanza:

> Astraddle on the dolphin's mire and blood,
> Spirit after spirit! The smithies break the flood,
> The golden smithies of the Emperor!
> Marbles of the dancing floor
> Break bitter furies of complexity,
> Those images that yet
> Fresh images beget,
> That dolphin-torn, that gong-tormented sea.

The dolphins, the smithies, the marbles and the gong (the *semantron* of Byzantine churches), opposed to the mire and blood, the flood, the dancing floor, the furies of complexity and the sea allude to the gradual liberation of the soul in its flight from circle to circle: 'Neither between death and birth nor between birth and death can the soul find more than momentary happiness; its object is to pass rapidly round its circle and find freedom from that circle.'[3] Similar

---

[1] ibid., p. 237. [2] *W. B. Yeats, Man and Poet*, p. 260.
[3] *A Vision*, p. 236.

images, with the same meaning, appear in 'News for the Delphic Oracle':

> Straddling each a dolphin's back
> And steadied by a fin,
> Those Innocents re-live their death,
> Their wounds open again.
> The ecstatic waters laugh because
> Their cries are sweet and strange,
> Through their ancestral patterns dance,
> And the brute dolphins plunge
> Until, in some cliff-sheltered bay
> Where wades the choir of love
> Proffering its sacred laurel crowns,
> They pitch their burdens off.

The perfect image of beauty is found when the soul has freed itself from impurities, beyond the psychological and historical circles.

There is no purification, however, without evil, and many poems of Yeats's last period are, not an acceptation, but an affirmation, of evil, which corresponds to his desire for a rehabilitation of the senses. This attitude induced him to write two kinds of poetry: the poetry written when his energy was at a low ebb, in which he displays a patient craftsmanship, and the passionate poetry written in moments of physical health. The Byzantium poems may be included in the first category, and Keats may be chosen as a representative, whereas the Crazy Jane poems are typical of a passionate poetry in which sensuality is curiously mixed with spirituality. Although he lacked the vision of evil,[1] Shelley might serve as an example of an impulsive poet as opposed to a craftsman, but he might also illustrate the conflict between the solitary and proud poet who praises intellectual beauty and the gregarious man who writes humanitarian pamphlets.

Without his system Yeats could not have extended the scope of his poetry to such a dramatic diversity of expression, and Eliot's dismissal of the system as a minor philosophy[2] comes from a prejudice against Yeats's ideas, but does not impair the fact that these ideas contribute to a great poetry.

[1] cf. H. W. Häusermann: *W. B. Yeats's Idea of Shelley*, (*The Mint*, Routledge, 1946, p. 179); and *The Crooked Road*, by F. O. Matthiessen (*The Southern Review*, Winter 1941, p. 467).

[2] *The Poetry of W. B. Yeats*, by T. S. Eliot (*The Southern Review*, Winter 1941, p. 442).

CHAPTER II

THOUGHT IN EDWIN MUIR'S POETRY

MUIR AND HIS TIME

IN order to place Edwin Muir in his time, it is convenient to use the method he employs in *Transition, Essays on Contemporary Literature.*[1]

Muir's criticism is linked with his poetical thought. According to him the works of art express their time, through which they define themselves, and yet should be sufficiently detached from their time to be able to watch it objectively.

The literature of our time, according to Muir, is a literature of transition, which questions the validity of every aspect of life because no one knows where we are going to: 'There is hardly an aspect of life, hardly a feeling or a general conception, which the universal questioning of our age has left untouched.'[2] Our time is so uncertain that we are unable to see it clearly, and writers become puzzled and unstable: 'If poetry is conditional and ironical, affirming and denying in one breath, what response could be more natural to a world which has changed so rapidly that no one knows where he stands?'[3] To certain changes in life, however, some definite trends in modern literature correspond, as for example: 'In the main, English poetry has been a poetry of the English country; it is now a poetry chiefly of the town.'[4] Muir is not much influenced by new literary trends: he accepts his time because he sees it in relation to the past, although he proposes that 'we must shape here a new philosophy':

'When a force determining men's lives is indefinable, inescapable, and overpowering, it will arouse hostility in those who realize its power, and this hostility will be the more intense the more intense the realization.'[5]

Muir accepts this force because he is able to withdraw from it and

[1] Hogarth Press, London, 1926.   [2] *Transition*, p. 194.   [3] ibid., p. 185.
[4] ibid., p. 182.   [5] ibid., p. 4.

consider it as an object. He knows that he cannot change it and, besides, that its significance changes in proportion as his attitude changes:

'Without this hostility against itself, the spirit of no age could come to realization; it would remain undifferentiated and unawakened; it could never be objectified, for all objectivation implies separation.'[1]

The word 'spirit' is used here to suggest a materialist notion, since spirit and matter, in this connotation, are not opposed to each other: the 'Zeit Geist' fights against itself:

'Yet it is the "Zeit Geist", the mass of suggestion, desire and suffering of the time, which differentiates one literary period from another; by presenting a new resistance it provokes a new response.'[2]

The struggle of a force against itself is not a fight of two different enemies: Muir's dualism is not the opposition, in his thought, of two different realities, but of two different conceptions of the same reality, and of two different attitudes towards the same reality. 'The force determining men's lives is indefinable, inescapable, and overpowering', and the poet escapes it all the more because he is conscious of it. By being conscious of it, he objectifies it, and is free to confer a meaning upon it, so that it depends, after all, upon his attitude, which allows for a free vision of a mechanical world.

Although Muir rarely deals in his poetry with modern subjects and, when he does, avoids an original, sarcastic, and hostile treatment, he reacts by opposing to the deliquescence of his time a coherent thought and an established tradition. He is not upset by actual circumstances, which do not seem to mean anything new to him:

> I could neither rise nor fall
> But that Adam fell.[3]

The stable equipoise between his thought and his time excludes Muir from the categories described by him in the following passage from *Transition*:

'If Mr. Huxley is our best example of the fashionable writer, and Mr. Joyce of the artist expressing the age by an uncompromising opposition to it, there is a figure equally significant as a writer of escape.'[4] (D. H. Lawrence.) And: 'All the important writers of our time belong to these categories. In some there is a divided allegiance,

---

[1] ibid., p. 5.   [2] ibid., p. 12.
[3] *The Voyage*, London, Faber and Faber, 1946, p. 18.   [4] *Transition*, p. 14.

in Mr. Eliot most strikingly, who in his poetry sets side by side the response of the poet who desires to escape from his environment, and that of the critic of life who wishes to come to terms with it. The rank of these writers will be determined by the thing which at present determines their value for us: the profundity, comprehensiveness and truth of their criticism of contemporary life.'[1]

In order to criticize his time, a writer must be detached from it. This does not mean that he is an escapist. It implies, however, that a writer should give way to a force strong enough to resist the pressure of events and to bring order and meaning to life: such is the task which Muir sets before him as a poet, and, considering the growing mastery of his thought, we might infer that he is rather successful. Muir's opinion of modern poets in that respect is negative:

'The response of the poet to this world is not pessimism, for pessimism is a reasonable and traditional thing; it is rather a bewilderment and distress of mind. The poet is not concerned because ideals do not correspond to realities (a great source of pessimistic poetry); he is hardly concerned with ideals at all. His bewilderment springs from something far more complex: the feeling that reality itself has broken down, that even the simple emotions, the instinctive reactions, are disorientated and lead us astray. This bewilderment has not the absoluteness of pessimism, but it is nevertheless more completely without consolations.'[2]

The world is changing so much that we utter relative truths and see passing, unconvincing beauties, either because we are blind and unable to think or because the world is inconsistent and unseizable: according to Muir, we are blind because we live in an epoch of transition, in 'the modern world which has risen silently around us'. Modern poets lack assurance and, if they have enough assurance, they lack persuasion, for their thought is without basis:

'The present dislike for "the pathetic fallacy" and for *catharsis* is peculiar to a society which is not integrated. Once postulate a great order and these things become inevitable, for any enduring belief, the belief of a civilization in God, in humanity, or in itself, makes certain things pathetic and tragic, giving its meaning naturally and involuntarily to the varied accidents of life.'[3]

Muir finds a basis in the rigidity of his main theme, time, and his perpetual effort to break time's fixity and to redeem time's lack of

[1] ibid., pp. 15 and 16. [2] ibid., p. 188. [3] ibid., p. 193.

meaning is his own solution of the problem of how to strengthen one-self against life, of which he writes about James Joyce: 'That problem must needs have been the problem of all the things from which he suffered, for the sincere artist is distinguished from the rest by the fact that his essential concern is with the things which make him suffer, the things, in other words, which stand between him and freedom.'[1]

Muir's preoccupation with the destiny of our time incited him, in 1946,[2] to draw a comparison with the time of Shakespeare, which was also a time of transition and which may be seen objectively. The tragedy of King Lear results, according to Muir, from the struggle of tradition against opportunism, of society against individualism and of moral conscience against nature: 'the medieval world with its communal tradition was slowly dying, and the modern individualist world was bringing itself to birth. Shakespeare lived in that violent period of transition.'[3] The old world is represented by Lear: 'he sets against the idea of natural freedom the sacred tradition of human society.'[4] The new world is not unknown to us: 'We know, too, that Shakespeare was acquainted with the Renaissance man, and that his plays abound in references to "policy", which stood in his time for what the Germans dignify by the name of *Realpolitik*, that is political action which ignores all moral considerations.'[5] Edmund is the pro-totype of the ambitious man without scruples, and Lear's daughters are not less representative of the new generation: 'Their life in the moment, their decisions based on what the mere moment presents, their want of continuity, their permanent empty newness, are suffi-cient in themselves to involve them with nature, for nature is always new and has no background: it is society that is old. Their position may be defined by saying that they claim a liberty which is proper to nature but not to society.'[6] Free choice in an established society is opposed to arbitrary power in a weak society, and it is the irony of life to transform natural liberty into fate.

MUIR'S VISION

The idea of time occupies a large place in Muir's thought, and his poems express his various impressions and ideas about the same real-

[1] ibid., p. 23. [2] *The Politics of King Lear*, Glasgow, Jackson, 1947.
[3] ibid., p. 7. [4] ibid., p. 19. [5] ibid., p. 16. [6] ibid., p. 18.

ity. Time, however, does not appear, in Muir's poems, as a fixed object or as a definitive abstraction: it is modified by the various standpoints and attitudes of the poet, so that the unity of his works consists in the coherence of his interpretation of time rather than in the recurrence of the same theme. Although he did not base his poems upon a philosophical system, or group them according to the thought they express, he presents in each of them one aspect of a complex and solid vision, although the object of the vision is elusive and deceitful. It would be impossible, indeed, to group the poems according to their themes, because there is almost no succession; they are all mature fruit of the same seed, and it is the task of the analyst to relate their individual characteristics to their common origin.

Each poem could be considered separately, but the whole is so coherent that it is better not to lose sight of it. The most explicit and comprehensive poems expose and solve a duality which is the spring of Muir's poetical tension. Two images are struggling against each other: a fatal and unbreakable chain of events, and an obscure path leading to a bright destination.

Besides his poems, Edwin Muir has written on such practical questions as *Social Credit and the Labour Party* (1939). Idealism is balanced in him by a broad-minded materialism, and his poems attempt to blend these two views and to mark their intersection. His idealism is controlled by his materialism and his materialism is enlightened by his idealism: he never surrenders to one conception: he unites them in the poetic experience, which is the perpetual creation of a balance.

As a Scot, he feels in himself the racial and historical forces which formed his nation and which become the symbol of a pre-ordained fate. He describes the hardness and perseverance of his race in a little book entitled *The Scots* and in *Scott and Scotland: the Predicament of the Scottish writer* (1936, Routledge).

It should be emphasized that Muir does not vacillate between materialism and spiritualism, and that the struggle of his interacting conceptions is not developed in philosophical terms, but in concrete images. His conception might be summarized as a blending of the feeling of tragic necessity in the Greek manner, and of the Christian conceptions of the Fall, of Grace and of Resurrection. That conception is very complex and comprehensive. Some would say contradictory instead of comprehensive, but they would think of a philosophical system instead of looking at the solution proposed by the poems. Muir's poetry is not the exposition of two opposed systems, but the expression of two visions converging on the same object. The first vision is objective, whereas the second starts from a high and broad plane of consciousness and requires the intervention of intuition and personal judgment. Both visions are valid, but one is finally substituted for the other, for they are two degrees of awareness indicating a spiritual progress (in 'The Three Mirrors',[1] Muir distinguishes three stages of awareness).

Muir is perhaps, among contemporary poets, the one who shows best the profound difference between philosophical speculation and poetical vision. He does not try to explain the world, adapting his conceptions to the characteristics of their objects: he integrates the world in his images and transforms or transfigurates it according to the progress of his vision.

THE GROWTH OF MUIR'S POETICAL THOUGHT

Muir's poems are coherent as a whole and achieved in a process of growth. Some of the *First Poems*[2] contain elements which tend to disappear in the last ones, and some contain elements which are more and more emphasized. The development of Edwin Muir is not simply a change from luxuriance to restraint, from richness to power, as happens with some other poets, it is also a shifting of themes and a gradual acquisition of a firm thought.

It has been noted that young poets are often rhetorical and exaggerated. Muir's *First Poems* were published when he was thirty-eight (in 1925): they are already poems of maturity, and to some extent less rhetorical than the later poems. But they are more rhetorical in that they are more contrasted: the *First Poems* are bursts of poetry, the later ones are a slow, cohesive gestation. They are full of contrasts: the later ones are built on oppositions and crystallize in a vision which, like the earth, has two poles.

Some of the *First Poems*, like 'Salsburg—November' (1939), are without a single abstract idea: Muir's career has been a gradual capture of his thought, and a gradual infusion of his thought into his impressions. His first ideas are complex and shy enough to 'betray some

[1] *The Voyage*, p. 26.
[2] London, Hogarth Press, 1925

79

influences, among which two inseparable poems seem to predomin-
ate, Coleridge's *Ode to Dejection* and Wordsworth's *Ode on Intimations of
Immortality*.[1] The two romantic poets regret that they are no longer
able to see the visions of childhood (cf. Herbert Read's 'innocent
eye'): 'there hath past away a glory from the earth': beauty springs
from nostalgia. Muir's beginning is a romantic one, he is tossed between mythological dreams and reality:

> Ah, this is not my haven; oft before
> I have stood here and wept for the other shore.[2]

Beauty comes from his recollections of early childhood, it is a desperate reminiscence of what is lost. Such an attitude recurs in *Journeys and Places*,[3] where beauty is often identified with the age of innocence in Eden, before the Fall.

The attempt, which the poet was bound to make, to unite dreams
and reality, and to present them as a coherent whole, is successful in
some later poems which will be examined at the end of this study.
The first poems enunciate the problem which is solved in the later
ones. The key of the solution is Muir's dualism and, more particularly, his ambiguous conception of time, for time is both binding and
loosening, it is the accomplishment of destiny and the sign of deliverance from fate. In the *First Poems*, however, the deliverance is not yet
apparent:

> For still she smiles, and does not know
> Her feet are in the snaring lime.
> He who entrapped her long ago,
> And kills her, is unpitying Time.[4]

As long as he does not possess the key, the poet, yearning for beauty,
can find peace only in such a convincing evasion as the 'Ballad of
E ernal Life'.[5] But he is nevertheless aware of man's double nature:
'lust for the unmoving mire' and spirit; soul and body are separated,
but the soul is not stained by the body:

[1] Begun on 27 March 1802, the second half was written after Wordsworth had
read Coleridge's poem.
[2] *First Poems, The Lost Land*, p. 11.
[3] *Journeys and Places*, London, Dent, 1937.
[4] *First Poems, Betrayal*, p. 30.
[5] ibid., p. 51.

> But my soul hovered, trembling still,
>   On the bleak empty air,
> Waited, and feared, and knew full well
>   What still must happen there.

The contrast is heightened in the last stanza of the *Ballad of Rebirth*:

> My limbs are strong as the deep hills,
>   Set on the enduring slime,
> But my eyes were forged in Paradise,
>   And have forgotten Time![1]

A comparison between 'When the Trees Grow Bare on the High Hills'[2] and the poem entitled 'The Narrow Place'[3] would show the difference between first and mature poetry, between spontaneous, flowery poetry on the one hand and austere, controlled poetry on the other. The setting of the early poem is romantic and autumnal, and the substance is made of impressions:

> The wrinkled sun-memoried leaves fall down
> From black tall branches
> Through the gleaming air,
> And wonder is lost,
> Dissolving in space,
>
> .   .   .   .   .
>
> And in mere memory, mere dream,
> Attainment breathes itself out,
> Perfect and cold.

On the other hand, 'The Narrow Place' is more austere, cogent, less florid and less dazzling, but more suggestive of thought:

> It is your murdering eyes that make
> The sterile hill, the standing lake,
> And the leaf-breaking wind.

A small highland tree is a sufficient symbol in 'The Narrow Place': a forest is needed in the early poem.

[1] ibid., p. 48.
[2] ibid., p. 35.
[3] *The Narrow Place and Other Poems*, London, Faber and Faber, 1943, p. 20.

THOUGHT IN EDWIN MUIR'S POETRY

THE FORMULATION OF TIME'S AMBIGUITY

The key to Muir's thought, his discovery of the double aspect of time, and the transition between the *First Poems* and the later poetry are represented mainly by *Variations on a Time Theme*.[1] The predominant idea of this poem-sequence could be expressed thus: man is enslaved by time, but time is but an agent of a superior justice. The poet, however, does not seem to be quite satisfied with the solution he has found, for in each variation he utters a cry of desolation. The thought of each variation will be summarized under its corresponding number.

1 Time and imperfection are synonymous. The poet who, in youthful enthusiasm, sang of eternity, of gods and dragons, now turns to time, limitation, isolation:

> We have walked
> In radiance and in darkness. Now this twilight.

2. Time is symbolized, in the second variation, by mortal horses who perpetually turn around the same spot and we as their riders fall off. Our fate and duty is to live in time as if it were eternity:

> So we must mourn or rejoice
> For this our station, our inheritance
> As if it were all. This plain all. This journey all.

3. Time appears as a whole: Adam, Noah, and the poet are one, but Eden is lost and, as long as time lasts, man will be searching for eternity:

> . . . now I walk the sand
> And search this rubble for the promised land.

4. When history is taken as a whole, time is transformed into eternity because time is a repetition of the same acts; time, as a whole, is fixed, eternal.

5 Men are stationary, whereas the world changes around them; the past of mankind is forgotten, but lives in us, if death can be said to live.

6. Yet there are brief intermittences of revelation in the fixity of time and destiny, where a superior reality makes itself known as if we

[1] London, Dent, 1934.

82

were moving towards a goal. Moses' laws and Christian hope announce our deliverance:

> . . . when we shall leave this sand
> And enter the unknown and feared and longed-for land.

7. The promise of salvation haunts the poet who thinks that, if we are time's prey, eternity, although 'lost and empty', exists.

8. The poet identifies himself with Sebastian, tortured and his eyes full of visions, or with Socrates at Marathon contemplating the defeat of struggling time.

The only stratagem to win in the battle against time is to retreat, to escape. Even Plato and Shakespeare were nourished by time and did not avoid its verdict.

The poet wishes he could rob time of sparkles of eternity, but

> It is not I but Time that is the fisher.

Man is caught in the nets of time, but time is a flame which burns itself out, leaving eternity, which some men, although caught in time, have the strength to contemplate.

9. The poet tells of his two visitors, indifference, for whom everything is a matter of time, and the soul, who pities all:

> On these double horns
> I take my comfort, they're my truckle bed.

The two opposed attitudes, indifference and pity, live by each other; the death of pity would be the triumph of indifference, but the death of indifference would be the death of pity. It is convenient, therefore, to consider life, or time, as a tragedy which excites pity:

> A mimic stage where all the day
> A phantom hound pursues a phantom prey,
> Where the slain rise and smile upon the slayer.

When pity prevails over indifference, when pity that is, invents a stage to play with time's indifference, then the soul is at rest:

> Oh, then, at such deceitful art,
> Tears, real and burning, from my lids would start,
> And peace would burst into my heart.

10. The last variation introduces a new symbol: the lion. The lion

declares war on time, he has a supernatural strength, he becomes
Christ and even as such he is derisively fixed on the wheel of time,
like the Lion of the Constellation. His strength was once quenched by
a wave of time, the revolt against time was subdued by a storm: it is as
if the revolt had not happened and as if it had to be stirred again:

> Ignorant that the dragon died
> Long since and that the mountain shook
> When the great lion was crucified.

The revolt of the lion, like the pity of the soul, lasts as long as there
is time; the two opposite forces are still struggling, and mock at each
other. In this poem-sequence, Muir's thought is already crystallized
around two poles: time, involving all mortals, and eternity.

Variations on a Time Theme implies all the ideas of opposition and
struggle which are developed in *The Narrow Place* and *The Voyage and
Other Poems*. The same theme is diversified and amplified in *Journeys
and Places*. 'The Stationary Journey'[1] marks a retrogression of the poet's
thought, for there he considers only the fixity of destiny. He imagines that he travels back in the past, as if past and present were one,
only to emphasize the invincible strength of destiny:

> A dream! the astronomic years
> Patrolled by stars and planets bring
> Time led in chains from post to post
> Of the all-conquering Zodiac ring.

The same theme is handled in 'The Mountains'.[2] The mountains are
the symbol of time: they close the horizon and hide what is beyond,
what can be dreamt of:

> Dreaming of a peak whose height
> Will show me every hill,
> A single mountain on whose side
> Life blooms for ever and is still.

The same idea is suggested by 'The Road':[3]

> There is a road that turning always
> Cuts off the country of Again.

Hope, the idea of the original sin, and recollections of the anterior
life of Eden, dominate the second part of the volume, entitled *Places*.

[1] p. 3.   [2] p. 6.   [3] p. 9.

THE FORMULATION OF TIME'S AMBIGUITY

'The Fall'[1] situates our life in a world of transition oscillating between good and evil:

> And so I build me Heaven and Hell
> To buy my bartered Paradise.

The Fall (in its orthodox meaning) is the cause of man's weakness:

> Before I was a slave, long, long ago,
> I lost a sword in a forgotten fight,
> And ever since my arm has been too light
> For this dense world, and shall grow lighter still.
> Yet through that rage shines Troy's untroubled hill,
> And many a tumbled wall and vanished tree
> Remains, as if in spite, a happy memory.

For the first time since 'Logos',[2] the Word is presented as a source of redemption.

In spite of their titles, implying a static notion, the last poems of *Journeys and Places*[3] are new variations on the theme of time. The titles are justified by Muir's frequent identification of time with destiny. 'The Unfamiliar Place' is the present time, that is, a continuation of unvarying destiny, yet something emergent and new:

> But I am balked by fear
> And what my lips say
> To drown the voice of fear.
> The earthly day waits.

'The earthly day' is terrible because it departs from fate: although destiny is unbreakable, something new is to come.

'The Place of Light and Darkness',[4] 'The Solitary Place' and 'The Private Place' renew the central theme of *Variations* and of 'The Mountain':

> O I shall miss
> With one small breath these centuries
> Of harvest-home uncounted![5]

and:

> the thief Time will steal
> Soft-footed bit by bit this boundless treasure
> Held in four hands.[6]

[1] p. 23.　　　[2] *First Poems*, p. 33.　　　[3] p. 39.　　　[4] p. 41.
[5] p. 43, *The Solitary Place*.　　　[6] *The Private Place*, p. 45.

85

The theme of man's limitation in time leads to the theme of man's aspirations, treated in *The Unattained Place*:[1]

> We have seen the world of good deeds spread
> With its own sky above it
> A length away
> Our whole day,
> Yet have not crossed from our false kindred.

Muir deplores that human condition should be fixed, that we cannot break with time:

> if we could break
> This static hold with a mere blank, with nothing,
> But man is entangled in contradictions:
> The one hand bound, the other fighting.

We revolt against destiny and accept it at the same time. 'The Original Place'[2] contrasts again the freedom in Eden and the servitude on the earth, whereas 'The Sufficient Place'[3] is the place where man situates his memories of his existence before the Fall. 'The Dreamt-of Place'[4] is Paradise:

> Every height
> On earth was thronged and all that was stared upward.
> I thought, This is the reconciliation,
> This is the day after the Last Day.

An earthly paradise is impossible: Muir affirms his dualism:

> And then I thought, Where is the knife, the butcher,
> The vic.im? Are they all here in their places?
> Hid in this harmony? But there was no answer.

There is a slight looseness of thought in *Journeys and Places*: the same themes recur in almost the same form; hence a certain monotony. On the other hand, Muir is anything but dispersed. It is better to have a certain monotony and a strong unity, for we know what Muir means: he is clear because the reader finds, in Muir's coherent (although contrasted) thought, sufficient points of reference and support. He may allow himself to use remote similes and indirect hypotheses: we know their direction, and we realize that his poems are

[1] p. 47.   [2] p. 51.   [3] p. 53.   [4] p. 54.

concentric. If the centre is already pointed to, in the poems we have considered, the sphere is not yet suggested.

It is convenient to analyse Muir's poems, whatever may be their subject, according to the intensity and scope of their thought. There is a difficulty in doing so: few poems represent only one degree of awareness, and most of them mark a progression.

If we proceed according to the intensity of the vision, we distinguish three kinds of poems, those which express a realistic vision (poems emphasizing destiny), those which end in elevation (poems emphasizing eternity and freedom), and finally those which show the most complete development achieved by the poet.

The struggle between time and eternity is the theme of nearly all the later poems. The originality of Muir is that he describes the battle as seen from each camp, discusses various aspects and speculates on the causes and issues of the conflict. If, at times, he focuses his attention on one particular aspect, he situates it in the whole. This unity of thought enables him to deal with any subject.

POEMS EMPHASIZING DESTINY

(a) Historical Themes

The Scottish poems are a pretext for Muir to display his deep sense of history. He entertains no illusions about Scottish history: the past is dark and the poet can hardly pick up a spark in it. 'Then'[1] is an evocation of the past, a past of blind strife without soul, the only witness of which is blood without grief. The poem is built upon the antithesis between cold cruelty and wounded sensibility revolting against blood and shaking the wall of enmity and struggle:

> The wall was haunted
> By mute maternal presences whose sighing
> Fluttered the fighting shadows and shook the wall
> As if that fury of death itself were dying.

In another poem, 'The Ring',[2] the poet thinks gloomily of the earlier times of Scottish history, of the fabulous age:

> We were long since a family, a people,
> The legends say; an old kind-hearted king
> Was our foster-father, and our life a fable.

[1] *The Narrow Place*, p. 12. [2] ibid., p. 35.

Although the Scots were dispersed, massacred, and lost their national entity, they remember their origin:

> We have heard
> Our fathers or our fathers' fathers say
> As in a dream the half-remembered word
> That rounded again the ring where sleeping lay
> Our treasures, still unrusted and unmarred.

Scotland is the symbol of mankind; the early times of Scotland the symbol of Paradise.

The substance of what Muir has to say about Scottish history is concentrated in 'Scotland 1941'.[1] The first part is an evocation of the early history of Scotland, of the 'tribe', and of the desolation which followed the religious wars. It is a dim past:

> Out of that desolation we were born.

Frustration is, according to Muir, the main characteristic of the destiny of the Scots:

> We with such courage and the bitter wit
> To fell the ancient oak of loyalty
> And strip the peopled hill and the altar bare,
> And crush the poet with an iron text,
> How could we read our souls and learn to be?

A pitiless description of the Scottish character follows:

> Here a dull drove of faces harsh and vexed,
> We watch our cities burning in their pit,
> To salve our souls grinding dull lucre out,
> We, fanatics of the frustrate and the half,
> Who once set purgatory hill in doubt.
> Now smoke and dearth and money everywhere,
> Mean heirlooms of each fainter generation,
> And mummied housegods in their musty niches,
> Burns and Scott, sham bards of a sham nation,
> And spiritual defeat wrapped warm in riches,
> No pride but pride of pelf.

[1] ibid., p. 15.

This is the portrait of a nation without hope or sincerity, and yet of a brave and enduring nation:

> Such wasted bravery idle as a song,
> Such hard-won ill might prove Time's verdict wrong,
> And melt to pity the annalist's iron tongue.

Muir finds a certain nobleness in the perseverance of the Scots, in spite of defeat and privation. The idea of a superior justice, that of the Word, hinted in 'Logos'[1] and mentioned in 'The Fall',[2] as well as the meaning attributed to pity in the tenth *Variation*, help to interpret 'Scotland 1914'.

The peculiar pessimism of Scottish people is expressed in 'The House',[3] a poem opposing youth to old age. It is the complaint of an old woman who envies youth's bliss and ignorance, and who is comforted by her knowledge that we are all the servants of an impartial and unbreakable necessity.

Historical themes of a wider scope (not necessarily dealing with Scotland) are treated in a series of poems, three in *The Narrow Place* and three in *The Voyage*. Their symbolism has a more general meaning.

'The Return'[4] is the return of the Greeks without Ulysses, while Penelope is weaving:

> Here I do nothing
> Or less than nothing, making an emptiness
> Amid disorder, weaving, unweaving the lie
> The day demands. Ulysses, this is duty,
> To do and undo, to keep a vacant gate
> Where order and right and hope and peace can enter.

Penelope is the symbol of fidelity, and fidelity is a victory over time. There is no philosophical digression, the symbol is just hinted.

Because we consider first the poems included in *The Narrow Place*, let us proceed to an actual subject: 'The Refugees'.[5] Muir sees in the arrival of refugees the judgment of an epoch without moral conscience. Evil has been shared and suffered not only by the refugees, but also by those who lived without reacting against evil:

> We bear the lot of nations,
> Of times and races,

[1] *First Poems*, p. 33. [2] *Journeys and Places*, p. 23. [3] *The Voyage*, p. 30.
[4] ibid., p. 7. [5] *The Narrow Place*, p. 13.

Because we watched the wrong
Last too long
With non-committal faces.

Then, the idea of divine punishment through the bombing of
cities is introduced:

. . . Tenement roofs and towers
Will fall upon the kind and the unkind
Without election,
For deaf and blind
Is rejection bred by rejection,
And where no counsel is what will be will be.
We must shape here a new philosophy.

The conclusion is abrupt and firm: unless we assume our responsibilities, and unless we act according to our conscience instead of
accepting cynically whatever happens, there will be wars, bombed
cities and homeless refugees.

The variety of Muir's poems is such, and yet their unity is so
strong, that, from the immediate and actual themes to the visionary
and irrational ones, he diffuses the same atmosphere and confirms
the same thought.

'The City'[1] is a regular poem, seven stanzas of four lines, narrating
the symbolical expedition of the pilgrims to Jerusalem, who find but
blood:

And centuries of fear and power and awe,
And all our children in the deadly wood.

'The Castle'[2] tells the medieval story of people besieged in a strong
castle, who could resist victoriously, were they not bought by gold:

We could do nothing, being sold;
Our only enemy was gold,
And we had no arms to fight it with.

The same theme is treated in a more general and more complex
way in 'The Town Betrayed':[3]

Our homes are eaten out by Time,

[1] ibid., p. 28.   [2] *The Voyage*, p. 11.   [3] *Journeys and Places*, p. 37.

The scenes of desolation are more enlarged upon in the earlier poem:

> Yet there is no word, no sigh
>> But quiet murder in the street.
> Our leaf-light lives are spared or taken
>> By men obsessed and neat.

The younger poet shows his literary knowledge:

> There our ancestral ghosts are gathered,
>> Fierce Agamemnon's form I see,
> Watching as if his tents were Time
>> And Troy Eternity.
> We must take order, bar our gates,
>> Fight off these phantoms. Inland now
> Achilles, Siegfried, Lancelot
>> Have sworn to bring us low.

'Moses',[1] and his vision, on Pisgah hill, of the tribulations of Israel, 'Sappho'[2] and her violent death, are other examples of Muir's conception of the dark destiny of mankind.

(b) Philosophical Poems

Other poems, with the same outlook, are philosophical rather than historical. *The Prize*,[3] under the form of a tale, expresses man's hard destiny and his vague aspirations. We come from eternity and are lost on the earth; we try to forget our origin and to regain Paradise, but in vain:

> While all around each trivial shape exclaims:
> 'Here is your jewel; this is your longed-for day,'
> And we forget, lost in the countless names.

What is in germ in 'The Prize' is developed in 'The Face',[4] where the contradiction is extended from human nature to nature. The theme is the deceptive, double aspect of things, the symbol of which is the antithesis between the destructive power of the sea:

> See me with all the terrors on my roads,
> and the external aspect of the sea:

[1] *The Voyage*, p. 12.   [2] ibid., p. 14.   [3] *The Narrow Place*, p. 33.
[4] ibid., p. 26.

And the untroubled oval of my face
That alters idly with the moonlike modes
And is unfathomably framed to please
And deck the angular bone with passing grace.

The second stanza does not alter the theme, but amplifies it:

I should have worn a terror-mask, should be
A sight to frighten hope and faith away,
Half charnel field, half battle and rutting ground.
Instead I am a smiling summer sea
That sleeps while underneath from bound to bound
The sun- and star-shaped killers gorge and play.

The tragic feeling is heightened, in Muir's poems, by the suggestion of another feeling, that of a possible escape. 'The Escape'[1] describes the impossible, dreamy escape from the life in which we are imprisoned:

Like dialogue in a dismal dream
Where right is wrong and wrong is right.

The antinomies of necessity and freedom confront each other. In the poem, the 'besieged' were strong, but did not know their enemy. Now, they cannot escape destruction, and they will recognize their enemy:

I must pass through that fiery wall,
Emerge into the battle place,
And there at last, lifting my eyes,
I'll see the enemy's face.

Necessity is not, for Muir, a materialistic conception: it may as well be the meaning and the substance of art's fixity. A work of art may have the same rigour as history. These ideas are implied in 'The Rider Victory.'[2] There is nothing to win or to lose, but victory and defeat are eternal gestures traced by an eternal hand. Our acts have a consequence, an issue, not in this world, but in eternity. These views are expressed in two successive stages. First, there is nothing to conquer:

The rider Victory reins his horse
Midway across the empty bridge
As if head-tall he had met a wall.
Yet there was nothing there at all,

[1] *The Voyage*, p. 9.   [2] *The Voyage*, p. 28.

> No bodiless barrier, ghostly ridge
> To check the charger in his course
> So suddenly, you'd think he'd fall.

Secondly, victory is not decisive: it is an eternal gesture:

> Suspended, horse and rider stare,
> Leaping on air and legendary.
> In front the waiting kingdom lies,
> The bridge and all the roads are free;
> But halted in implacable air
> Rider and horse with stony eyes
> Uprear their motionless statuary.

The poem might have been inspired by one of those equestrian statues erected on the market-places of small towns. It expresses the meaninglessness of life's issues and changes as well as the truth and eternity of the work of art.

POEMS EMPHASIZING ETERNITY AND FREEDOM

(a) Poems Inspired by Circumstances and by Reading

If there is progress in Muir's thought, this progress does not consist in the shifting of themes, but in the gradual expression of his whole thought. The poems emphasizing eternity are not necessarily a more complete expression of Muir's thought; they are so when they do not exclusively emphasize eternity, as many of them do. Like the preceding ones, they deal with a great variety of subjects.

'The Wayside Station' [1] is apparently one of the least philosophical of Muir's poems. Although it is made of familiar images (a railway station at daybreak, a farm and its inhabitants), it produces an intense and profound effect heightened and crystallized at the end:

> The lonely stream
> That rode through darkness leaps the gap of light,
> Its voice grown loud, and starts its winding journey
> Through the day and time and war and history.

The unexpected complexity of the last statement (it is impossible

[1] *The Narrow Place*, p. 9.

93

to attribute to it a precise meaning; it suggests nature's indifference, with something more) gives an impression of completeness and awakes a feeling of serenity. The connection between the stream and 'the day and time and war and history' is so surprising, and yet so evident, that it gives the rare satisfaction of seeing mystery and reality united. The same effect is produced by Yeats's last poems.

Contemporary events are alluded to in 'Reading in Wartime'.[1] The poet is reading, at the end of 1943, and he justifies his serenity and his inaction by hinting that war is fruitless, that nothing comes out of war except confusion, and that art tells more about life than events. Art is not only a source of information, but also a means of transformation, of shaping the eternal face of the world:

> Boswell's turbulent friend
> And his deafening verbal strife,
> Ivan Ilytch's death
> Tell me more about life,
> The meaning and the end
> Of our familiar breath,
> Both being personal,
> Than all the carnage can,
> Retrieve the shape of man,
> Lost and unanimous, . . .

There is another poem inspired by reading: 'Isaiah',[2] probably written after a reading of the Bible. Here, Isaiah's vision is not as dark as Moses's vision of the future:

> Isaiah from his ledge could see
> Angel and man and animal
> At their everlasting play.

With Muir, the broader a vision is, the brighter. Isaiah sees the world as a struggle between good and evil, between the shadow and the wall. Let us notice here that the image of the wall is used in 'The River':[3]

> The enormous frontier walls fall down,

and the image of a shadow against a wall has been used in 'Then':[4]

[1] *The Voyage*, p. 36.   [2] *The Narrow Place*, p. 37.   [3] ibid., p. 10.
[4] ibid., p. 12.

> The wall was haunted
> By mute maternal presences whose sighing
> Fluttered the fighting shadows and shook the wall
> As if that fury of death itself were dying.

The theme of 'Isaiah' is the destruction of the world, but the catastrophe bears the shape of Trinity:

> But the triple shadows crossing
> Framed an image in their fall,
> A shape against the breaking wall.

The atmosphere, not the facts, of antiquity, is evoked in 'The Old Gods',[1] which brilliantly expresses the eternity of beauty. But it is better not to analyse that poem, for according to Read's words: Poetry 'cannot be dissected unless it is first killed.'[2] 'The Guess'[3] is a poem suggesting resurrection. The poet sees the victims of war coming back home again:

> . . . Yet there seemed
> Nothing more natural than blessedness,
> Nor any life as true as this I dreamed,
> So that I did not feel that I had willed
> These forms, but that a long forgotten guess
> Had shown, past chaos, the natural shape we take.

(b) Poems Expressing an Elevation of the Soul

'The Annunciation'[4] expresses the transfiguration, by love, of the two lovers:

> Forgetting love was born
> Here in a time and place,
> And robbing by such praise
> This life we magnify.

'The Confirmation'[5] and 'The Commemoration'[6] have similar themes. Sleep is the theme of 'The Lullaby'.[7] Sleep becomes the symbol of eternity and the lullaby the symbol of art, art being a bridge between life and death, time and eternity.

'Dejection'[8] expresses the poet's refusal of reality. It is midnight, the

---

[1] ibid., p. 45.   [2] *Annals of Innocence and Experience*, p. 93.
[3] *The Narrow Place*, p. 47.   [4] ibid., p. 42.   [5] ibid., p. 43.   [6] ibid., p. 44.
[7] *The Voyage*, p. 38.   [8] ibid., p. 39.

poet is disgusted with life, with the perpetual return of the seasons, and he feels abandoned and separated from the world:

> My melancholy
> Folds me beyond the reach of care
> As in a valley
> Whence long ago I tried to sally,
> But dreamt and left my dream upon the air.

He wants to be nowhere and contemplates, with his nostalgic mood, the dull spectacle of nature, an accumulation of meaningless facts and events, out of which nothing comes, until the hour of destruction. That we are made for joy, but have to make a pact with sorrow, is the meaning of 'Sorrow'.[1] The counterpart of the two preceding poems is to be found in 'Song':[2] it is the moment of happiness and of illumination, when all is right and man is in the right place. In that moment, the world and history disappear or are transformed, and it is good to live and easy to work. Sorrows and suffering have left:

> Keep fast your mystery,
> Time has no history,
> All things are clear,
> Fear not your fear,
> You cannot away.
>
> Then wrap and lap you within the long day,
> And drop no tear
> For the star or the sphere,
> There's no anywhere
> But here, but here.

'All We'[3] is the glorification of God. We who can make only tools or machines cannot but take pleasure in the work of the Creator.

Other poems express elevation in a more philosophical way. Thoughts lead to another world, and the poet wishes, in 'The Day',[4] that he may find one day the other world, and that his present life may be recorded in God's mind or in the book of fate. Moreover, he asks for the freedom to accept destiny or to revolt against it. The stoics already wanted destiny to become their will:

[1] *The Voyage*, p. 43. [2] ibid., p. 42. [3] ibid., p. 51.
[4] *The Narrow Place*, p. 50.

Oh give me clarity and love that now
The way I walk may truly trace again
The in eternity written and hidden way;
Make pure my heart and will, and me allow
The acceptance and revolt, the yea and nay,
The denial and the blessing that are my own.

The whole poem is in one sentence, in one breath, and is built, like some others, on the construction: 'if . . . Then . . .'. The title, 'The Day', suggests the poet's wish to walk in the light, in certainty, and his horror of nothingness, of darkness and of abandon. The main idea could be expressed thus: if I have to walk in nothingness, may my journey be the will of God or the will of fate, may it be preordained. The thought is involved and not very clear.

'Thought and Image'[1] is much more explicit. It conveys the idea of the double origin of the soul. Before the Fall, thought was born free and had to look for its images on the earth, but became prisoner of earth. Christ came and the contrary process took place:

It's said that to reverse its doom
    And save the entangled soul, to earth
God came and entered in the womb
    And passed through the gate of birth;

Then Christ was crucified and:

There all at last with all was done,
    The great knot loosened, flesh unmade
Beyond the kingdom of the sun,
    In the invincible shade.

So in the earth, in which the soul is kept in servitude, and in earth's damnation only, can the soul 'know itself and be to itself revealed':

All that had waited for his birth
    Were round him then in dusty night,
The creatures of the swarming earth,
    The souls and angels in the height.

The souls are born again, but their perfect image is Christ crucified 'in dusty night'. The poem is somewhat conventional.

[1] *The Voyage*, p. 16.

97

Less conventional and less explicit, but more beautiful, is 'In Love for Long'.[1] The object of the poet's love is neither a woman nor beauty nor pelf: it is anonymous, it is something beyond this world and yet something actually living, it is an untouchable vision and yet something real, constant, and fleeting, something which is over and over again destroyed and massacred, and yet immortal:

> This love a moment known
> For what I do not know
> And in a moment gone
> Is like the happy doe
> That keeps its perfect laws
> Between the tiger's paws
> And vindicates its cause.

Muir's dualism is obvious here:

> It is not even a name
> Yet is all constancy,

and here:

> It is not any thing
> And yet all being is,

There is, in Muir's vision, a kind of transfusion, an exchange of values according to which life appears alternatively as unbearable ('Dejection',[2] 'Song of Patience'[3]) and beautiful ('Song', 'All We'). This dualism is solved in most poems, where it is presented as two different aspects of the same thing. Sometimes, however, there is a frightful gap between the two ('The Window'),[4] which heightens the effects by opposing them. We shall finally consider the poems in which the anti-thesis is more acute and better resolved.

POEMS OF RECONCILIATION

(a) *Poems Inspired by Circumstances, History, and Personal Feelings*

Some poems, though inspired by circumstances, display a great intensity of thought progressing along two opposite lines. Among them is 'To J. F. H.' (*1897–1934*).[5] Written in memory of a friend who

[1] ibid., p. 52. [2] ibid., p. 39. [3] ibid., p. 42. [4] ibid., p. 29.
[5] *The Narrow Place*, p. 7.

was killed in a motor-cycle accident, this poem is centred on two themes: the reappearance of the friend and death. The poet sees a young soldier dashing by on a motor cycle, and resembling his dead friend.[1] The strange feeling of the communion of the dead and of the living man in the poet's memory prevails over the beginning of the poem:

> . . . Had I cracked the shell
> That hides the secret souls, had I fallen through,
> I idly wondered, and in so falling found
> The land where life's untraceable truants run
> Hunting a halting stage? Was this the ground
> That stretched beyond the span-wide world-wide ditch,
> So like the ground I knew, yet so unlike,
> Because it said 'Again', all this again,
> The flying road, the motionless house again,
> And, stretched between, the tension of your face—

The event, as the preceding lines indicate, transfigures the landscape and endows it with a meaning. The motorist, symbol of man, darts along the road (the world) as if the world were perforated with a tunnel (death). The presence of death is so near, so evident, that it becomes a tragic commonplace, a hole personified by the motorist, an immediate, timeless hole in which the poet recognizes his friend seven years after the death (in 1941).

The poet looks once more at his friend through the hole, with a questioning and anguished glance, and here is the answer:

> I knew at last
> The sight you saw there, the terror and mystery
> Of unrepeatable life so plainly given
> To you half wrapped still in eternity,
> Who had come by such a simple road from heaven;

The transfiguration is at its climax when the road appears as the meeting place of the two appearances of the friend: his last run in life, seven years ago, and his coming back to the memory of the poet in the form of another man.

It is as if the friend, like the criminal who returns to the fatal place, comes twice to the fatal spot: once from the earth, then from heaven.

[1] These particulars have been kindly indicated to the author of the present essay by Edwin Muir in a letter of 10 June 1949.

When he comes back from heaven, the truth is revealed and the fatal scene takes new proportions:

> So that you did not need to have the story
> Retold, or bid the heavy world turn again,
> But felt the terror of the trysting place,
> The crowning test, the treachery and the glory.

The poem illustrates, in a circumstantial and tragic way, Muir's double vision, an absolute and a relative vision, and his conception of man as being the common object of both.

That idea of man is exposed in more general terms in 'The Fathers',[1] which opens with considerations on the historical past:

> Our fathers all were poor,
> Poorer our fathers' fathers;
> Beyond, we dare not look.

It is a dim past, and what we now have is a result from that past, an accumulation of efforts and gold. Only when history will cease shall we see the light:

> We, the sons, keep store
> Of tarnished gold that gathers
> Around us from the night,
> Record it in this book
> That, when line is drawn,
> Credit and creditor gone,
> Column and figure flown,
> Will open into light.

But the past is heavy upon us: we cannot avoid its burden and we live in darkness. The third stanza contains again a statement of the double origin of man, the terrestrial origin symbolized by the fathers, and the divine origin. When destiny's circle will be closed, when all the times will be accomplished, then eternity will come, and we shall see the light (this is a restatement):

> Panics and furies fly
> Through our unhurried veins,
> Heavenly lights and rains

[1] *The Voyage*, p. 24.

100

Purify heart and eye,
Past agonies purify
And lay the sullen dust.
The angers will not away.
We hold our fathers' trust,
Wrong, riches, sorrow and all
Until they topple and fall,
And fallen let the day.

Muir does not mean that, one day, time will end and let in eternity; he says that time dies with every man's death, that the past is abolished with every passing day. Life has a meaning: through its own destruction, it reveals eternity, 'the day'.

It is significant that the first poem with a comical touch we come to is 'Epitaph':[1]

His vastest dreams were less than six feet tall;

That man did not fully live: 'he crept in himself alone.' Now, he has become something true:

Since he was half and half, now let him be
Something entire at last here in this night
Which teaches us its absolute honesty
Who stray between the light and the half-light.

Let him be something or nothing, for we are dust and spirit, not only dust:

If now is Resurrection, then let stay
Only what's ours when this is put away

There is an antithesis of another kind in 'Suburban Dream':[2] activity and leisure, and in 'Comfort in Self-Despite':[3]

So I may yet recover by this bad
Research that good I scarcely dreamt I had.

However detestable we may be, there is something pure in us.

Linked with the poems inspired by circumstances are the poems expressing personal feelings, like the preceding one and 'Time Held in Time's Despite'.[4] Muir's duality appears here under another form: the blending of temporal and spiritual feelings:

[1] ibid., p. 44.   [2] *The Voyage*, p. 35.   [3] ibid , p. 45.   [4] ibid., p. 47.

> The hours that melt like snowflakes one by one
> Leave us this residue, this virgin ground
> For ever fresh, this firmament and this sun.

The same theme is developed in 'The Transmutation'.[1] Man is in the middle between the eternal and the changing. We gather eternity in time:

> ... That we who fall
> Through Time's long ruin should weave this phantom ground
> And in its ghostly borders gather all.

We are moving with mortal steps in an eternal mould:

> As in commemoration of a day
> That having been can never pass away.

The link between time and eternity is love: this is the meaning of 'Song of Patience'.[2] The poet is tired of life, his only strength is worn-out patience. But patience is impatience too, it means waiting for something else to happen, and suddenly the poet sees life as a whole, life with its surroundings:

> Die in pain, be born in pain,
> And to love at last attain:

At that moment, life is transformed, life becomes again bearable under the spell of love:

> Love to whom all things are well,
> Love that turns all things to ease,
> The life that fleets before the eye,
> And the motionless eye of death;
> That tunes the tedious miseries
> And even patience makes to please;
> Love to whom the sorrows tell
> Their abysmal dreams and cry:
> 'Weave the spell! Weave the spell!
> Make us well!'

'The River'[3] is the symbol of life flowing nowhere. In that poem, life's antinomy is expressed by the contrast between a soldier looking at the present and his grandmother; each is unable to share the

---

[1] ibid., p. 46.   [2] ibid., p. 40.   [3] *The Narrow Place*, p. 10.

other's grief. Then, time's negative value is symbolized by the destruction of the town, which soldiers come to conquer. Nature's indifference, already hinted in 'The Wayside Station'[1] (last lines), is suggested by the river eroding the frontier wall,[2] flowing on and leaving nothing:

> The enormous winding frontier walls fall down,
> Leaving anonymous stone and vacant grass.
> The stream flows on into what land, what peace,
> Far past the other side of the burning world?

There is only one thought behind all the images and symbols and the poetic unity of such a complex poem comes from it. In most of his poems, Muir is thinking in terms of Scottish history because the remoteness and multiplicity of events allows him to seize them as a whole and to draw a conclusion, if there is any. In 'The River', history appears to him like a stream in which all shapes disappear, like a flux causing ravage. Will this go on for ever or will the stream reach some definite place, is there an end to history, will there be an era of peace? Muir does not answer that question, but he feels the necessity of a conclusion, of a decisive turn, of a change. *There is an answer,* and for Muir it is enough to suggest the existence of the answer, and the presence of something transcendental which has to fulfil the needs of his thought. For Muir as well as for Yeats, it does not matter if his thought is not justified by an external representation, provided that his thought is justified by itself, feeds on its own substance and creates.

'The Myth'[3] is a meditation on the poet's past life, an analysis of his feeling of time in the three successive stages he has lived through (childhood, adolescence, and maturity), until he finally emerges to guard the sheaves of eternity.

In the two preceding poems, the ideas or the themes are presented in a state of progress, without solution or continuity: we shall now consider the poems displaying a dialectical process.

[1] ibid., p. 9.

[2] 'This poem was written during the war, soon after the invasion of France, which brought images of universal disaster to so many of us. Frontier walls seemed to be beyond saving just then, and I had an image of a Europe quite featureless, with all the old marks gone'. (Letter of 10 June 1949 to the author of the present essay.)

[3] cf. *Childhood* (*First Poems*, p. 9).

(b) *Poems with a Dialectical Architecture*

'The Voyage' (for Eric Linklater[1]) belongs to a group of poems in which the thought is covered with a coat of images.

It is the story of mariners lost at sea. The earth is out of sight, and they think they will never see it again. They see only their own ship and the sea; no sail is in sight.

Then, they think of the land they have left and of the one to which they were bound. They think of their home as if they will never see it again. What had been real for them becomes a dream and they feel happy; they feel happy to be separated from the earth and to see it from afar, they feel safe and blessed. They have the sensation of living in eternity, and their memories of reality, of their homes, are transformed, embellished:

> The words we knew like our right hand,
> Mountain and valley, meadow and grove,
> Composed a legendary land
> Rich with the broken tombs of love.
>
> Delusion or truth? We were content
> Thenceforth to sail the harmless seas
> Safe past the fate and the Accident,
> And called a blessing on that peace.
>
> And blessing, we ourselves were blest,
> Lauded the loss that brought our gain,
> Sang the tumultuous world to rest,
> And wishless called it back again.
>
> For loss was then our only joy,
> Privation of all, fulfilled desire,
> The world our treasure and our toy
> In destitution clean as fire.

They saw eternity, but they were not yet in eternity: it was a delusion, earth appears, and:

> The dream and a truth we clutched as ours,
> And gladly, blindly, stepped on earth.

[1] *The Voyage*, p. 20.

This poem illustrates Muir's conception of the double life of man: conditioned life and eternal, visionary life.

The same conception is more explicitly revealed in 'The Human Fold'.[1] Like 'The Narrow Place',[2] it is a meditation on man's limitations:

> Here penned within the human fold.
> Man may contemplate the huge machine of the sky; he cannot move.

However stationary we are, we kindle around us fantastic visions:

> The dragon with his tears of gold,
> The bat-browed sphinx
>
> .   .   .   .   .
>
> Hell shoots its avalanche at our feet,
> In heaven the souls go up and down,

(the last line is perhaps a reminiscence of Dante through Blake). We are entangled in those visions through our moral life.

But those visions evolve in another world. The idea of the fall is introduced here: even those who enjoy those visions cannot escape this world, they are here but to suffer, life is a burden:

> All this, but here our sight is bound
> By ten dull faces in a round,
>
> .   .   .   .
>
> I read this burden in them all:
> 'I lean my cheek from Eternity
> For Time to slap, for Time to slap.
> I gather my bones from the bottomless clay
> To lay my head in the light's lap.'

The theme of the burden is developed in the continuation and repeated as the conclusion of the poem. It expresses man's double origin or the two contrary movements which meet in life: first the divine origin, which makes men resemble fallen angels grounded on earth (this simile was beautifully used by Baudelaire in *L'Albatross*); secondly, the terrestrial origin of man, man made of ashes and ascending to light, that is, spiritual life.

Then, Muir considers man's duality, not as two contrary move-

[1] *The Narrow Place*, p. 18.   [2] ibid., p. 20.

ments, not as two opposite poles, but as a co-existence of two different elements in the present situation. There is a struggle in man between flesh and spirit, between the mortal and the immortal man, and everything happens as if both could never be reconciled, as if the soul were always dying and falling on the earth:

> Forward our towering shadows fall
> Upon the naked nicheless wall,
> And all we see is that shadow-dance.

The prevailing idea at the end of the poem is the constant dis-appearance of the ideal, disenchantment:

> They loved and might have loved for ever,
> But public trouble and private care
> Faith and hope and love can sever
> And strip the bed and the altar bare.

The only idea which is certain and all-embracing is the myth of man's double origin.

'The Narrow Place',[1] which gives its title to one volume, implies all the intuitions which give birth to most of the poems. It is marked with the antithesis of limitation (the human condition) and eternity (man's aspirations); servitude and freedom. Most of Muir's poems, as we have already seen, and especially those we are going to analyse, are built upon an antithesis.

'The Narrow Place' evokes a hamlet in the Highlands, with its 'creeping roads', its 'bleak mountain wind' and its meagre vegetation. It is universalized and chosen as the symbol of life, parsimonious and yet generous life.

Sometimes it seems that a single small Highland tree has more to give than a wood:

> Yet under it we sometimes feel such ease
> As if it were ten thousand trees
> And for its foliage had
> Robbed half the world of shade.

However small it may be, the Highland tree is enough to man, there is something complete even in that smallness.

Life answers the double needs of man, needs of the real and needs

[1] ibid., p. 20.

of the imaginary. The tree of life gives enough to protect man waking or sleeping. At this point of the poem, nature presents itself under its objective, aggressive aspect on one hand:

> It is your murdering eyes that make
> The sterile hill, the standing lake,
> And the leaf-breaking wind.

On the other hand, the visionary, eternal aspect:

> Then shut your eyes and see,
> Sleep on and do not wake
> Till there is no movement in the lake
> And the club-headed serpents break
> In emerald lightnings through the slime,
> Making a mark on Time.

The image of the serpent is obviously borrowed from Scottish popular imagination. The symbols are not rich or extraordinarily suggestive; there is a certain dryness (already in the title), but no heaviness, no insistence. There are some vigorous lines:

> How all the roads creep in.

and some banal ones:

> And keep but what they have.

The three main symbols of this poem are: (*a*) the narrow place, a Highland hamlet, symbolically the earth; (*b*) the 'faces', the inhabitants of the hamlet; sharp, grave faces of hard mountaineers, symbolically of all men; and (*c*) the tree, a thin, fragile tree, symbol of life, frail and yet sufficient to protect man.

The Recurrence[1] is the poem in which Muir's metaphysical vision is most sharply distinguished from that of Yeats. The image of the wheel has approximately the same significance as in Yeats, but Muir sees something beyond: freedom. (With Yeats, freedom, 'the thirteenth circle', is integrated in the system of cones and wheels.)

The two first paragraphs deal with the idea and the symbols of fate as they have again and again been expressed by the Greek tragedies and philosophy, by the stoics, by the determinists and, under the form of the eternal return, by Nietzsche, who is mentioned in Muir's

[1] *The Narrow Place*, p. 23.

poem and from whom Muir borrowed, in *Transition*, the notion of 'Zeit Geist'. There is no escape from fate, everything which happens is inevitable:

> What is ill be always ill,
> Wretches die behind a dike,
> And the happy be happy still.

(The same idea, in a different connection, is expressed in *Revelation*.) The stock of illustrations of that idea is inexhaustible; Muir does not choose new or striking ones, but uses them as disillusioned warnings: man cannot achieve anything, he is always defeated.

After having strongly expressed that idea, Muir declares that it is not the absolute truth: it is the truth of the eye; the truth of the heart and of the mind is different. Muir's dualism appears here under another form. What the eye sees, without understanding it, is the wheel of necessity; the eye is unable to look beyond the astronomical wheel:

> Quarterings on the turning shield,
> The great non-stop heraldic show.

But the truths of the heart and of the mind are in complete contradiction to fatalism: they are a 'revolutionary' truth, the vision, not of something coming back again, but of something entirely new:

> What has been can never return,
> What is not will surely be
> In the changed unchanging reign,

There is something beyond necessity or fate, let us say even that necessity or fate are unreal for the heart. Fatality is impossible because there is no creation in it, and in such a system nothing would really happen or exist, for there would be no maker. Such a system would take God for an actor who pretends to be God, but who is a mere joker, miming life and doing nothing:

> Else the Actor on the Tree
> Would loll at ease, miming pain,
> And counterfeit mortality.

Mortality is not a mere appearance, everything being changeless and unchangeable: there is death and resurrection, we are not in a closed circle, death is a reality and something is to issue from mortal life.

'The Good Man in Hell'[1] is a poem, condensed, philosophical and of great speculative richness, on the alternative of salvation from evil or the inevitability of sin.

Two things might happen 'if a good man were ever housed in Hell': he might surrender to evil,

> Feeling the curse climb slowly to his throat

and that would prove the inevitability of sin and eternal damnation; or would he

> Kindle a little hope in hopeless Hell,
> And sow among the damned doubts of damnation,
> Since here someone could live and could live well?

Thus he might save others from evil, and damnation would not be eternal. The fifth and last stanza of this perfect poem contains a reflection on the second part of the alternative, redemption, and it expresses, like the last part of 'The Recurrence', Muir's own conception: destiny is not fixed, evil is not eternal, life can be changed, old Adam may become a new man:

> One doubt of evil would bring down such a grace,
> Open such a gate, all Eden could enter in,
> Hell be a place like any other place,
> And love and hate and life and death begin.

The whole is expressed with reserve, without redundance, in the form of generalities and philosophical concepts. It is highly poetical, the thought is unflinching, self-sufficient.

'The Wheel'[2] has the same theme as 'The Recurrence' and an analogous turn at the end. Muir's fundamental dualism, however, is not illustrated here by the opposition between the truth of the eye and the truth of the heart (between passive objectivity and creative intuition), but by opposing the order of grace to the order of fate.

1. The power of fate is again expressed. Nothing matters to us if we are under the unavoidable influence of the past, of the dead, of our ancestors, if everything is to go on for ever without change, if there is no end to struggle and no reward to love. What is the point of loving or of hating if we are not the lovers, the haters, if love and hate do not change anything? Muir is once more confronted with and rebuked by the same absurdity: everything is eternal (this is

---

[1] *The Narrow Place*, p. 24.   [2] *The Narrow Place*, p. 25.

Nietzsche's eternal return), every changing thing is a repetition, and the world is settled once for all (*nihil recens sub sole*):

> . . . Loves and hates are thrust
> Upon me by the acrimonious dead,
> The buried thesis, long since rusted knife,
> Revengeful dust.

Only the appearances are changing: they are a mask of the unchanging reality, and, supposing this is true, our life is a comedy or a tragedy played by the dead (we are not far from Yeats, but Muir takes the idea only as a likely conjecture to be finally refuted):

> A stony or obstreperous head,
> Though slain so squarely, can usurp my will
> As I walk above it on the sunny hill.

2. Such a conjecture is unacceptable. If we accept it, we assume that there is no purpose in life, and it excludes any reason to justify our individual and actual life. The lack of a rational, deterministic justification of actual life constitutes a refutation: no individual can accept fatalism unless he claims no longer to be an individual, in other words our very existence is the refutation of determinism.

But we can do nothing about this apparently changing, but unchanging world. We can neither change it, nor escape from it. It would be vain to look at it from afar or to try to do something new. Whatever may be said against them, necessity and the dark influence of the past exist and cannot be removed:

> How can I here remake what there made me
> And makes and remakes me still?
> Set a new mark? Circumvent history?
> Nothing can come of history but history,

and this is followed by a series of equivalent similes illustrating the idea that the things which happen are absurd, since their happening cannot change anything:

> The stationary storm that cannot bate
> Its neutral violence,
> The transitory solution that cannot wait,

The indecisive victory
That is like loss read backwards and cannot bring
Relief to you and me,

The climax of those similies, perhaps the most terrible feature of
necessity, is the universal conflict of nature originating in the isolation
and limitation of things and beings:

The jangling
Of all the voices of plant and beast and man
That have not made a harmony
Since first the great controversy began,
And cannot sink to silence.

3. In proportion as we reach the climax, however, we reach the
turning point: the acceptation of destiny is at the same time the negation of destiny; the idea of all-including fate is unacceptable, grace is
necessary, grace which remakes us. Something must die in ashes and
something must be born from ashes. Muir postulates here, if not free
will, the double nature of man, death dividing one part from the other:

Unless a grace
Come of itself to wrap our souls in peace
Between the turning leaves of history and make
Ourselves ourselves, winnow the grudging grain
And take
From that which made us that which will make us again.

The symbol of the wheel is an obsession, against which the poet
struggles. When the idea of grace is introduced, the problem is
solved, the obsession removed, and the poem justified.

The same idea as in 'The Recurrence' is implied in 'Twice-Done,
Once Done'.[1] The difference is that the two opposite truths (of the eye
and of the heart) which, in 'Recurrence', appeared as opposed to each
other, are reconciled and united in 'Twice-Done, Once-Done'. In a
way, determination and freedom exist at the same time. Our destiny
is preordained, our days are counted, but each day matters, each soul
matters, each is independent, although belonging to the chain. The
poem is so coherent that it has to be quoted fully.

The idea expressed in the three first stanzas is *nihil recens sub sole,*

[1] *The Voyage,* p. 18.

nothing is unique, all things happen many times, repeat themselves, the same happens always, there is no individuality, all has already been done, old Adam lives in us:

> Nothing yet was ever done
>   Till it was done again,
> And no man was ever one
>   Except through dead men.
>
> I could neither rise nor fall
>   But that Adam fell.
> Had he fallen once for all
>   There'd be nothing to tell.
>
> Unless in me my fathers live
>   I can never show
> I am myself, ignorant if
>   I'm a ghost or no.

But, in the three following stanzas, the poet turns from the depressing contemplation of man lost in uniformity, and starts from the less pessimistic of the preceding considerations:

> Had he fallen once for all
>   There'd be nothing to tell.

There is something positive in actual, individual life, otherwise the story would cease to repeat itself. If, therefore, the poet turns once more to Adam and Eve, it is to learn from them how to believe in life, how to take the present life seriously, to believe in what is unique in it:

> Father Adam and Mother Eve,
>   Make this pact with me:
> Teach me, teach me to believe,
>   For to believe's to be.

It is as if life were beginning again, as if something new had happened. The world is a feast to many young women and love has the power to enchant it, to make it as beautiful as a legend:

> Many a woman since Eve was made
>   Has seen the world is young,
> Many and many a time obeyed
>   The legend-making tongue.

Let us, therefore, forget Adam and Eve, forget the past, for the past is invisible, and even if it exists and influences us, it exists only through us, it owes its existence to us: it would not be the past, did we not come after:

> Abolish the ancient custom—who
> Would mark Eve on her shelf?
> Even a story to be true
> Must repeat itself.

The two last stanzas are devoted to the vision of eternity in the present time, eternity in man. Each human life is universal and decisive, we are the measure of everything. It is not the Greek 'everything is in everything', but: all the past is met in the present, human life is at the same time unique and universal:

> Yet we the latest born are still
> The first ones and the last,
> And in our little measures fill
> The oceanic past.

> For first and last is every way,
> And first and last each soul,
> And first and last the passing day,
> And first and last the goal.

'Dialogue'[1] is even more concise, simple and short than 'Twice-Done, Once-Done'. The extreme simplicity of the poem arises from the fact that, short as it is (three stanzas of five lines), it takes its unity from the harmonious repetition of the same words with three different meanings.

The first stanza proposes the following hypothesis: suppose that we complete or close the circle of destiny, suppose that destiny is accepted without revolt or contest, suppose that the human will is of no importance, that destiny rules without encountering any resistance:

> Now let us lover by lover lay
> And enemy now to enemy bring,
> Set open the immaculate way
> Of everything to everything
> And crown our destiny king.

[1] *The Voyage*, p. 19.

There is an answer to that hypothesis. If destiny's rule were absolute, there would be no life, nothing would happen any longer, everything would be accomplished and there would be no food for thought, no problem for the will. If destiny's rule were absolute, there would be nothing to love or to hate. Destiny's power is relative, and exerts itself on beings who otherwise are free:

> If lover were by lover laid,
>   And enemy brought to enemy.
> All that's made would be unmade
>   And done would be the destiny
>   Of time and eternity.

But destiny is not absolute, not complete, never fully accomplished. Love's and hate's circle is not closed. Events repeat themselves, but they are always new, as if their goal were never reached: there is another life beyond this one, this one is incomplete and must be fulfilled elsewhere. These thoughts could lead to various fruitful philosophical developments only suggested by Muir. Two conceptions are here confronted: (1) the hypothesis that eternity is stationary, immobile and does not depend on the flux of time (this recalls Zeno's problems); and (2) the reality, that is, eternity involved, engaged in time:

> But love with love can never rest,
>   And hate can never bear with hate,
> Each by each must be possessed,
>   For, see, at every turning wait
>   The enemy and the mate.

Other facets of the theme of the double truth shine in 'The Window'[1] and 'The Three Mirrors'.[2] The first of these poems presents two, the second three, facets of Muir's dualistic conception. Muir's poems are like a kaleidoscope in which the same images are presented in various positions.

Eternity is symbolized, in 'The Window', by a tower including everything:

> In endless change on changeless ground

Time appears as a glass, in the tower, on which all the changes of the world are reflected.

[1] *The Voyage*, p. 29.   [2] ibid., p. 26.

Suddenly, when looking in the glass, the poet notices that there is a crack, that something escapes the tower of eternity. All things which appear in the glass are destroyed, they pass and go nowhere, they are excluded from eternity:

> And there one day we looked and saw
> Marsh, mere and mound in anger shaken,
> The world's great side, the giant flaw,
> And watched the stately forests fall,
> The white ships sinking in the sea,
> The tower run toppling in the field,
> The last left stronghold sacked and taken,
> And earth and heaven in jeopardy.

Eternity, fixed perfection, is balanced by disaster, destruction; eternity does not hold everything in its fixity, time flees from it. The poet takes, first a universal point of view, then a relative point of view. Baudelaire expressed Muir's intuition, saying: 'Le monde est fêlé.' There is a break in the wall of eternity, it is Satan's work, whose kingdom of torments is established beyond the tower of eternity. The world is rent in two, man is attracted by both eternity and destruction:

> Then turning towards you I beheld
> The wrinkle writhe across your brow,
> And felt Time's cap clapped on my head,
>
> .   .   .   .   .

A contemplation of the gap of non-being, destruction and fury and awe ends the poem:

> Across the towering window fled
> Disasters, victories, festivals.

More dialectical, although not less intuitive and beautiful, speculations are offered in 'The Three Mirrors'.[1]

The first mirror (the first stanza), is the mirror of objective reality, or that part of reality which falls under sensory experience, and the main feature of that reality is that it is incomplete: there is something wrong, something unfinished and unrevealed about it. Objective reality is not all, and it is ill done, ill arranged: its character is

[1] ibid., p. 26.

disorder. In the first mirror, therefore, appears a distorted, unfinished image:

> I looked in the first glass
> And saw the fenceless field
> And like broken stones in grass
> The sad towns glint and shine.
> The slowly twisting vine
> Scribbled with wrath the stone,
> The mountain summits were sealed
> In incomprehensible wrath.
> The hunting roads ran on
> To round the flying hill
> And bring the quarry home.
> But the obstinate roots ran wrong,
> The lumbering fate fell wrong,
> The walls were askew with ill,
> Askew went every path,
> The dead lay askew in the tomb.

The second mirror is, let us say, the reverse of the first. The same things step over the threshold of the finite:

> Tel qu'en lui-même enfin l'éternité le change[1]

The same things, the same beings change, appear as if time had stopped, as if they were facing eternity, as if all actions were decisive and leading to a solution, as if there were an end to mortal things. That mirror shows finality. The earth is torn and there is a crack through it, there is an issue. Things and beings pass through that issue and take their eternal, definitive form:

> I looked in the second glass
> And saw through the twisted scroll
> In virtue undefiled
> And new in eternity
> Father and mother and child,
> The house with its single tree,
> Bed and board and cross,
> And the dead asleep in the knoll.
> But the little blade and leaf

[1] Mallarmé: *Le Tombeau d' Edgar Poe.*

By an angry law were bent
To shapes of terror and grief,
By a law the field was rent,
The crack ran over the floor,
The child at peace in his play
Changed as he passed through a door,
Changed were the house and the tree,
Changed the dead in the knoll,
For locked in love and grief,
Good with evil lay.

The third mirror no longer shows finality leading to eternity, but eternity itself. The poet is not claiming that he actually sees eternity, he suggests what he would see if he could look in the mirror of eternity.

In eternity, each gesture is perpetuated and immobile, the rebels are eternally revolting and the rulers eternally governing (this is what happens, in a way, in Dante's *Inferno*). There is no change from good into evil or from evil into good: everything is settled, unchanging, fixed.

The second mirror was the reverse of the first: the third one is the synthesis of both; we have here a kind of Hegelian trilogy which is far, however, from being explicit and logical enough. There is perhaps, in this poem, nothing else than in the others, but 'The Three Mirrors' supposes a greater complexity and range of thought than any other poem does.

The third mirror is the mirror of completeness, of the final achievement of God's will, and of perfection:

If I looked in the third glass
I should see evil and good
Standing side by side
In the ever standing wood,
The wise king on his throne,
The rebel raising the rout,
And each so deeply grown
Into his own place
He'd be past desire or doubt.
If I could look I should see
The world's house open wide,

> The million million rooms
> And the quick god everywhere
> Glowing at work and at rest,
> Tranquillity in the air,
> Peace of the humming looms
> Weaving from east to west,
> And you and myself there.

That image of peace is the climax of Muir's achievement. It is not the only vision to which his thought leads him, but it is the last one: the eternity of hardship and loss is replaced by eternal peace.

The two conflicting conceptions which result in a crystallization of Muir's poetry, first the idea of a pre-ordained destiny, secondly the image of an obscure path leading to a bright destiny, are reconciled in his new volume, *The Labyrinth*.[1] With a first sentence of thirty-five lines, the title-poem develops the first of these conceptions, that of a world without issue. And yet the poet is not satisfied with this vision, for he has emerged from the labyrinth and dreams of a world of transcendental freedom. Two worlds co-exist, and the bright one, in which all is permissible and acceptable, lies elsewhere than on the earth:

> There's no prize in this race; the prize is elsewhere,
> Here only to be run for.[2]

It would be bold to assert that Muir's thought is a reconciliation of Greek necessity with Christian freedom, and yet both conceptions are present in his work. The second one dominates *The Labyrinth*:

> Then he will come, Christ the uncrucified,[3]

Nothing could end this chapter better than this note of hope, for a poet who has long explored the depth of destiny is entitled to utter this promise of freedom.

[1] London, Faber and Faber, 1949.
[2] ibid., 'The Journey Back,' p 24
[3] ibid , 'The Transfiguration' p 56

CHAPTER III

THOUGHT IN T. S. ELIOT'S POETRY

ELIOT AND THE TRADITION

WHAT strikes most readers and critics who have followed the development of Thomas Stearns Eliot is the consistency of his work. It is not the consistency of a personal, extravagant or revolutionary attitude, as might be expected in a period where culture is separated into disconnected fields, it is an effort towards re-uniting our fragmentary culture. It is strange that the poet who was considered as one of the most revolutionary of our time is the one who is perhaps the most deeply anchored in tradition. After a first, apparently negative, period in which he launched a satire against our decadent civilization, he indicated the source of unity which he found in the tradition and which may save us from chaos. His poetry as well as his life are turned towards accepting the authority of religion. His conversion to Anglo-Catholicism is one of the aspects of his pursuit of religious experience and of his reliance on extra-temporal guidance. His poetry may be considered as a means for discovering something beyond poetry which accounts for the transparency of his later poetry.

Eliot maintains the traditional distinctions between soul and body, spirit and matter, and holds, like Pascal, that man is helpless without God. His devotion to asceticism and his contempt for the world relate him to a tradition which is regarded as wide, significant and again powerful to-day, although it has been dwindling and superseded for five centuries. The characters described by Eliot are pictures of man as religion and humanism conceived him, that is, man with a conscience. 'Instead', writes Edwin Muir, 'there has emerged a new species of the natural man firmly dovetailed into a biological sequence and a social structure. This new natural man is capable of improvement but, unlike the natural man of religion, has no need for regeneration.'[1] The natural man, according to Edwin Muir, is nothing else than the primitive man or a return to the primitive man, so that the modern wars are a consequence of this degeneration. Eliot opposes to the prevailing ideas of our time an idea of man similar to that of Milton and Racine. For Eliot, life is not a development: it is conflict between reason and passion or impulse, and we are not surprised by his praise of Dante.

The eternal element in life has been neglected in literature and philosophy since the end of the nineteenth century, man has been animalized and his life has become insignificant:

> I have measured out my life with coffee spoons;

Eliot sees in the decay of spiritual authority the doom of our civilization. 'No less central in his mind', writes F. O. Matthiessen, 'is the doctrine of God become man through the Saviour, since Eliot holds that the nineteenth-century substitution of Deification, of man becoming God through his own potentialities, led ineluctably through hero-worship to dictatorship. Here Eliot has found a solider basis for his politics, as he demonstrated in his play, *Murder in the Cathedral* (1935), where he contrasted Christian law with violent usurpation of the fascist kind.'[2]

There is no doubt that in his later poems the aesthetic faculty of Eliot is placed under the authority of his religious convictions. One feels that his austerity checks his lyrical impulse, explains the laconism of his work and forces him into a narrow path where he has already described all that he has discovered, so that there is little more to add. His sense of humour, his irony and his contempt for the world are closely related to the puritan element of his character, which is well described by Mr. Van der Vat: 'Eliot still shows an attitude, an extra-poetical consciousness of ethical problems, which tends to mar the purity of his poetry. We feel everywhere his puritan sense of sin and sordidness, his preoccupation with evil, which also shows itself in the way he is fascinated by the more vulgar aspects of life. . . . The beauty of his poetry is never meek or humble as it was

[1] Edwin Muir: *The Natural Man and the Political Man* (*The Penguin New Writing*, p. 25).

[2] *American Poetry*, 1920–40, by F. O. Matthiessen (The *Sewanee Review*, Winter 1947).

in Verlaine or Rilke. It should be remembered especially that it is the puritan element in Eliot's make-up which is largely responsible for the frequent bitterness of his poetry. That is undoubtedly the reason why he has felt himself attracted by the bitterness (due to other reasons, it is true) of La Corbière and Laforgue. We shall also see that this puritanism and the resulting struggle with beauty will lead to Eliot's poetical undoing in the end. The taste of ashes, so familiar to the readers of Joyce and Lawrence, is equally prominent in Eliot.'[1]

Poetry is for Eliot a means to convey a religious experience, and there is nothing to say against this process since poetry itself may be considered as an essentially religious experience, but according to Mr. Van der Vat, Eliot makes a clear distinction between religious and purely aesthetic experience: 'Verlaine could combine contrition with the love of earthly and poetical beauty, so could many others. But the puritan has to pay his own price. The harshness of his religious asceticism abhors the allurements of beauty which is closely allied to sin.'[2]

In spite of his contempt for the senses, Eliot has been able to propose a coherent aesthetic doctrine. It should be noted here that his need for authority reappears in the fact that he does not regard poetry as an individual experiment. The form of his earlier poetry is in contrast with his theory that the poets should accept the tradition and the knowledge of their time. There is, under the title *T. S. Eliot and Philosophical Poetry*, an enlightening article by Luciano Anceschi[3] which deals especially with the relation between the thought and the poetry of Eliot. In spite of his modesty, Anceschi has successfully elucidated what doctrine can be drawn from Eliot's poems and prose works. According to Anceschi, the basic axiom of that doctrine is that individual perceptions have a universal value and consequently may be used to express not so much the poet himself as his own time and, through his own time, the cultural background of society. Here is a long passage from Anceshi's article: 'Eliot's conception of the *impersonality of art* does not and cannot deny the individuality of the

[1] *The Poetry of T. S. Eliot*, by D. G. Van der Vat (*English Studies*, June 1938, p. 110).

[2] ibid., pp. 116 and 117.

[3] Published in *T. S. Eliot, a Symposium Compiled by Richard March and Tambimuttu*, Editions Poetry, London, 1948, pp. 154–66. Tr. by Kathleen Noth.

artist—how could it indeed? Rather it redeems that individuality in a special pointed sense. But if we are to get near to the inner meaning of such a conception, we must dwell on a fundamental consideration: on the fact that this poet is a man whose whole cultural background has made him believe in the fundamental epistemological truth of the senses, and whose point of departure is therefore a theory of perception; and in fact he has re-echoed the famous Aristotelian proposition, interpreted in the philosophical light which is predominant in the English tradition, and said that "Not only every kind of cognition but every feeling has its location in perception".

'Within the ambit of this general conception he has essayed a modern revival of the old idea of the poet as a *medium*, and interpreted the poet's mind as a *means of combining* sensations and thoughts into a new unity according to a law by which neither the special personality, nor the private history and particular emotions of the poet-as-man, nor even his individual outlook, are finally determinant in favouring the rare act of poetic generation.'[1]

It should be remarked that Anceschi is not discussing a doctrine, but 'an organic system of poetic creation'. If Eliot is a conformist, he conforms to the purest and highest forms of culture: Dante, St. John of the Cross, etc., and organizes his experience of the modern world with reference to the achievements of religious poetry. The more the external images are assimilated by a cultural tradition the more poetry is universal, and the more emotions are transfused into and embodied in sensual perceptions, the more poetry is intense: 'The poetic operation is made actual only in the endlessly rich internal articulation of a relation between the emotive and the sensuous which, according to Eliot, who has studied it in various aspects, resides in the words themselves, when they are purified from all purposes of ordinary intercourse.'[2]

Visible objects acquire a poetic value when they are the embodiment or the personification of emotions, and philosophical thought is transformed into poetry if it succeeds in being invested with concrete, actual symbols derived from immediate perception. This point is important because it justifies the introduction of philosophical thought in poetry. Eliot goes even as far as saying that the validity of the thought as thought may influence our appreciation of poetry: 'When the doctrine, theory, belief or "view of life" presented in a

[1] ibid., p. 155.   [2] ibid., p. 157.

poem is one which the mind of the reader can accept as coherent, mature, and founded on the facts of experience, it interposes no obstacle to the reader's enjoyment, whether it be one that he accept or deny, approve or deprecate. When it is one which the reader rejects as childish or feeble, it may, for a reader of well-developed mind, set up an almost complete check.' According to Eliot, it is convenient that a poet should rely upon accepted or recognizable ideas. Eliot attacks Blake's mythology because it is strictly personal. In Dante and Lucretius, writes Anceschi, 'we can see that a *concept*, an *objective truth*, becomes something which can be *perceived*. It is not accidental that I have used the words, *concept, objective truth*: philosophically, the poets, according to Eliot, have nothing to add to the knowledge of their time, to the thought which happens to be the living expression of the form in which truth is offered to their time; they are competent only to work it out according to the possibilities granted to their natural disposition, to give to thought some sort of imaginative concreteness.'[1]

It may be objected that the history of a particular period may call for a truth that is not accepted in that time, and that the truth proposed by Eliot is rejected and forgotten by almost everybody. The answer is perhaps that we live in a period of decadence, in a world already empty of any meaning, and that two attitudes are possible: a rejection of the world and a call for an unearthly truth. These two attitudes correspond roughly to the two main periods in Eliot's poetical work, a first in which satire and irony are predominant and the last in which a religious experience is expressed.

Several critics have sufficiently shown that the second period is the logical conclusion of the first. The weak point, however, in Eliot's thought, is perhaps the relation between his asceticism and his classicism, for his aesthetic theory emphasizes the importance of the technical achievement of the poets and disregards almost completely the contents; the style, which is used only as a means in his poems, is regarded as an end in his theory. This tendency might be ascribed to his sympathies with the Imagists and especially to the influence and friendship of Ezra Pound. Perfect technique is what Eliot appreciates most in poetry and emotion for emotion's sake what he most repudiates. He rejects Wordsworth's definition of poetry because he thinks that poetry must be the creation of something which does not exist in

[1] ibid., p. 160.

life, of a new object or reality: 'The business of the poet is not to find new emotions, but to use the ordinary ones and, in working them up into poetry, to express feelings which are not in actual emotions at all.'[1] However vague may be the words 'ordinary emotions', these considerations lead Eliot to a distinction between emotions of life and artistic emotions as well as between two realities: the realities witnessed by the sensations, perceptions, and reason on the one hand and the realities created by a poem on the other. This is the consequence of his theory of impersonality. Some critics have objected that Eliot is not impersonal at all, especially in his critical works,[2] and reject his interpretation of life. Even if they do not share his thought, they should admit that he is not concerned with his personal sensations and reactions, even with his particular ideas. Even in the *Quartets*, where the poet is the protagonist, he is concerned with what is universal in man; he projects his thoughts and his feelings against a cultural background and they are less his thoughts and his feelings than the experiences of any man transformed and elaborated in poetry: 'Impressions and experiences which are important for the man may take no place in the poetry, and those which become important in the poetry may play quite a negligible part in the man, the personality.' The categories of art are different, for him, from the categories of life: art is a creation. What Eliot writes about Donne might be applied to him: 'Jules Laforgue, and Tristan Corbière in many of his poems, are nearer to the "school of Donne" than any modern English poet. But poets more classical than they have the same essential quality of transmuting ideas into sensations, of transforming an observation into a state of mind.'[3]

When applying this process to his own poetry, Eliot justifies his allusive, oblique style: 'The poets of our time, writes Eliot in his essay on Dryden, must be difficult. Our civilization is very complex and varied, and this variety and complexity, operating on our refined sensations, must give rise to complex and varied results. The poet has to become always more *compressed*, more allusive, more indirect, even doing violence to language, in order to express himself.'

[1] *Tradition and the Individual Talent*, from *Selected Essays*, London, Faber and Faber, 1932, p. 21.

[2] Hamilton Fyfe, in *John o' London's Weekly*, 21 January 1949, in a review of *Notes towards the Definition of Culture*, maintains that culture is an individual possession and is not inseparable from religion.

[3] *The Metaphysical Poets* (*Selected Essays*, p. 290).

The preceding passage certainly deserves notice, and it has been quoted many times. It does not, however, describe all the relations between subject-matter and style in the poetry of our time. It considers poetry in relation to the external world and leaves aside the interior life with which Eliot deals elsewhere. In that respect it is interesting to consider what he says about Racine and Baudelaire: 'The greatest two masters of diction are also the greatest two psychologists, the most curious explorers of the soul.'[1] The importance attached by Eliot to the subjective aspect of life can be shown by the two following quotations: 'Racine and Donne looked into a good deal more than the heart.' On the contrary, 'two of the greatest masters of diction in our language, Milton and Dryden, triumph with a dazzling disregard of the soul'.[2]

Eliot has a very sharp notion of the problems of the soul, and connects them with his notions of classicism and authority. In order to understand these notions better, let us consider his ideas on culture. Eliot claims to be a European, and for him European civilization is a product of the classical culture: 'But Donne would have been an individual at any time and place; Marvell's best verse is the product of European, that is to say Latin, culture.'[3] The following passages show the relation which exists, in Eliot's view, between classicism and catholicism, two attitudes which spring directly, as we have seen, from his notion of authority: 'With Mr. Murry's formulation of classicism I cannot agree; the difference seems to me rather the difference between the complete and the fragmentary, the adult and the immature, the orderly and the chaotic. . . .' 'Mr. Murry makes his issue perfectly clear. "Catholicism", he says, "stands for the principle of unquestioned authority outside the individual; that is also the principle of Classicism in literature. . . ." Those of us who find ourselves supporting what Mr. Murry calls Classicism believe that men cannot get on without giving allegiance to something outside themselves.'[4] That principle of authority is the Church: 'I prefer to think of the Church as what I believe it is more and more coming to be, not the "English Church", but national as "the Catholic Church in England".'[5]

A result of these opinions is that Eliot stands against the English tradition of spontaneity and the German tradition of pantheism.

[1] ibid., p. 290.   [2] ibid.   [3] *Andrew Marvell* (*Selected Essays*, p. 293).
[4] *The Function of Criticism* (*Selected Essays*, p. 26).
[5] *Thoughts after Lambeth* (*Selected Essays*, p. 371).

'The English writer, the English divine, the English statesman, inherit no rules from their forebears; they inherit only this: a sense that
in the last resort they must depend upon the inner voice. . . .' 'The
inner voice, in fact, sounds remarkably like an old principle which
has been formulated by an elder critic in the now familiar phrase of
"doing as one likes".[1] The same principle of authority influences
Eliot's opinion about pantheism: 'Pantheism', writes Eliot, and he
certainly alludes to German pantheism, 'is not European.'[2]

The bulk of his work, his method of composing and his theory of
the creative process make him stand against spontaneity: 'Probably,
indeed, the larger part of the labour of an author in composing his
work is critical labour; the labour of sifting, combining, constructing,
expunging, correcting, testing: this frightful toil is as much critical as
creative.'[3]

Except in his poems written after 'The Hollow Men', the Christian
attitude and thought which are the foundation of Eliot's works are
not explicit, but they dominate the poems and exist in the form
of characters or objective symbols. His thought cannot be wholly
rejected and it has to be taken as a whole. His conversion to the
Catholic branch of the Anglican Church does not split his work into
two parts; on the contrary, it reinforces the significance of both
periods. It is dangerous to consider the first Eliot as a satirist and the
Eliot of the later period as a mystic: the same thought and the same
tradition inspire both.

To-day, Eliot no longer appears extravagant and revolutionary as
he appeared to the English public of the 'twenties. Those who have
intensely felt, beyond their private miseries, the profound misery of
Europe (and, indeed, Eliot is a European, as many cultured Ameri-
cans can claim to be) understand Eliot's complexity, his indirectness
and his final rejection of the world. They understand it better now,
and the young generation of poets is more disillusioned[4] and goes
further than Eliot in irony, in pity and in distress.

---

[1] *The Function of Criticism* (p. 27). This view of the English tradition is corrobor-
ated by Charles Morgan's opinion that 'the artist should listen to his voices'.
(Rencontres internationales, Geneva, September 1948.)

[2] *The Function of Criticism* (p. 28).   [3] ibid., p. 30.

[4] Herbert Read, in a lecture at Geneva University in 1946, said: 'Je crois en
cette nouvelle génération, parce que ses membres ont commencé leur vie sans
illusions: sans illusions religieuses, sans illusions politiques, sans illusions person-
nelles.' (*Présence*, avril 1946.)

PRUFROCK

PRUFROCK

'The Love Song of J. Alfred Prufrock'[1] begins a series of poems dominated by irony. The title itself is ironical. Prufrock is the personification of unredeemed life. Prufrock himself is partly aware that his life is insignificant, he is conscious of his ridiculousness and has much self-pity. He is a failure because he always postpones the decision of changing his life. He seems unable to disentangle himself from the net of banalities and pettiness in which he is caught, so that his hesitation is a sign of great sin.

If there is any affirmation in this poem, it is the affirmation that Prufrock is lost; correspondingly, the beauty of the poem consists in the picture of what Prufrock might have been and in his self-irony. Most poems of the first period are satirical poems. 'The Boston Evening Transcript', 'Aunt Helen', 'Cousin Nancy', 'Mr. Apollinax' and 'Conversation Galante' are satires of Boston. These poems should not be taken separately, for the same mood, the same technique and the same thought unites them. Whatever may be his subject, the poet expresses the deep sadness he feels in a decadent world. The reader feels that the world described by Eliot has lost its meaning and is not controlled by the mind; before *The Waste Land,* however, the poet will not denounce explicitly that deficiency, so that the reader of the early poems has the feeling of frustration brought by a purely destructive work. In the four 'Preludes', Eliot is experimenting in his method and his approach of his major subjects without the intermediacy of characters. They are all city landscapes and symbols of desolation. The images are chosen so as to suggest the barrenness of life:

> With the other masquerades
> That time resumes,
> One thinks of all the hands
> That are raising dingy shades
> In a thousand furnished rooms.

There is, however, in the fourth 'Prelude', a short apparition of beauty quickly swept away by an hysterical gesture indicating that Eliot's disgust overwhelms his pity:

[1] *Collected Poems,* 1909–35, London, Faber and Faber, 1936, p. 11.

> I am moved by fancies that are curled
> Around these images and cling:
> The notion of some infinitely gentle
> Infinitely suffering thing.
>
> Wipe your hand across your mouth, and laugh;
> The worlds revolve like ancient women
> Gathering fuel in vacant lots.

The desolation of a modern city is also expressed in 'Rhapsody on a Windy Night', which produces the effect of a similar intense sadness.

The same capacity for correlating and adapting landscapes and characters to his critical mood is displayed by Eliot in 'Poems—1920', including four poems in French. It is a pity that Eliot should have left his French poems to the appreciation of the public, for they are ridiculous rather than satirical and many expressions in them are not correct. The self-irony of 'Mélange Adultère de Tout' is a disguised and unconfessed boasting.

It is not enough to give a general idea of the meaning and purpose of 'Prufrock'. The poem has been closely examined by the critics who have devoted themselves to the interpretation of the character. It is a dramatic character, who is on the verge of tragedy but who never makes the final jump. He is inhibited, full of self-pity, unable to answer the call of his secret voices and to force the situation to its climax; he is bound to live in a kind of mediocrity, in a kind if 'no-man's-land':

> Streets that follow like a tedious argument
> Of insidious intent
> To lead you to an overwhelming question . . .
> Oh, do not ask, 'What is it?'
> Let us go and make our visit.

A method which is frequently used in the earlier poems is that of announcing something beautiful and of presenting instead something ludicrous. Through that process, Eliot contrasts the sadness of our time with a half-suggested beauty.

In order to determine Prufrock's problem and the virtual tragedy which it involves it is necessary to leave the wonderfully worked-out scenery in the background and to follow the narrow path which leads from the concrete images—the body or the sensual substance of the poem—to the emotion—the tragic sense of pity and fear perfectly incarnated in the character. The result will not be an explanation, but it will enable us to present the metaphysical aspect of the theme. The end of that path is indicated by the six lines from Dante following the title:

> S'io credesse che mia riposta fosse
> A persona che mai tornasse al mondo,
> Questa fiamma staria senza piu scosse.
> Ma perciocche giammai di questo fondo
> Non torno vivo alcun, s'i'odo il vero,
> Senza tema d'infamia ti rispondo.

If this interpretation is right, the motto reveals that Eliot considers 'Prufrock' as a confession, but not a personal confession like Oscar Wilde's *De Profundis*: it is the *De Profundis* of our time. The abyss into which Prufrock is pushed, in spite of the comic, but intensely depressing, atmosphere of the poem, might well be suggested by these words:

> giammai di questo fondo
> Non torno vivo alcun,

This interpretation throws some light on all the similes and on the haunting hesitation of the rhythm.

Prufrock's love, if his feeling may be termed so, is 'the love of created beings' and, more exactly, the love of a life without meaning, of a social life which appears to him as inevitable, dreadfully limited and mean:

> For I have known them all already, known them all—
> Have known the evenings, mornings, afternoons,
> I have measured out my life with coffee-spoons,

and inevitably reduced to the measure of common thought:

> (They will say: 'How his hair is growing thin!')

'Inevitable' was not the right word: it did not take account of the unfinished drama which Prufrock's hesitation and failure involves:

THOUGHT IN T. S. ELIOT'S POETRY

> There will be time . . .
>
> .   .   .   .
>
> And time yet for a hundred indecisions
> And for a hundred visions and revisions,
> Before the taking of a toast and tea.

And:

> Do I dare
> Disturb the universe?

It would be easy to follow Prufrock's hesitation: it pervades the poem to the end.

The essential inconsistency shown by Eliot in Prufrock's character is well described by Dilys Powell: 'The poem is, in fact, concerned with fitting together incongruities. Prufrock cannot reconcile his own character with the romantic situation into which he foresees himself drawn; he cannot reconcile either with the anti-social passions of which he is momentarily aware.'[1]

'The second poem, "Portrait of a Lady", reverses the situation; here it is the woman who makes tentative advances to a man younger than herself.'[2]

According to Dilys Powell, the main point in Eliot's earlier poems is to denounce the decay which attacks society. 'Mr. Robert Graves and Miss Laura Riding have ingeniously explained the poem "Burbank with a Baedeker; Bleistein with a Cigar" as dealing with the decline of Venice under the usurping Jew.'[3]

There is no flesh on the bones of philosophy to-day and poetry has fallen into disrepute; religion and the Church, too, are involved in the dryness of the waste land.

Some of Eliot's characters belong to a certain class of people, 'les déracinés', 'les blasés', the cosmopolitan society of half-leisurely people whose culture is a make-up and a futile refinement. This would apply as well to 'Mr. Apollinax', 'Conversation Galante', 'Gerontion' and 'Burbank'. They are all already inhabitants of the waste land. F. O. Matthiessen points out that 'Prufrock, the fastidious and futile middle-aged product of the genteel tradition, and

---

[1] *Descent from Parnassus*, London, The Cresset Press, 1934, p. 62.
[2] ibid., p. 63.
[3] ibid., p. 67. 'Dear me! I should never have thought so, myself,' exclaims Eliot on a marginal note in a draft of this chapter.

Sweeney, the tough Irishman "assured of certain certainties", are Eliot's chief response to the decadent Boston he knew as a young man.'[1]

Many interpretations of Prufrock have been proposed, and this may be due to the fact that the character is not built upon an abstract or artificial type, but on mere observation, later rearranged and interpreted. It is difficult to reduce observation to theories. The weak point of Eliot's idea of 'the objective correlative' is perhaps that it may prevent the poet from saying exactly what he means, especially when the poet wants to convey a truth which does not necessarily find its support in the external world. Yeats's attitude is much less ambiguous in that respect. 'I believe', he writes, 'that all men will more and more reject the opinion that poetry is a "criticism of life", and be more convinced that it is a revelation of a hidden life.'[2]

Louis MacNeice, in *Eliot and the Adolescent*,[3] gives an example of a distorted view of Prufrock and makes clear that Prufrock, who is presented in a moment of crisis—crisis without solution—is neither an exception nor an artificial product: 'For us it was merely a case of Prufrock (meaning Us) versus Society; that Prufrock himself is a product of that society was something we chose to ignore. So when he says, "Do I dare disturb the universe?" we assumed that he could if he wanted to.'

It is unnecessary for our purpose to give a more detailed analysis of Prufrock's character, and yet the passage where the 'objective truth' and the 'revealed truth' are mixed should not pass unnoticed:

> We have lingered in the chambers of the sea
> By sea-girls wreathed with seaweed red and brown
> Till human voices wake us, and we drown.

Prufrock's self-pity and self-knowledge are darkened by a presentiment of another life; the solution of this dramatic situation is that Prufrock chooses to listen to human voices. By refusing to listen to the voices of the mermaids he rejects the call of the life beyond, the call of beauty, and drowns. He knows that there is another way,

---

[1] *American Poetry, 1920–1940* (*The Sewanee Review*, Winter 1947, p. 33).

[2] Quoted in Matthiessen's *The Achievement of T. S. Eliot*; London, O.U.P., 1935, p. 90.

[3] Published in *T. S. Eliot, a Symposium*, p. 148.

another life, but he avoids them and, closing his eyes, he abandons himself to a life 'measured out with coffee-spoons', hopeless, un-redeemable.

The other characters make the same mistake, the mistake of the ostrich. They are symptoms of the blindness of our time. It can be easily guessed from that remark that for Eliot the antidote is mysticism, and the clinging to a social order and institution which would save us from the danger which we do not want to see or to prevent. Maybe the wide diffusion of Eliot is not due to the fact that we recognize Prufrock or the other characters. Other non-poetical factors, like the Nobel Prize bestowed upon him in 1948, recently increased his popularity, and this rush towards books for external reasons is just one more sign of our blindness, who need an external incentive to discover works to which we would otherwise never pay attention.

THE WASTE LAND

All the ideas of Eliot on impersonality, culture, history, politics, and authority find their poetic expression in *The Waste Land*. The development of the poem tends to show the need for a spiritual regeneration of man.

As the same argumentation is more apparent in 'The Hollow Men', where there are fewer literary allusions, it is convenient to examine this poem first. The emptiness of modern man suggested by 'The Hollow Men' awakens in the reader a spiritual longing; the subjective aspect of the poem is sustained by its objective justification. The junction of these two aspects produces a compelling effect, for the emptiness expressed in the poem is not without grandeur; the men whose actions are paralysed or sterile, whose will is inefficient and whose mind is blind are the medium of a religious feeling. This summary does nothing to give an idea of the poem, but it succeeds perhaps in defining the theme, for the theme is not important, it is but a whimper, stuffed men in a desolate landscape where there is nothing to see but the shadow which brings human life to nothing. The atmosphere of the poem, however, is not filled with despair, it is a solemn atmosphere, for the poet succeeds in expressing, through the medium of his exotic images of modern life, the necessity of a divine presence rather than the futility of the hollow men. The strong rhythm and the harmony of the form contribute to that solemnity. Eliot takes advantage of a similar process in his later poems, especially in the wonderful choruses of *The Rock*.

The theme of *The Waste Land* is similar to that of 'The Hollow Men', but it would require a very long interpretation and indeed it provokes an abundance of comments. Such work has already been done by various hands. Eliot himself has been urged to accompany the text with a certain number of 'Notes' which supply the references and elucidate the frequent allusions to Dante, The Bible, Webster's *White Devil*, Shakespeare, Ovid's *Metamorphoses*, the *Brihadaranyaka Upanishad* and various other sources. The most important of them are Frazer's *The Golden Bough*, and above all Miss Weston's *From Ritual to Romance*.[1] This abundance of sources makes the style extremely indirect and lessens the pleasure of reading. The most laborious interpretation of the poem is the one by Cleanth Brooks,[2] who elucidates all the allusions and literary associations which, according to him, succeed in forming a whole. That poetry and meaning survive beneath the heap of allusions is a miracle. We shall not try to establish all the connections between all the passages and sources of the poem, for it would lead us far from our subject. Let us, however, quote a passage from Brooks which shows the complexity and the technique of the poem: 'The Hanged Man, who represents the hanged god of Frazer (including the Christ), Eliot states in a note, is associated with the hooded figure who appears in "What the Thunder Said". That he is hooded accounts for Madame Sosostris's inability to see him.'[3]

Brooks's interpretation proves that the text is compact and forms a logical sequence; it does not prove that there is both unity and emotional, dramatic progression in the poem. The second section, for example, is a 'concrete illustration' of the first. The whole poem is the development of a philosophical thought, and the ideological element is perhaps as important as the technical element. The most important features of the latter are characterized by Brooks as follows: 'Of hardly less importance to the reader, however, is a knowledge of Eliot's basic method. *The Waste Land* is built on a major contrast—a device which is a favourite of Eliot's and is to be found in

[1] Cambridge University Press, 1920.
[2] *Modern Poetry and the Tradition*, The Univ. of N. Carolina Press, 1939
[3] ibid., p. 143.

133

many of his poems, particularly in his later poems. The contrast is between two kinds of life and two kinds of death. Life devoid of meaning is death; sacrifice, even the sacrificial death, may be life-giving, an awakening to life. The poem occupies itself to a great extent with this paradox, and with a number of variations upon it.'[1] In other words, Eliot's purpose is to propose a Christian interpretation of life and to prove the human need for regeneration (provided that we accept that man is endowed with a spirit, and is not 'the natural man' of Edwin Muir). The reason why Eliot's faith had to be clothed in esoteric symbols is explained by Brooks in the following passage: 'The Christian material is at the centre, but the poet never deals with it directly. The theme of resurrection is made on the surface in terms of the fertility rites; the words which the thunder speaks are Sanscrit words.'[2] Brooks's conclusion is that 'in this way the statement of beliefs emerges *through* confusion and cynicism—not in spite of them'.[3]

Eliot's attempt in this poem is similar to the attempt of neo-scholasticism to blend revealed and objective truth in a philosophical system based on the work of Thomas Aquinas but taking account of the progress of science. Eliot's 'objective correlatives', as we have already seen, are interpreted in the light of faith, some would say of preconceived ideas. If we accept that faith we accept the connections Eliot establishes between the fertility rituals, the Grail Legends, Dante, Shakespeare and the aspects of contemporary life described by Eliot. Otherwise we may claim that the work is inconsistent.

The numerous allusions to the past and to esoteric ritual are interspersed with sudden allusions to the present, and the poem, in its chaotic form, suggests the disintegration of modern civilization, to which the visions of the Hindoo sacred books, of the Ecclesiastes and of Dante can be applied.[4]

We shall try, however, to divest the poem from its literary implications in order to extract its metaphysical meaning. But it is impossible to do so without first examining the references to Miss Weston's *From*

[1] ibid., p. 137.   [2] ibid., p. 171.   [3] ibid., p. 172.

[4] Eliot would justify his constant use of fragments of poetry by the following considerations: 'I have tried to point out the relation of the poem to other poems by other authors, and suggested the conception of poetry as a living whole of all the poetry that has ever been written.' (*Selected Essays, Tradition and the Individual Talent*, p. 17.)

Ritual to Romance. The waste land, or the land of death-in-life, is the earth in all its aspects: nature, men, and cities. The first section of the poem, entitled 'The Burial of the Dead', conveys not so much the idea of a burial as the fear of death-in-death and consequently of resurrection. April is the month of which men are most afraid, for it involves a rebirth:

> April is the cruellest month, breeding
> Lilacs out of the dead land, mixing
> Memory and desire, stirring
> Dull roots with spring rain.

The word 'nature' takes a different meaning if we relate it to the primitive Aryan cult of nature, and the seasons have a different meaning if we try to imagine what they meant for the singers of the *Rig-Veda*. More than a disguise of Eliot's convictions as a Christian, the allusions to Indian rituals are the whole foundation of the poem. These rituals have never been completely lost, they still exist in various, isolated manifestations of folk-lore, they have been observed and transmitted by the Templars and the Knights of the Grail, they were preserved by the early Grail legends, then they are forbidden by the Church and they make a last literary appearance with Tennyson, Wagner, E. A. Robinson and Matthew Arnold. The disappearance of these rituals in Western Europe coincides with a weakening of religious belief and with the corresponding meaninglessness of our life. The waste land, or our epoch, is a dry land, that is, a land deprived of its connections with and help from supernatural forces and fertilizing deities.

In order to understand why water occupies such an important place in *The Waste Land*, it is necessary to remember the meaning of water for the Indian populations where the 'nature cult' and the 'vegetation ceremonies' took place.

'We must first note that a very considerable number of the *Rig-Veda* hymns depend for their initial inspiration on the actual bodily needs and requirements of a mainly agricultural population, i.e. of a people that depend upon the fruits of the earth for their subsistence, and to whom the regular and ordered sequence of the processes of Nature was a vital necessity.'[1]

This passage throws an intense light on our first quotation from

[1] *From Ritual to Romance*, pp. 23 and 24.

The Waste Land. The 'dryness', meaninglessness of modern life which
is the theme of the first paragraph of the poem:

> I read, much of the night, and go south in the winter

helps at the same time to elucidate Eliot's main purpose, which is to
show the necessity of giving a meaning to life, of turning back to the
profound and elementary sources of life, of restoring religion in its
original spontaneity and efficacy, and of reuniting our culture,
'these fragments' (line 430).

Throughout the poem, the present time is projected against a
background of defunct civilizations, as if the thread of history had
been lost and as if we were deprived of the eternal sources of inspiration and left with a heap of reminiscences which we no longer
consider as part of our life:

> O O O O that Shakespehearian Rag—
> It's so elegant
> So intelligent
> 'What shall I do now? What shall I do?'
> 'I shall rush out as I am, and walk the street
> 'With my hair down, so. What shall we do to-morrow?
> 'What shall we ever do?'

The man of our time is lost because he has lost his origin out of
sight.

After allusions to Ezekiel ('Son of man' . . .) and to *Tristan und
Isolde* ('Frisch . . .' and 'Oed'und leer das Meer'), the poet leads the
readers to the room of

> Madame Sosostris, famous clairvoyante,

where the ancient cultures still survive in their most corrupted form.
There the past, the buried life, makes a shadowy appearance and two
figures stand out, the 'Phoenician Sailor' and the 'Hanged man':

> Here, said she,
> Is your card, the drowned Phoenician Sailor,
> (Those are pearls that were his eyes. Look!)

These ghosts, together with the most important of them, Tiresias,
appear several times in the poem. They are haunting us to-day, for

they are symbols of the loss suffered by mankind, of the break with our origins and of the artificial way in which historical continuity is preserved. The allusions to Baudelaire, Dante, and to the Dirge in Webster's *White Devil* strengthen the feeling of frustration which pervades this section:

> And each man fixed his eyes before his feet.

The second section of the poem, entitled 'A Game of Chess', marks one more step towards the revelation of utter dryness and the urgency of death. Every simile is used to suggest the immediate presence of death and the quick disintegration of life, as if life were but a short interval before the end. This last point is made clear by the recurrence of the customary command:

> HURRY UP, PLEASE, IT'S TIME!

and by the last greetings:

> Goonight Bill. Goonight Lou. Goonight May. Goonight.
> Ta ta. Goonight. Goonight.
> Good night, ladies, good night, sweet ladies, good night,
> good night.

These greetings suggest that there is for us nothing else to do than to lose awareness, that life has no longer any purpose:

> What you get married for if you don't want children?

The picture of spiritual emptiness in 'A Game of Chess' is completed by allusions to Shakespeare, Virgil, Milton, Ovid's *Metamorphoses*, and Webster:

> The wind under the door.
> 'What is that noise now? What is the wind doing?'
> Nothing again nothing.

The theme of the third section, 'The Fire Sermon', is lust, purposeless sensuality symbolized by fire. Tiresias, the main protagonist, is a man in whom two sexes meet, and Eliot warns the readers that 'he sees the substance of the poem'. That assertion might be explained by saying that Tiresias, through his anomaly, outlives himself and undergoes successive metamorphoses which enable him to see the past in the present:

> (And I Tiresias have foresuffered all
> Enacted on this same divan or bed;
> I who have sat by Thebes below the wall
> And walked among the lowest of the dead.)

'The Fire Sermon' is full of London imagery and scattered with interludes such as the meeting of two lovers, the 'typist' and the 'small house agent's clerk', and a party of Queen Elizabeth and Leicester recorded in Froude's *Elizabeth*. The last allusion is to St. Augustine:

> To Carthage then I came
>
> Burning burning burning
> O Lord thou pluckest me out
> O Lord thou pluckest
> burning

The fourth section of the poem, 'Death by Water', calls for reference to Miss Weston's book. What death by water meant for the early Indians is well explained by Miss Weston: 'Tradition relates that the seven great rivers of India had been imprisoned by the evil giant, Vitra, or Ahi, whom Indra slew, thereby releasing the streams from their captivity. . . .'[1] 'The *Rig-Veda* hymns abound in references to this feat. . . .

> 'Indra has filled the rivers, he has inundated the dry land.'
> 'Indra has released the imprisoned waters to flow upon the
> earth.'[2]

The second appearance of the 'Phoenician Sailor', or 'Phlebas the Sailor', in 'Death by Water' is elucidated by another passage in *From Ritual to Romance*: 'The worship of Adonis . . . was originally of Phoenician origin.'[3] Phlebas, 'who was once handsome and tall as you', is mentioned in one of the poems in French, 'Dans le Restaurant'. The story of the death of Phlebas, which constitutes this short section:

> A current under sea
> Picked his bones in whispers

---

[1] *From Ritual to Romance*, p. 24.   [2] ibid., p. 25.   [3] ibid ,. p 40.

is the symbol of divine judgment. It is the story of the doom of Phlebas and it adds very little to the theme of the preceding sections, except that the symbol of water is more general in its implications than the symbol of fire. Brooks's interpretation of this section is too hypothetical and far-fetched, as all detailed interpretations of *The Waste Land* are bound to be. It is possible to find new and unsuspected connections between the works and facts alluded to, but it would be quite legitimate also to find discrepancies and divergences. The only advantage of the allusive style is that it enables the reader to make a cultural synthesis. But it may mislead him as well. It is difficult to find support in the text for the following remark: 'At least, with a kind of hindsight, one may suggest that "Death by Water" gives an instance of the conquest of death and time, the "perpetual recurrence of determined seasons", the "world of spring and autumn, birth and dying" through death itself.'

The fifth and last section, 'What the Thunder said', may have been inspired indirectly by some passages of the Grail legends: 'Perceval, seeking the Grail Castle, rides all day through a heavy storm, which passes off at nightfall, leaving the weather calm and clear. . . .' 'At a much later point Manessier tells how Perceval, riding through the forest, is overtaken by a terrible storm. He takes refuge in a Chapel which he recognizes as that of the Black Hand.'[1]

The prevailing symbol of this section, however, is that of aridity (the same theme and the same symbol are used in 'The Hollow Men') which brings a longing, a sickness and hallucinations. As this section contains direct allusions to an Indian source, the *Brihadaranyaka Upanishad*, it is convenient to pick out some passages from Miss Weston's book which present us with the symbol of the dryness of the waste land; first some passages referring to Indian mythology, especially that of the *Rig-Veda:* 'Their hymns and prayers, and, as we have strong reason to suppose, their dramatic ritual, were devised for the main purpose of obtaining from the gods of their worship that which was essential to insure their well-being and the fertility of their land—warmth, sunshine, above all, sufficient water. . . .' '. . . It is Indra to whom a disproportionate number of the hymns are addressed, . . . it is from him the much desired boon of rain and abundant water is besought . . . the restoration of the rivers to their channels, the "Freeing of the Waters".'

[1] ibid., p. 166.

Here is a passage on the god Mithra: 'His beneficent activities might seem to afford a meeting ground with the vegetation gods—"Il donne l'accroissement, il donne l'abondance, il donne les troupeaux, il donne la progéniture et la vie".'[1]

These myths appear in the Grail Legends: 'As a result the springs dried up, the land became waste, and the court of the Rich Fisher, which had filled the land with plenty, could no longer be found.

'For 1000 years the land lies waste, till, in the days of King Arthur, . . .'

Eliot's allusions are usually precise, but, as the unity of the theme obliges us to take them as a whole, they are so compressed and indirect that, even if we find that they are connected with one another, we cannot help thinking that the whole is chaotic and we question the validity of Eliot's syncretism.

The incident of the storm in the Grail Legends is accidentally related to the episode of the Chapel Perilous, whereas Eliot establishes an intellectual or a rational connection between his various, independent sources. Here is one of his references: 'Students of the Grail romances will remark that in many of the versions the hero—sometimes it is a heroine—meets with a strange and terrifying adventure in a mysterious Chapel. . . . The details vary: sometimes there is a Dead Body laid on the altar; sometimes a Black Hand extinguishes the tapers.[2]

This passage helps us to understand the second theme of 'What the Thunder said', as Eliot himself writes that the three themes opening this part are '1 the journey to Emmaus, 2 the approach of the Chapel Perilous, 3 the present decay of eastern Europe'. These three themes are but illustrations of one single theme: the falling down of the temporal world and the promise of a revivification through the spirit. This section of *The Waste Land* marks a turning point in Eliot's work since the satire of the world is accompanied for the first time by a message of hope; the poem is no longer ironical, destructive, and negative. The relation between the scene of universal desolation, the symbols of the cock,[3] the sensual symbol of the hair, the notion of sympathy and the religious exhortation at the end of the

---

[1] ibid., p. 156, from Cumont: *Les Mystères de Mithra*.

[2] ibid., p. 166.

[3] 'Another form which the corn spirit often assumes is that of a cock.' (Frazer: *The Golden Bough*, London, Macmillan, 1890, vol. 2, p.7.)

poem is made clearer by this remark: 'We have already seen in the Naasene document that the Mystery ritual comprised a double initiation, the Lower, into the mystery of generation, i.e. of physical life; the Higher, into the Spiritual Divine Life, where man is made one with God.'[1]

The episode of the Journey to Emmaus is an opportunity for Eliot to repeat the theme of Dante's Limbo, or death-in-life:

> He who was living is now dead
> We who were living are now dying
> With a little patience.

Since the Hanged God (i.e. Christ) died, life is unreal and men sometimes catch glimpses of an unknown reality. The hallucination or mirage related in this section is a symbol of the supernatural beside which life fades away; it is derived from the account of an Antarctic expedition: 'it is related that the party of explorers, at the extremity of their strength, had the constant delusion that there was *one more member* than could actually be counted.'[2] Not less nightmarish is the approach of the Chapel Perilous, which appears as a destroyed chapel:

> In this decayed hole among the mountains
> In the faint moonlight, the grass is singing
> Over the tumbled graves, about the chapel
> There is the empty chapel, only the wind's home.
> It has no windows, and the door swings,
> Dry bones can harm no one.

Then we hear the cock crying, we see the clouds gathering over the dry Ganga and finally the thunder speaks. The first word in Sanskrit means: 'Give', and the scenery is taken from the *Rig-Veda* and the *Brihadaranyaka Upanishad*:

> Ganga was sunken, and the limp leaves
> Waited for rain, while the black clouds
> Gathered far distant, over Humavant.
> The jungle crouched, humped in silence.
> Then spoke the thunder
> DA
> Datta: what have we given?

[1] ibid., p. 172.   [2] 'Notes on *The Waste Land*.'

There is, in the answer to the preceding question, an allusion to the mysteries of generation, to the 'lower initiation':

> My friend, blood shaking my heart
> The awful daring of a moment's surrender
> Which an age of prudence can never retract
> By this, and this only, we have existed.

The commentary to the word *Dayadhvam*, 'sympathize', is provided by Dante, F. H. Bradley, and Shakespeare; they explain that we are living in a prison without communication with the external world, except for a key which is the symbol of the surrender to something outside the self.[1]

The third word of the thunder is: *Damyata*, 'control':

> DA
> *Damyata*: The boat responded
> Gaily, to the hand expert with sail and oar
> The sea was calm, your heart would have responded
> Gaily, when invited, beating obedient
> To controlling hands

The Fisher King makes his last appearance in the poem on the shore of a land which is still the waste land, but he is resolved to fight its sterility:

> I sat upon the shore
> Fishing, with the arid plain behind me
> Shall I at least set my lands in order?

Cleanth Brooks relates this passage to the last sentence of Eliot's 'Thoughts after Lambeth'. The comparison is not implied by the poem, but it is provoked: 'The World', writes Eliot, 'is trying the experiment of attempting to form a civilized but non-Christian mentality. The experiment will fail; but we must be very patient in awaiting its collapse; meanwhile redeeming the time: so that the Faith may be preserved alive through the dark ages before us; to renew and rebuild civilization, and save the World from suicide.'

In connection with these opinions of the episode is a fragment of Dante's *Purgatorio* quoted at the end of *The Waste Land*, where

---

[1] The allusion is to F. H. Bradley's *Appearance and Reality*, in which the author claims that external sensations, thought, and feelings are 'a circle closed on the outside' and that 'every sphere is opaque to the others which surround it'.

Arnaut joyfully leaps back into the purifying fire. The last eight lines contain allusions to fragments from *Pervigilium Veneris*, Nerval's 'El Desdichado', Kid's *Spanish Tragedy*, and finally the benediction ending the *Upanishads:* 'Shantih shantih shantih', which means: 'The peace which passeth understanding.'

The paradoxes, contrasts, and developments which are the foundation of *The Waste Land* could be reduced to the simple thought that life is empty without an external, divine help. There is an emotive, poetic argumentation which leads to that single thought. For Eliot, 'there is a logic of the imagination as well as a logic of concepts'. We understand the themes of *The Waste Land* and of 'The Hollow Men' better when we relate them to Eliot's view that 'poetry not only must be found only *through* suffering but can find its material only *in* suffering'. The longest part of *The Waste Land* is a picture of sterility, and at the end the poet exhorts us to rely upon God.

Now that single thought is clothed in a multiplicity of variations and illustrations, some of which are not necessarily connected with the theme and with the exhortation to belief which it implies. Some allusions are far-fetched and some variations are loose. Whether or not Eliot succeeds in conveying his thought through his allusions to various sources, the method itself, or the attempt, has to be discussed. The principle underlying and justifying Eliot's process in *The Waste Land* is that the poet should return 'to the most primitive and forgotten' and combine 'the most ancient and the most civilized mentality'. The sense of one's age is the sense of what is permanent in one's age, and in that respect Eliot is qualified in blending together images of antiquity and of the contemporary waste land. But is it really necessary to make precise allusions and to refer to precise sources, so that the poem depends on other poems and does not itself convey its whole meaning? The allusions of *The Waste Land* enable the reader to extract various meanings from one single image, but these meanings have a scholarly smell, they are made of special comparisons of a rather logical kind and they do not endow the image with that bright and pervading quality of an infinite meaning which might be described as 'magical'. The pleasure derived from the knowledge and interpretation of sources and allusions is not a poetic pleasure, for they are not part of the poem. This is why the best passages of *The Waste Land* are those which are beautiful in spite of their allusions and without reference to anything else. When all the

poetic substance is inside the poem, the method of combining sensations and emotions and of associating symbols of various cultures,
from the most primitive to the most recent, is perfectly adequate.

We have applied an aesthetic criterion to the thought implied in
The Waste Land, but this process is not so irrelevant as it seems
since Eliot himself insists that thought and form are one and the
same. Moreover, the images of the poem are all the more vivid and
convincing because they are closer to the thought and emotion; they
support one another and the poem fails only when they are separated.
In other words, the poem is good in proportion as the images are perfectly adapted to the thoughts and emotions which they represent.
Poetry is therefore all the more beautiful because it expresses a wider
and more convincing view of life and the enjoyment of poetry cannot
be wholly divorced from the beliefs it expresses. This explains why
Eliot prefers Dante to Shakespeare and why in his later poems he is
more specially concerned with religious experience.

LATER POETRY

'Ash-Wednesday' (1930) is a continuation of *The Waste Land* as
far as the theme is concerned. It is more intimate than the preceding
poems, and the protagonist, as in the *Four Quartets*[1] is the poet
himself. The six sections of the poem correspond to six states of mind:

1. The poet gives up any hope, owing to the limitations of
time and space:

> Because I know that time is always time
> And place is always and only place
> And what is actual is actual only for one time
> And only for one place
> I rejoice that things are as they are and
> I renounce the blessed face.

The poetry is bare and the mood is that of calm resignation which is
commanded by circumstance.

2. Something, however, springs from that resignation: memory;
the oblivion of the earth calls for the memory of God; through the
intercession of the Virgin, 'bones shine with brightness'.

3. The symbol used in the third section is that of the stair in Dante's

---

[1] London, Faber and Faber, 1944.

Purgatorio. After rising above 'the deceitful face of hope and despair' the poet, in his spiritual ascent, discovers that he is unable to go further, that the reach of the human spirit is limited. Therefore he calls for a superior spirit:

> Lord I am not worthy
> but speak the word only

4. The fourth section marks a progression in the poet's meditation: he experiences a moment of eternity in the middle of time, symbolized by a sister in the middle of a garden:

> The silent sister veiled in white and blue
> Between the yews, behind the garden god,

The theme and the mood anticipate the *Four Quartets*.

5. The next step is an expression of the poet's faith, or his belief in Incarnation. The symbol of the wheel of the first section is completed by the symbol of the centre. The wheel of the temporal world has an axle or a still point which represents eternity or Incarnation within the world. The same symbol is further developed in the *Four Quartets*:

> And the light shone in darkness and
> Against the World the unstilled world still whirled
> About the centre of the silent Word

'The veiled sister', symbol of faith, prays for those who are caught in the limitations of time and space.

6. The last section recapitulates the vision of solitude implied in the preceding sections and ends in a cry:

> Suffer me not to be separated
> And let my cry come unto Thee.

The profound change which makes the difference between the early, ironical poems and the later ones is in the nature of the images, rather than in their thought, and their symbolic value is more and more extended until they express spiritual realities. The corresponding reduction of and control over the materials used by the poet enable him to endow his images with a wider and more intense meaning. The 'heap of broken images' is more and more eliminated from Eliot's works, and this is certainly a gain for his

poetry, which becomes meaningful, purer and more creative instead
of being based on mere destructive observation. This effort culminates in the *Four Quartets* with an attempt to go even beyond the
images.

'The Journey of the Magi', a narrative poem, leads to the same
dilemma as 'Ash-Wednesday': to resign or to die. The Magi, after
having suffered long hardships, find their discovery both reassuring
and disconcerting:

> this Birth was
>
> Hard and bitter agony for us, like Death, our death

The birth of Christ means, indeed, death to the world, and the
narrator foresees the necessity of Christ's agony:

> We returned to our places, these Kingdoms,
> But no longer at ease here, in the old dispensation,
> With an alien people clutching their gods.
> I should be glad of another death.

Both 'A Song for Simeon' and 'Animula' illustrate the death of
those who refuse to take the last step:

> Not for me the martyrdom, the ecstasy of thought and
>
> > prayer,
>
> Not for me the ultimate vision.

'Animula', especially, is the tragedy of the closed souls:

> The pain of living and the drug of dreams
> Curl up the small soul in the window seat
> Behind the *Encyclopedia Britannica*.

'Marina', the last of the 'Ariel Poems', and perhaps one of the most
beautiful of Eliot's poems, is full of a nostalgia for an existence
beyond earth, where lives the lost daughter, and which is indicated
by the shores, the whispers and the feet: images of the temporal
world are in this poem symbols of the spiritual world and a direct
expression of the poet's longing.

If, in this survey of some of Eliot's later poems, we have noticed a
crystallization of the themes, we should not conclude that it is a sign
of sterility. On the contrary, the use which the poet makes of his
theme is more important than the theme itself, and the thought is
inseparable from the images. Even the *Four Quartets*, after all, are

crystallized around Eliot's experience of plenitude. 'In dealing with Eliot, as with Yeats, there is always the danger that several writers will say the same thing, choosing different examples of the repeated ideas or images of the poets to illustrate their own comments.'[1]

The originality of Eliot, and of all poets, lies in the freshness and intensity of their perception of things already known, and more particularly in the constantly renewed and progressing use of the images which, in Eliot's case, from chosen sensory experiences, become more and more symbolical until they directly express a reality which transcends them.

It is not important if the subject-matter is thin; the poetry lies in the working and transforming of the subject-matter, and it implies a considerable effort of thought. The poet operates a transfiguration of the world by conferring a meaning upon it, and his task is not to represent anything: there lies another thought than philosophical thought, a thought which is not made of statements, an operating thought which really creates. The discipline of poetical thought endows with a fruitful meaning things which otherwise are distressing, hopeless, blank, and mute.

The preceding insistence on the handling of the themes justifies Eliot for using a musical form in the *Four Quartets*. The best account of this form is to be found in Raymond Preston's *Four Quartets Rehearsed*[2] and in Helen Gardner's *Four Quartets: a Commentary*.[3] Let us quote from the last work the following passage: 'The structure of the poems is seen very clearly when they are read together, and can be recognized as being essentially the same as the structure of *The Waste Land*. It is far more rigid than we should suspect from reading any of the poems by itself. In fact, Mr. Eliot has invented for himself, as the word *Quartets* suggests, a kind of poetic equivalent of "sonata form", containing what are best described as five "movements", each with an inner necessary structure, and capable of the symphonic richness of *The Waste Land* or the chamber-music beauties of Burnt Norton. The five movements suggest the five acts of a drama, and the poems are built on a dialectical basis, employing deliberate reversals and contrasts in matter and style. . . .' 'The first movement

---

[1] *English Studies*, vol. XXIX, No. 6, December 1948, review of *T. S. Eliot, A Study of his Writings*.

[2] London, Sheed and Ward, 1946.

[3] *The Penguin New Writing*, 29, p. 123.

in each of the *Quartets* consists of statement and counter-statement in a free blank verse. . . .' 'The second movement shows the most striking similarities from poem to poem. It opens with a highly "poetical" lyric passage. . . .' 'This is followed by an extremely colloquial passage, in which the idea which had been treated in metaphor and symbol in the first half of the movement is expanded, and given personal application, in a conversational manner. . . .' 'The third movement is the core of each poem, out of which reconciliation grows; it is an exploration, with a twist, of the ideas of the first two movements. . . .' 'The fourth movement is a lyric in all four poems. The fifth is again in two parts, but the change in manner and metre is slighter than in the second movement and it is reversed. Here the colloquial passage comes first, and then, without a feeling of sharp break, the rhythm tightens and the manner becomes graver for a kind of falling close. The whole movement recapitulates the themes of the poem, with personal and topical applications, and makes a resolution of the discords of the first.' Miss Gardner draws attention to the similarity between the structure of the *Quartets* and that of *The Waste Land* and stresses the preoccupation with time which is alike expressed in *The Family Reunion*, in the choruses of *The Rock*, and in 'Ash-Wednesday'. ' 'Burnt Norton', 'East Coker', 'The Dry Salvages' and 'Little Gidding' are poems on one theme, or rather on different aspects of the same theme, and they are closely linked with *The Family Reunion*, which is a dramatic treatment of the subject. The theme can be variously defined, since we are speaking of poetry, not of philosophy or theology. It might be called the relation of time to eternity, or the meaning of history, or the redemption of time and the world of man.'

The sources of the *Four Quartets* have been equally well traced by Miss Gardner: 'Mr. Eliot is here writing in the tradition of those mystics who followed the negative way. It is a tradition that goes back beyond Christianity to the Neoplatonists, who turned what had been a method of knowing—the dialectical method of arriving at truth by negations of the false—into a method of arriving at experience of the One. This doctrine of the ascent or descent ("the way up is the way down") into union with reality, by successively discarding ideas which would limit the one idea of Being, found a natural metaphor in darkness and night. It was a double-edged metaphor, since night expressed both the obliteration of self and all created things, and also the uncharacterized Reality which was the object of contemplation. The anonymous English mystic who wrote in this tradition in the fourteenth century used for his symbol a cloud, and called his book *The Cloud of Unknowing*. He taught that the soul in this life must be always between two clouds, a cloud of forgetting beneath, which hides all creatures and works, and a cloud of unknowing above, upon which it must "smite with a sharp dart of longing love". . . .' 'The actual phrase "a cloud of unknowing" occurs in *The Family Reunion*, and a line of 'Little Gidding' comes directly from the book, but in 'East Coker' the great paradoxes of the negative way are taken from its most famous doctor, St. John of the Cross. The riddling paradoxical statements at the close of the third movement are an almost literal rendering of the maxims under the "figure" which stands as frontispiece to *The Ascent of Mount Carmel* and which appear in a slightly different form at the close of Chapter XIII of the first book of that treatise.'[1]

If we know the philosophical and mystic tradition in which Eliot places his later works, our interest shifts from the thought to the form which he gives to that thought. It is good for our purpose to consider only one of the *Quartets* since we are bound to repeat ourselves in an analysis of all four. The repeated handling of the same theme allows for the mastery of the poet in his field and an analysis should be confined to a few specific points and should bear upon the treatment and value of a few images, since the thought lies in the handling and meaning of a few images.

Let us choose 'Burnt Norton', not because it is richer in images or thoughts, but precisely because in it we may leave aside philosophical or circumstantial data more boldly than in any other poem, and concentrate on the creative process, for 'Burnt Norton' has no special connection with historical data or with Eliot's family history. Most of the imagery of the first part of the poem is taken from the garden of a deserted Cotswold manor house, but the poem is not confined to this setting. All the imagery, however, is an imagery of the land in opposition to the sea imagery of 'The Dry Salvages' (islands off the coast of Massachusetts). The need for a definite field of reference in nature comes from the double or paradoxical aim of the poet: to express an experience of timelessness and yet to situate it in place and above all in time, in other words to reconcile time and eternity, for time is both vain and necessary; it is vain in proportion as it splits life into past,

[1] ibid.

present, and future, and it is necessary because man could not bear to live in eternity, although past, present, and future meet in eternity. This contrast and this reconciliation, which could be expressed differently, make the harmony of all the *Four Quartets*, which are variations with two opposed themes, an opposition which is solved at the end, or, philosophically, applications of the same thought and mood to various places and circumstances.

Eliot's double interpretation of time may be said to derive from two points of view, the point of view of man, for whom time appears in the categories of past, present, and future, and the point of view of the Creator, for whom past and future are present. There are certain men, however, who may operate a synthesis of both views:

> Men's curiosity searches past and future
> And clings to that dimension. But to apprehend
> The point of intersection of the timeless
> With time, is an occupation for the saint—
>
> ('The Dry Salvages', V.)

The intervention of human and divine persons in Eliot's conception allows for the dramatic tension of the *Four Quartets* and enables him to develop his ideas in dramas like *Murder in the Cathedral*, *The Rock* and *The Family Reunion*. The synthesis, that is, Incarnation, is more important for Eliot than the two ideas taken separately, and he would only partly accept Dunne's and Ouspensky's 'theory of a Serialistic Universe, that all time is one', as Hermann Peschmann hints.[1] It is a mistake to envisage 'Burnt Norton' or any of the *Quartets* in the perspective of a philosophical theory; the attitude of the poet might best be described as that of a dramatist who ascribes a value to external objects only as far as they are related to a character, to a man who thinks and feels, so that all the images have a common focus. The things represented by the images are relative, and they acquire a value only in relation to a man who lives and suffers, so that the thought is somewhat autonomous, that is, independent from the objects which are projected by it instead of being represented. Owing to this autonomy, a wide freedom is left to Eliot in his use of subject-matter and imagery, whereas the combination of his themes fits in a rigorous form which is the same in the four *Quartets*.

[1] *The Later Poetry of T. S. Eliot* (*English*, Autumn 1945).

If we accept that all the *Quartets* aim at expressing the perception of eternity in time or point to a goal outside time and yet including time, we find that a passage from the works of St. John of the Cross, in relation to the second epigraph to *Four Quartets*, is a remarkable introduction: 'Communications which are indeed of God have this property, that they humble the soul and at the same time exalt it. For upon this road to go down is to go up, and to go up to go down; for he that humbles himself is exalted and he that exalts himself is humbled.'[1]

The first section of 'Burnt Norton' contains a negative and a positive statement of the theme. The first half is the affirmation that past, present, and future are unreal, that they exist only in relation to eternity, which contains them. Temporal life is therefore essentially negative, and yet it is part of the eternal scheme, for eternity involves change and change points to eternity. These ideas are directly expressed in philosophical, abstract terms, then illustrated and applied to the image of the rose-garden. The unreality of time and the absence of eternity create a rarefied atmosphere. The second half of the section leads to a positive statement. The poet is trying to combine the metaphors offered by the garden and thereby to give a hint of the oneness of time. He discovers, however, that he is unable to trace the 'echoes' to their source:

> Go, said the bird, for the leaves were full of children
> Hidden excitingly, containing laughter.
> Go, go, go, said the bird: human kind
> Cannot bear very much reality.

The poet is on the verge of experiencing eternity, at least he is certain of its existence. He realizes, however, that he is unable to go further and he is satisfied with the proof and the guess. The whole imagery suggests an invisible presence:

> And the bird called, in response to
> The unheard music hidden in the shrubbery,

With the second section of 'Burnt Norton' the poet leaves the garden and develops the symbol of the wheel, first in a symbolical passage, secondly in the conversational manner. The opening of the section:

[1] *Dark Night*, II, xviii, 2.

151

> Garlic and sapphires in the mud
> Clot the bedded axle-tree.

reminds us of Mallarmé:

> Dis si je ne suis pas joyeux
> Tonnerre et rubis aux moyeux
> De voir en l'air que ce feu troue
>
> Avec des royaumes épars
> Comme mourir pourpre la roue
> Du seul vespéral de mes chars[1]

The idea of the reciprocity of natural phenomena culminates in the recognition of both fixity and movement:

> The dance along the artery
> The circulation of the lymph
> Are figured in the drift of stars

The second half of the second section, where the poet presents the personal, that is to say, dramatic aspect of the theme, is a development of the notion of 'dance' introduced in the preceding quotation. The dance is what protects us from timelessness and at the same time enables us to escape from time. We consume and destroy time by living in it:

> Only through time time is conquered.

The allegory of the wheel in the first part of section two implied that the whole of nature can be interpreted as a symbol of the divinity, a conception which would find support in the theory of analogy and correspondences (Fourrier, Swedenborg, and De Maistre). In section three, Eliot no longer regards nature as a living symbol and indicates only one way to the 'heart of light' or the stillness at the heart of movement: a descent 'into the world of perpetual solitude'. The 'internal darkness' of St. John of the Cross is the solution to an unfulfilled, meaningless, distracting and eccentric life, and this explains the antithesis of the two parts of this section, London and the world of the mystic night. The London imagery is brought

[1] Tercets of 'M'introduire dans ton histoire' (*Oeuvres Poétiques*; Lausanne, Kaeser, 1943, p. 158).

into relation with the symbol of the wheel, for there seems to be no
centre in the disconnected movement observed in London:

> Men and bits of paper, whirled by the cold wind
> That blows before and after time,

London appears in a dim light which is 'neither daylight' 'nor darkness' symbolic of an irresolution which is solved in the second half
of the section:

> World not world, but that which is not world,
> Internal darkness, deprivation
> And destitution of all property,
> Desiccation of the world of sense,
> Evacuation of the world of fancy,
> Inoperancy of the world of spirit;

The fourth section is a short lyric without anything explicit in it
but suggesting again the two ways towards truth: the negative (time
destroys reality):

> Time and the bell have buried the day,

and the affirmative, hinting that there is no change, although we
cannot see the Deus absconditus:

> the light is still
> At the still point of the turning world.

The fifth section of the four *Quartets* begins with considerations
on art. In 'Burnt Norton' Eliot lays stress on form and composition.
The perfect form is the one in which the details and the words co-
exist, so that each word or musical note is integrated in the whole, so
that the work may be experienced as a whole which is both progressing and still, like the figures of a dance. The tension between time and
eternity cannot be maintained by the poets who fail to harmonize
their words:

> Words strain,
> Crack and sometimes break, under the burden,
> Under the tension, slip, slide, perish,
> Decay with imprecision, will not stay in place,
> Will not stay still. Shrieking voices
> Scolding, mocking, or merely chattering,

153

> Always assail them. The Word in the desert
> Is most attacked by voices of temptation,
> The crying shadow in the funeral dance,
> The loud lament of the disconsolate chimera.

The idea in the background of the end of the last section is that only love justifies and redeems change and time. Love marries time and eternity and all moments besides the moment of plenitude seem vain:

> Sudden in a shaft of sunlight
> Even while the dust moves
> There rises the hidden laughter
> Of children in the foliage
> Quick now, here, now, always—
> Ridiculous the waste sad time
> Stretching before and after.

The themes of 'Burnt Norton' may give way to various developments. In 'The Dry Salvages' the symbol of the sea is the starting point of a philosophy of history. When the human point of view is abandoned, history is no longer a succession of events, periods, civilizations, and ages, each of them having a birth and a death, nor is it a progression, an upward development of mankind: 'the sea is all about us', and the profound rhythm of the sea may find a response in the rhythm of our life, for all time is one:

> And the ground swell, that is and was from the beginning,
> Clangs
> The bell.

The human response to reality should not be indifference or the fatalism of the Stoics for whom the will of Fate is their own will; it should be love, which is at the same time attachment and detachment:

> Thus, love of a country
> Begins as attachment to our own field of action
> And comes to find that action of little importance
> Though never indifferent. History may be servitude,
> History may be freedom.

> ('Little Gidding', III.)

Love gathers all that is lost in history, and all shall be well when the fire of purgation meets the rose of beauty and love:

All shall be well and
All manner of thing shall be well
When the tongues of flame are in-folded
Into the crowned knot of fire
And the fire and the rose are one.
                    (End of 'Little Gidding'.)

The ironical poems of the first period are far from 'Little Gidding', but there is no gap and we may safely assume that, if Eliot's thought arrives at full maturity in the last poems, it is nevertheless already prefigured in 'The Love Song of J. Alfred Prufrock'.

The philosophical element in Eliot's poetry consists mainly in his criticism of contemporary life, and his satire is—perhaps arbitrarily—related to his religious convictions. Eliot is the witness of a world which is crumbling down because it has lost its foundations, of a world which exploits its resources but no longer creates. He is moved to write poetry partly by a desire to show an evidence of both the decadence of Europe and the necessity of a superior truth. He does not pretend to attain plenitude or perfection in his poems, but only an indication of his ideal perfection; his style is essentially allusive, his thought implied and, as it were, outside his poetry.

Thought, however, commands his work. Any of his poems gives an impression of profundity. There is no penumbra in his poems, but either utter darkness or blinding light; a realism tinged with cynicism or an ardent mysticism. If there is any penumbra it is the penumbra of the Purgatorio.

His thought is never impassioned, and it is not simply an element of the subject-matter, but lies in the treatment of the subject-matter, in his attitude and in the peculiar light in which the images appear. Before his contempt for the world is dictated by his faith, it is urged by his aesthetic attitude. If the critic in Eliot is mainly concerned with certain traditional values, the poet in him is mainly an artist, that is, a man who introduces an order in his vision of the world, an order which, in Eliot's case, has become more and more precise and static. Time and change have an eccentric place in the symbol of the wheel, and the centre of his thought has crystallized around his religious faith. Whatever his convictions may be, however, his achievement as a poet is in the formal arrangement—in the music—of his poetry.

The origin of that poetry is always an emotion, the artistic emotion spurred by the deformity of the world and the religious emotion inspired by human suffering. These emotions are translated into images and thoughts, so that Eliot's ideas are not the foundation of his poetry, but an equivalent and a substitute for a stirring passion which elevates the poet and his readers to a superior being and assumes the hieratic form of a traditional thought.

CHAPTER IV

THE PHILOSOPHICAL POETRY OF HERBERT READ

I. READ'S IDEAS

(a) His Philosophy

THE general title of this essay implies that we are going to confine our study to a particular aspect of the works of Herbert Read: his poetry as far as it reflects or applies, consciously or unconsciously, his ideas. A survey of those among his ideas which lie behind his poetry should come before an analysis of his poems.

'Philosophy' is an assuming word for what will be part of an introduction to the poems. Although Read has stated many times that aesthetics is the basis of his philosophy,[1] we shall devote the first section mainly to Read's ontology, that is, to his interpretation of nature. Generally speaking, Read is a pantheist, and his theory of art may be considered as a *superstructure* or a complement to his philosophical and poetical interpretation of nature. The fact that Read does not recognize any other laws than the laws of nature accounts for his anarchism, that is, his denial of arbitrary power and authority.

The words 'ontology' and 'pantheism' may be misleading when used in connection with Read's ideas. His image of the 'Tree of Life' represents both the correlation and the unity of reality, of nature. This symbol is an illustration and an extension of Whitehead's concepts of 'relatedness' and 'uniformity'. This is not the place for tracing Read's extensive reading in philosophy. One of his sources, however, should be mentioned here: the recent developments of physical

---

[1] 'If I begin with aesthetics, it is because I have accumulated most evidence of this kind, and found it a sufficient basis for a general philosophy.' (*Annals of Innocence and Experience*; London, Faber and Faber, 1946, p. 225.)

science. The suggestive power of that science upon a poet may be guessed from the following passage: 'What I immediately heard was the song. The birds only enter perception as a correlation of more ultimate data of perception, among which for my consciousness their song is dominant.'[1] The belief in the perfect harmony (Whitehead would say 'totality') of nature is the foundation of Read's poetry. As a consequence of his interpretation of relativity he denies the existence of objects as separate entities[2] and postulates that the essence of nature expresses itself through the 'self'.[3] The word 'self', when used in his poetry, means the subject to whom nature is related and in whom the laws of nature manifest themselves: 'In a sense I am a solipsist: that is to say, I believe that the world I discover, as well as the philosophical interpretation I give to it, is contained within myself, and inevitably conditioned by my temperament.'[4]

The two main tenets of Read's philosophy are, first, that nature is ruled by the same laws as art—rhythm, balance, and proportion; and secondly that individual perception is a sufficient basis for knowledge. It is not convenient to examine here Read's distinction between 'character' and 'personality', which divides people into two categories, but it should be emphasized that whereas 'character is the product of disciplined education', 'personality' is an independent, creative individual who may express and manifest in himself the laws of nature. There is an apparent contradiction between Read's emphasis on the self, on personality, and his acceptance of the impersonal laws of nature, his deistic belief in immanence: 'Inspired by Whitehead, Read's philosophy is ultimately pantheistic, leading to a negation of the self-willed, independent personality.'[5] It is not surprising that the last step in Read's philosophy should be a communion with the *natura naturans*, 'the immanent will of the universe': 'The final leap can be only into Nirvana, into the Heaven of the Christians or into that more ideal and less individual immortality for which I have

[1] Whitehead: *The Principle of Relativity*, Cambridge University Press, 1922, p. 53.
[2] 'Furthermore, I hold that these permanent objects are nothing else than adjectives of events.' (Ibid., p. 58.)
[3] 'The artist must master the essence, the *natura naturans*, "which presupposes a bond between nature in the highest sense and the soul of man".' (*Coleridge as Critic*, p. 2.)
[4] *Annals of Innocence and Experience*, p. 225.
[5] H. W. Häusermann: *The Development of Herbert Read* (*Herbert Read*, ed. by Henry Treece; London, Faber and Faber, 1944).

used the symbol of the Tree of Life.'[1] In another passage we find that the only wisdom recognized by Read is 'that which the Taoists call the Way: the natural Truth.'[2]

Read's mystical experience, if a feeling of communion with nature may be termed so, is connected with a belief in the natural goodness of man. Both this belief and this feeling were shared by the 'philosophers' of the eighteenth century. According to that philosophy, evil is an artificial disturbance of the laws of nature caused by man. Read's philosophy, however, is more complex than it seems at first sight, and his 'mystical experience' may give way to a wider interpretation than the one given above: 'the essentially religious experience described by the great mystics of the East as well as the West, and now generally known in modern theology as the Kierkegaardian "instant", the Barthian "crisis" or "leap", is a surrender of the existential being only possible to a personality, a man of negative capability.

'To question the values of the personality, therefore, is to question the values of mysticism and of art.'[3]

The last paragraph of the quotation should prevent us from concluding that Read is either a pantheist or a mystic. He opposes 'instinct' or emotion to reason, religion to morality, and this dialectical interplay influences his aesthetics as well as his sociology. Although the personality is more important with respect to his poetry, his emphasis on reason should not be underestimated. Reason checks his impulses, controls his emotions or sustains and inspires them. It should be remarked that there has been a fluctuation in Read's evaluation of both reason and intuition. According to H. W. Häusermann, Read assigns a predominant part to reason in every field in the years 1925 to 1930 and, after 1931, advocates an unreflective art and praises spontaneity of feeling. To throw a bridge between intellect and intuition is the aim of Read's poetry: 'In this way poetry involves everything: it is the sense of integral unity without which, not only no poetry but no philosophy—even no religion— is ever possible.'[4]

So far we have considered Read's ideas on nature and on human

[1] *Annals of Innocence and Experience*, p. 234.
[2] ibid.
[3] ibid., pp. 90-1.
[4] *The Sense of Glory*, p. 77.

nature and we have remarked that in his view nature is by no means an entity apart from man, that the 'totality' is not apart from the individual, from the self. Read's advocacy of the individual, of both the character and the personality, is based on his faith in the goodness of nature and consequently of human nature. In other words, his relativism, or his reliance upon individual perception, is associated with a belief in the perfect unity of nature. It is inevitable that a man who thinks so much of the individual should be interested in psychology. Although Read, with considerable receptivity, has been able to assimilate the philosophies of Nietzsche, Schopenhauer, Kant, Hegel, Hume, Pascal, Plato, Bergson, Whitehead, Croce, Vico, Traherne, Kierkegaard, and Santayana,[1] his interests shifted, after 1925, to psycho-analysis, where he found a confirmation of his idea that the laws of nature manifest themselves in human nature and especially in art.[2]

The relations between art and nature are an important point of his philosophy. In his view music, poetry, painting, and architecture are manifestations of the laws of nature, so that the human mind is able to reflect or to reproduce the laws of nature in works of art. Works of art, however, differ fundamentally from natural phenomena because they are created by the human mind, and if they are different we must admit that the human mind is an independent power. According to Read, however, the mind is but a manifestation and an expression of the laws of nature. Why then should we be impelled to create? Read does not seem to have solved this problem. Whether the works of art are created by reason or by intuition they do not create natural phenomena. Now, according to Read, nature depends on the mind or, to put it in other words, there is no substitute for individual perception, and the human mind, after all, is not less than the same principle of order, rhythm, balance, and proportion regulating life and art. Why then are works of art different from nature itself? There is an answer in *Coleridge as Critic*, p. 37. Read

[1] cf. J. F. Hendry: *The Philosophy of Herbert Read* (*Herbert Read*, ed. by Henry Treece).

[2] Hence Read's admiration for Bergson, 'whose ambition it was to unite biology with metaphysics, the theory of life with the theory of knowledge'. This is quoted from *Coleridge as Critic*, p. 36, where Read admits that 'non-spatial inner data, or experiences of the INSIDE are . . . real'. Page 39, in the same book, Read ascribes to the German philosopher Woltereck a more complete reconciliation of inner with external data.

comments upon Woltereck's ontology, which 'insists that reality is one progressive flow of events, from which not only consciousness, but organic life itself has been disengaged or particularized—"life is a jump-like intensification of not-life, dying is a jump-like relapse into this prior form of reality".' However satisfactory this reconciliation of inner with external data may be, one may insist upon the radical separation of the mind from its biological and social soil, cling to another definition of the word 'consciousness', and raise on this point the only objection of this chapter. Read's solipsism is entirely different from Turner's.[1] Read does not pay much attention to the obvious difference between what man creates and what he sees, and does not seem to have answered satisfactorily the question: what is the mind, if it exists? In other words, there is no separation between spirit and matter in Read's philosophy. His subjectivism—what he calls his solipsism—is both an affirmation and a denial of the self. The point upon which he may disagree with us, is that for him consciousness implies no separation.

An interesting and entertaining study of this difficulty is to be found in *The Green Child*.[2] When Olivero lives with the green people, he finds that in that country art consists in making crystals which do not exist in nature. The green people agree 'that the mind is fed by the senses and only formed by the process of sensual perception' and consequently that there are no independent creations of the mind. The only function of the mind is contemplation and if the senses create a new reality—crystals or works of art—it is 'an illusion of human power sufficient to quell disorder'. In that theory, artistic creations are illusions, they belong 'to an intermediate state', they do 'not really exist' although we may find in them a reflection of reality. In *The Green Child*, Read avoids rather than solves the problem stated above. 'The order created by man and the order of the universe' are distinct, and only the order of the universe is real, but Read does not say why the order created by man should exist. Works of art, according to Read, are real in proportion as they may be identified with natural processes, for there is a profound relation 'between the reality of art and the reality of nature'. This theory ends in a negation of consciousness: 'only an art which rises above the conscious, only a transcendent or superreal art is adequate to reconcile the contradic-

[1] cf. p. 308. This answer has been suggested by Read to the author.
[2] *The Green Child*, London, Grey Walls Press, 1945, pp. 129 and 130.

tions of our experience.' These considerations are an introduction to Read's conception of 'romantic art', an art which 'uses the laws of nature as analogies for creative experiments'.[1]

(b) His Aesthetics

If nature and art are closely related to each other, artists are automata who transmit the sense of proportion 'which they have acquired through their purely visual and therefore physical response to their natural environment'.[2] What the poet expresses, then, is his own sense of nature: 'And we must understand by nature, not any vague pantheistic spirit, but the measurements and physical behaviour of matter in any process of growth or transformation.'[3] Many images in Read's poetry express a natural process, 'the seed that becomes a flowering plant, the metal that crystallizes as it cools and contracts'.[4]

Many other images, however, are a product of the imagination and, like the crystals of the green people, they exhibit forms and laws which are not to be found in nature. Read's distinction between 'characters' and 'personalities' is paralleled by his distinction between reason and imagination: 'The very bases of reason, the perceptions of an unclouded intellect, are continually contradicted by the creative fictions of the imagination, by a world of illusion no less real than the reality of our clear awareness. It is the function of art to reconcile the contradictions inherent in our experience; but obviously an art which keeps to the canons of reason cannot make the necessary synthesis.'[5] As we have already seen, this conflict takes various shapes in the course of Read's development and may be ascribed to the shifting values attributed by Read to the mind. Words like 'the reality of our clear awareness' are ambiguous: does it mean that the awareness is real (real in the etymological sense of the word) or that the things witnessed are real? Whatever may be our, or Read's, interpretation of these words, we are convinced that the mind has a creative function and is separated from reality. Read, on the contrary, thinks that the mind is embodied in nature, and he finds support for his belief in Whitehead's theory that sensations like colour are not subjective

[1] This definition has been suggested by Read on an earlier draft of this chapter.
[2] *Art and Crisis* (*Horizon*, May 1944, p. 338).
[3] ibid.
[4] ibid.
[5] *Annals of Innocence and Experience*, p. 212.

representations, but natural phenomena. Images, according to that theory, would not be determined by the mind, but by the same laws as matter. In aesthetics, however, Read's position is hardly tenable, for an artist is always conscious that his creations depend upon his attitude. It might be assumed that Read's purpose 'to hold the real design of life within the intenser light of the mind' is an arbitrary purpose, that the reality he represents is a fictitious reality created by him, and this would not impair the beauty of his poems. Whatever Read's conception of life may be, it is a product of both reason, which is objective and receptive, and imagination, which is subjective and creative. It is not surprising that his conception should culminate in what he calls the 'superreal', which has nothing to do with the organic processes of nature and which presupposes a free effort of creation; nor is it surprising that Read should have been attracted by surrealism or, as he likes to put it, superrealism, which, because it is not inhibited by abstract formulas, he conceives as a reaffirmation of the Romantic principle. The conflict we have studied, as it is illustrated in *The Falcon and the Dove*,[1] springs from the fact that Read's materialism is not and cannot be absolute. As a poet, his sense of reality is always determined by his own mind. The unconscious spontaneity which, according to Read, informs the products of his imagination is for him 'the immanent will of the universe', but it does not matter if that spontaneity is a natural or a human feature: it is a spiritual[2] activity.

This controversy impels us to inquire further into the distinction between reason and imagination, and their relation to classicism and romanticism. One of the best accounts of Read's theory in this respect is presented in *Annals of Innocence and Experience*[3]: 'Kierkegaard realized—was perhaps the first philosopher to realize—that there exists between reason and inspiration exactly the same unbridgeable chasm as between reason and faith. Art, like dialectics, can proceed a certain distance with the aid of measurable quantities —the quantities of rhythm and harmony, for example; but there comes a point at which the creative spirit must leap into the unknown. It is at this point that romantic art begins. I do not imply

---

[1] *Collected Poems*, London, Faber and Faber, 1946, p. 129.
[2] Read does not share this view, and would write 'psycho-physical' instead of 'spiritual'.
[3] pp. 122–3.

that there is any relationship between romantic art and religion; indeed, what I have implied is that they are totally distinct aspects of the universe. But the relationship of the creative artist to his art is analogous to that between the believer and his faith.' The basis of art is what Read calls the personality, the coherent thought of the artist who aims at glimpsing perfection by penetrating 'very deep and far'. In this search for perfection, the artist has to leave reason behind him and to be in accord with the universe. A poet should never abandon reason, 'the adamantine sickle' which cuts the fetters of doubt and superstition: he should make a synthesis of reason and inspiration.

Art requires another synthesis: of thought and form. In this respect Read tells us that by the end of World War One he had made an equation between emotion and image, between feeling and expression. The term 'equation' implies a precision of language which Read has partly learned from the Imagists. The first point of their Manifesto is indeed 'to use the language of common speech, but to employ always the *exact* word, not the merely decorative word'. Read shares with the Imagists another characteristic: to use mainly visual images. In connection with this tendency of visualizing objects is Read's theory of 'the innocent eye', which starts from the conviction that 'art is spontaneous, the unpremeditated act of an individual, but always innocent'.[1] 'Innocent' means conforming to the laws of nature. In order to understand this theory better, we must have recourse once more to the distinction between character and personality: 'Character is an impersonal ideal which the individual selects and to which he sacrifices all other claims, especially those of sentiments or emotions',[2] whereas personality expresses the laws of nature in the form of sentiments: the lyrical impulse is not inhibited. Read opposes elsewhere the visions of the innocent eye, or real poetry, to wit-writing, the poetry of Dryden, for example. There is another explanation of the words 'innocent eye': it is the virgin eye of childhood, the eye of the natural man of Rousseau, which is not yet corrupted by bad education. But Read's 'innocent eye' is an unconventional eye which is so much spontaneous that it transforms everything it sees.

[1] *Art and Crisis* (*Horizon*, May 1944, p. 338).
[2] *Form in Modern Poetry*, London, Sheed and Ward, 1932, p. 18.

(c) His Ideas of Society, Politics and Education

Read's philosophy, aesthetics and sociology have a common denominator: his affirmation of the natural self (of the validity of individual perception, of 'personality' and of the liberty of the person) and a rejection of artificial authority. He belongs to the liberal tradition and must be opposed to T. S. Eliot in that respect. We have seen, however, that Read recognizes one authority: the laws of nature, as far as they can be identified with the medieval 'universal' rhythm, order, balance, and that his philosophy ends in a negation of the individual will.

Anarchism is a negative term for a constructive sociology, for the observance of the natural laws is as important to Read as the rejection of authority: 'The only necessity is to discover the true laws of nature and conduct our lives in accordance with them.'[1] Read insists on the necessity of a religion (the religion of nature) and, although he endeavours to work for the practical objects of socialism,[2] he rejects any kind of artificial planning. His *credo* is formulated in the following manner: 'Faith in the fundamental goodness of man; humility in the presence of natural law; reason and mutual aid—these are the qualities that can save us.'[3] The main source of Read's political theory is not Marx, but Bakunin and Kropotkin. The ideal state would be the one in which 'the individual will is in unison with the general will'. For this reason Read advocates community of ownership and makes a distinction 'between the totalitarian conception of the State as a controlled herd, and the libertarian conception of society as a brotherhood'.[4]

For the establishment of a natural society Read does not see any better instrument than education through art. Besides, the analogy between his aesthetics and his conception of society is striking: to the synthesis of reason and intuition corresponds the synthesis, which the society of the future should make, of functionalism and craftsman-

[1] *The Philosophy of Anarchism*, London, Freedom Press, 1940, p. 24.
[2] cf. *The Sweated Author* (*The London Mercury*, February 1935, p. 333), where Read compares the income of modern authors with the much larger income of the writers of the eighteenth and nineteenth centuries, concludes that the author is being sacrificed in the interests of the middleman, and proposes an 'Authors' Co-operative Publishing Guild'.
[3] *The Philosophy of Anarchism*, p. 32.
[4] *Chains of Freedom 11* (now *9*, p. 20, July–August).

ship: 'We must . . . establish a double-decker civilization.' Functionalism, or machine-work and industry, requires an activity of the mind, of reason, whereas craftsmanship requires an education of the senses. This idea of a double-decker civilization is used in 'The Nuncio'.[1] The practical results implied by Read's anarchism[2] are extolled by other sociologists having different convictions, so that the most important point in Read's theory is what he calls 'the mystique of anarchism', that is, the building of a free society on a strong we-feeling rather than on economic efficiency, for an emotional impulse should always support society; the failure to recognize this fact explains the bankruptcy of historical materialism and of logical positivism.

It is obvious that Read's ideas are directed towards a goal in the future.[3] It makes no doubt for him that the collapse of both capitalism and communism, of artificial state-control, will coincide, in a distant prospect, with the birth of a natural society and with 'a rebirth of universal art in local communities'. There is no border between spiritual life and economic factors, and art may be regarded as a factor of prime importance. One of the most urgent tasks which confront us to-day is the establishment of 'an educational system which preserves and matures the innate aesthetic sensibility of man'.[4] Read's theory of education is based upon the assumption that art 'is not the by-product of a culture; rather, a culture is the end-product of the outstanding personalities of a number of artists'.[5] The State is an enemy of culture, which can flourish only in local communities. Read accepts the aims of the Bauhaus school, founded by Dr. Gropius at Weimar in 1919, for that school develops the child's emotional response to the outer world and regards life as an organic whole.

[1] *Collected Poems*, p. 189.

[2] cf. *On Justice* (*Horizon*, June 1945), where Read stands against clause 39A of the Code, forbidding anybody to persuade soldiers to quit the Forc ., that is, to speak of universal peace and brotherhood: Justice to-day has a sword, but no scales.

[3] 'Perhaps in some distant age anarchism and Christianity will come together again, as they were in the early days of the Church.' Both anarchism and Christianity, according to Read, converge in the same goal, although one 'is theistic and has a supernatural background, the other . . . humanistic and has a background of reason and natural law.' (*A Coat of Many Colours*, London, Routledge, 1945, p. 12.)

[4] *The Grass Roots of Art*, London, Lindsay Drummond, 1947, 'The Problem of Taste'.

[5] *Art and Crisis*, p. 342.

II. THE POETIC EXPRESSION OF READ'S IDEAS

(a) The Unity of Organic Life: 'Eclogues' (1914–1918)

Read's poetry is not the product of his philosophy; it is rather his philosophy which is the result of his poetry. Read dislikes abstraction; there is in his poems an equation between emotion and form, between thought and images, between subject-matter and the state of mind of the poet. Emotion, thought, and state of mind, however, play an important part in the longer poems; thought becomes explicit, but should not be taken for philosophical preconception. There is an alternation in Read between intuition and reason, between spontaneity and voluntary creation, but he expresses in all his poems what he calls the sense of glory: the immediate perception of the world's harmony. The short lyrical poems are intuitive expressions of the sense of glory, whereas the longer poems are more intellectual. The sense of glory supposes a philosophy which is rather the result than the cause of his poetry. His belief in the goodness of man is connected with his conviction that in a distant future the brotherhood of men will be an image of the harmony of nature, and that the sense of glory will pervade life.

The 'Eclogues', written during the first World War, when Read served as an officer in France, are for the most part impressionistic notations of rural scenes which may be explained as intuitive perceptions of 'the design of life'. The tragic circumstances in which the poems were written do not impair the serenity of the poet. The idea of death, to which soldiers are accustomed, becomes a pretence for illustrating Read's pantheistic feeling:

> The empty body broods
> One with the inanimate rocks.[1]

Life, on the contrary, appears as a painful waking from the slumber of death:

> The last rays are fierce and irritant.
> Then on the lonely hill my body wakes
> And gathers to its shell my startled soul.[2]

[1] 'Champ de Manoeuvres' (Collected Poems, p. 30). [2] ibid.

The communion of the poet with nature is the prevailing state of mind of these poems:

> A rising fish
>   ripples the still water
>
> And disturbs my soul. [1]

and:

> Rains wash the cold frail petals
> Downfalling like tremulous flakes
> Even within my heart. [2]

'Childhood' [3] is a poetical summary of the first part of *Annals of Innocence and Experience*; Read's childhood was spent in the country in communion with nature.

Our interpretation of Read's poems does not explain them, but helps to see them in the perspective of his ideas.

(*b*) *Eternity through Heroic Life: 'War Poems' (1916–32 and 1936–45)*

The serenity displayed in 'Eclogues' is unchanged in the 'War Poems': Read looks impartially at life and death. 'Kneeshaw Goes to War' [4] is the story of an innocent countryman who is involved in the horror of war; his impassibility and passivity keep him apart from the indignities of war:

> He plunged with listless mind
> Into the black horror.

The ruins acquire the aspect of beauty in Read's poems:

> Here and there
> Interior walls
> Lie upturned and interrogate the skies amazedly. [5]

Most of the 'War Poems' are narrative and descriptive; they are made of intuitions expressing, like the 'Eclogues', the poet's feeling of communion with nature; this feeling takes various shapes; in 'My Company' [6] it is represented by two different attitudes: mockery and humility:

---

[1] 'The Pond' (ibid., p. 18).   [2] 'The Orchard' (ibid., p. 19).   [3] ibid., p. 25.
[4] *Collected Poems*, p. 39.   [5] ibid., 'Villages Démolis', p. 44.   [6] ibid., p. 50.

From my giant attitude,
In godlike mood,
I laugh till space is filled
With hellish merriment.

Then again I assume
My human docility,
Bow my head
And share their doom.

'The End of a War'[1] contains some explicit ideas. The first episode, entitled 'Meditation of the Dying German Officer', reflects some of Read's ideas, especially his denial of life after death, of Paradise and Hell. The officer lives and dies for 'the Father and the Flag', and reprobates his friend whose face, after he has gone to church, is 'drained of sorrow as of joy':

God we create
in the end of action, not in dreams.

Agony is the beginning of nothingness, and the death of man is the death of God, so that the dying officer exults in the thought that everything fades and disappears with him.

The second episode of the poem is the 'Dialogue between the Body and the Soul of the Murdered Girl', a symbol of the martyrdom of innocence. The girl's faith in Christ and her sacrifice to France enable her soul to consider death as a blessing, for

Those who die for a cause die comforted and coy;
believing their cause God's cause they die with joy.

On the contrary, those who die without faith in a cause are confronted with an hostile fate.

In the third episode, 'Meditation of the Waking English Officer', Read has found a protagonist for his own feelings and ideas. After his life has been lost in the turmoil of war, the officer awakes, hearing voices of thanksgiving; in spite of the destruction which he could not resist he affirms that

the infinite is all
and I, a finite speck, no essence even
of the life that falls like dew

[1] ibid., pp. 58–74.

> from the spirit breathed on the fine edge
> of matter, perhaps only that edge
> a ridge between eternal death and life eternal,
> A moment of life, temporal.

The idea of the disappearance of the self into the great All is the key to the preceding passage. There must be, however, a relation between the self and the All, otherwise life would be meaningless, and the universe a machine. It is convenient to insist here on Read's rejection of a quantitative, mechanistic conception of the universe; about the quantum theory he writes: 'I was content with the fact that physics had apparently provided an escape from a situation that threatened to be wholly mechanistic.'[1] The poet does not want to abandon his life to a blind fate and asserts the necessity of connecting life with eternity:

> But whilst I cannot pray, I can't believe
> but in this frame of machine necessity
> must renounce not only God, but self.
> For what is the self without God?
> A moment not reckoned in the infinite.
> My soul is less than nothing, lost,
> unless in this life it can build
> a bridge to life eternal.

This passage marks the turning point between Read's philosophy and his aesthetics, between his ideas on nature as an impersonal entity and his perception of nature through the senses and the mind. Those who think in a warm room may easily believe in God, but 'the meek', those who put their beliefs to a test, come to a certitude: the officer does not regret having voluntarily engaged in the army, for there is a providence:

> we act
> God's purpose in an obscure way

Mr. Geoffrey Moore writes about 'Bombing Casualties in Spain': 'Not only has Mr. Read failed to escape from the imagist conception of poetry (of stuffed-trout fame, *vide* Mr. Henry Treece), but he is here guilty of loose thinking.'[2] This is not the place for examining the

---

[1] *Annals of Innocence and Experience*, p. 229.
[2] *The Poetry Review*, No. 1, vol. XXXVII, 1946, p. 80.

reproach levelled against Read's association of images, but it should be remembered that we cannot understand a poem by Read before we relate it to his own view of life: it is not fair to say that 'Bombing Casualties in Spain' 'is no spell-binder, but poetic reportage in Mr. Read's more familiar manner'. The essential point of the poem is the contrast between life and the stillness of death, and the mood of resignation and hopelessness. The same author writes about 'A Song for Spanish Anarchists': 'What real connection is there between the golden lemon growing on a green tree rather than being *made*, i.e. manufactured, and the main theme of the poem: that a strong man and his crystal eyes is a man born free?' The connection is obvious: the lemon grows naturally, of itself, freely, like the man who has his own ways, who is a self. The poem cannot be explained without reference to Read's philosophy of anarchism, although the thought is not explicit in the poem. 'Herschel Grynspan', 'War and Peace', 'To a Conscript of 1940' and 'The Contrary Experience' show the same attitude towards modern warfare. Although death is 'an irresistible rain', the poet is not in despair, for war is an evil and a failure, and the irresponsible soldiers are heroes if they know that their sacrifice is useless, in other words, if they preserve their honour by being detached from the act of killing:

> To fight without hope is to fight with grace,

'The Contrary Experience'[1] illustrates the struggle in the conscience of the poet between two attitudes towards war: a refusal to participate in it or action. The poet chooses the latter, like Arjuna in the *Baghavad-Gita* who, hesitating to fight against his brothers, is advised by Krishna to strike. War is the contrary experience against which spiritual forces are used and strengthened:

> Buffeted against the storm's sullen breath
> the lark rises
> Over the grey dried grasses
> rises and sings.

'Ode Written during the Battle of Dunkirk, May, 1940'[2] opens with a prelude where Read uses a storm as a symbol for lust and war. In the fourth section of the poem he analyses the causes of war in a

---

[1] *Collected Poems*, p. 84.   [2] ibid., pp. 86–93.

retrospective meditation on the twenty years between the two wars:

> Belief without action
> action without thought
> the blind intervention
> of years without design.

The break in the organic unity of life:

> The world our person
> the self the nucleus

is the cause of war, which comes as a just retribution. The climax of the poem is reached in the sixth section where the poet rejects despair and expresses his belief in the spirit of harmony and in the future of art:

> For against his symbol is the spirit and the spirit is
>   a breath
> that rises invincible to seek reincarnation
> in flesh that cannot be defeated in hearts that rescind
> the powers without persuasion the hands without art
> to reign in aeons that are ageless in worlds without end.

Read's faith in the harmony of nature and his anarchism are unshaken:

> The self, passively receiving
> illusion and despair
> excluding
> the unreal power of symbols
> the false shelter of institutions
> returns reluctantly upon its self

The poem ends in a vision of the future and illustrates Read's conception of poetry as a synthesis of reason and intuition:

> Reason and love
> incurved like a prow
> a blade dividing
> time's contrary flow
>
> Poetry a pennon
> rippling above
> in the fabulous wind.

The third of the great war poems, 'A World Within a War',[1] is as simple as the preceding ones. The first two sections are a description of the poet's seclusion and work in his country house during the war. In the third section, as in most of Read's poems, we find an image—this time a conscious image—of the pattern of life:

> In that peace
> Mind looks into a mirror pois'd
> Above body: sees in perspective
> Guts, bones and glands: the make of a man
> Out of that labyrinth
> The man emerges: becomes
> What he is: by no grace
> Can become other: can only seize
> The pattern in the bone, in branching veins
> In clever vesicles and valves
> And imitate in acts that beauty.

Not only the whole of Read's philosophy is suggested in the preceding passage, but his aesthetics are contained in germ in the last line. The connection between his aesthetics and his ethics is indicated by the following passage in which evil is presented as a failure of our aesthetic faculty; we should see, imitate the beauty of life, and act according to it:

> His nature is God's nature: but torn
> How torn and fretted by vain energies
> The darting images of eye and ear
> Veil'd in the web of memory
> Drifts of words that deaden
> The subtle manuals of sense.

War and death leave the poet unstirred, for they cannot prevent 'the source of love' to flow. There is no hope in the external world, but the solution is to be found inside, in the heart of men who are in communion with God and who will succeed one day in establishing a universal brotherhood; for them death is a step towards the accomplishment of their goal:

> There is a grace that fills the dying eye
> With pity for the wielder of the axe.

[1] ibid., pp. 94–100.

173

> There is a grace that lulls the pain
> Of martyrs in their hour of death.
>
> Death is no pain to desperate men.

The house in which Read lived in seclusion during the war becomes the symbol of the peace of death, and of the communion of the poet with nature. This communion is associated with the creation of a superreal and transcendental world of imagination which rises above the immediate reality and preserves mankind from despair and destruction:

> Vision itself is desperate: the act
> Is born of the ideal: the hand
> Must seize the hovering grail.

and:

> We shall build
> A crystal city in the age of peace
> Setting out from an island of calm
> A limpid source of love.

Except perhaps for the claim for the rights of the imagination and the feeling of pity for the offenders, the predominant note of the poem, which is full of rustic imagery, is a pantheistic feeling. The calmness, and the indifference towards death, is a pantheistic feeling. The vision of a future world of peace and harmony is a prolongation of Read's ideas on nature, but it is not wholly consistent with a pantheist doctrine since it presupposes more or less the transcendental nature of the human mind, which may act against natural laws or in concordance with them, but always independently.

(c) The Philosophy of the Concrete: 'Satirical Verses' (1919–34)

The 'Satirical Verses' are based upon unorthodox ideas of good and evil. For Read 'an ethical code is an imaginative and perhaps an irrational vision of conduct. It is an immediate or direct apprehension by the intelligence, and not the work of discursive reason.'[1] An ethical code is an abstraction, a set of arbitrary formulas which does not take facts into consideration; it is not a perception of organic life. In other words, it is an *a priori* conception. The first of the 'Satirical

[1] *Reason and Romanticism*, 1926; from 'The Attributes of Criticism', p. 24.

Verses', 'Equation a + b + c=x' has provoked many diverging interpretations. Michael Roberts, who writes about the last lines of the
poem: 'we feel that some acts are good and some are bad, although
we perceive no absolute ethical landmarks,'[1] does not seem to realize
that the poem involves a rejection of the ethic mind. The best interpretation of the poem is provided by Mr. Häusermann, who writes:
'The first three stanzas of this poem are three different statements of
one intuition, namely of the essential identity and totality of (a) the
world and God, (b) of man and woman, and (c) of the mind and its
biological soil, the human body. The other half of the equation (x) is
a query which might be formulated thus: How is it possible for the
mind to manufacture a system of ethics outside the totality of the
universe? Clearly, it is impossible. Any attempt to manufacture such
a system by the mind alone without taking full account of the mind's
opposite is condemned to inefficiency, like an engine 'accelerating in
the void'.[2]

Most significant are the lines which explain, in a way, the origin of
knowledge:

> All knowledge and ideality
> Are borne in the lapse of the menstrual sea

They imply not only Locke's theory that ideas come from sensations, but also a denial of revelation and of a supernatural or transcendental being. Read's satire is directed against both spiritual and
temporal arbitrary authority, and against artificial manners. It is,
however, by no means a philosophical satire and consists in short,
suggestive poems in which we find hints like the following:

> Intent on solemn inanities,
> They maintain a torpid demeanour.
> ('Lepidoptera', p. 104.)

> here we make artificial flowers
> of paper tin and metal thread.

> I have no power therefore have patience.
> ('A short Poem for Armistice Day', p. 110.)

Read's irony is all the more efficient because it is discreet.

[1] *Critique of Poetry*, p. 85.
[2] *Herbert Read's Poetry* (*Herbert Read, an Introduction to his Work*, ed. by H. Treece).

(d) The Essential Goodness of Nature: 'Lyrical Poems' (1919–34)

Most of the lyrical poems express a state of irrational exaltation; they should neither be analysed nor explained, for an analytical approach would miss their richness of evocation. The word 'evocation' should be stressed here, for Read's lyricism is descriptive and urged by a sense of relationship and communion rather than of solitude. Whether he borrows his imagery from Christian legends ('The Judgment of Michael'), Greek mythology ('The White Isle of Leuce') or other sources, the style is always descriptive and the mood an exaltation, but not a sophisticated exaltation: the poet is filled with the splendour of nature.

Other poems, in which the interest shifts from nature to the historical situation between the two wars, express the sadness and the mistrust of the poet:

> we wander our hearts lifted
> above the shadows and the dust
> secure in an alien light.[1]

But these feelings are counterbalanced by a strong belief in the essential goodness of nature:

> There is no other life than ours.
> God is good to us this September evening
> to give us a sun
> and a world burning its dross.[2]

Although there is no explicit thought in these poems, they are derived from a profound thought, which is all the more intense because it is not analytical, but loaded with a rich and complex feeling. Life appears as incomplete, broken, artificial and purposeless, but the poet finds a consolation in its very desolation:

> Ragged ends of time
> that no time will knit together.
> Death is the only even skein:
> Death that is both ghost and gain.[3]

[1] 'Inbetweentimes', *Collected Poems*, p. 124.
[2] 'September Fires', ibid., p. 125.
[3] 'The Even Skein', ibid., p. 126.

The feeling of desolation, however, prevails in 'Device',[1] where time is compared to a screen which prevents us from seeing the perfection and the unity of nature, instead of which the poet sees only a transitory, unreal world:

> Time that is a shrouded thought
> Involving earth and life in doubt.

The belief in a transcendental beauty beyond death is expressed by the myth of 'The Seven Sleepers'. Time does not matter to those who sleep ten thousand years, persuaded that beauty is eternal:

> Beauty when we wake will be
> a solitude on land and sea.'[2]

This conviction is based upon Read's belief in the immortality of the mind as far as the human mind may be considered as an embodiment of the spirit of harmony. The senses perceive the transitory beauty manifested in time, but the mind has a vision of its own, which time leaves intact. 'Time Regained' is built on the antithesis between sensual and mental memory. The mind forgets what the body remembers, the mind forgets what is mortal and looks through death:

> for the mind has reasons of its own
> for covering with an eyeless mask
> marks of mortality
>
> .   .   .
>
> for circumventing life and love's
> sodality[3]

The love of the harmony of nature can be defeated neither by life nor by death:

> wake cold
> to face the fate
> of those who love
> despite the world.[4]

The main theme of Read's aesthetics, the comparison of the respective values of reason and imagination, finds poetic expression in 'The Falcon and the Dove', where the Dove, symbol of the imagination, is hunted and caught through the intermediacy of the Falcon. Read's

[1] ibid., p. 130. [2] ibid., p. 131. [3] 'Time Regained', ibid., p. 132.
[4] 'Night Ride', ibid., p. 137.

belief that there must be a synthesis of both is implied in his assertion
that reason is ultimately the victor, yet must be dismissed at the end:

And now the falcon is hooded and comforted away.[1]

The conflict and the balance of the two faculties is well described by
Henry Treece: '. . . while the poem tells of the reason's triumph, the
language it uses is a tribute to romanticism, as in such words as *fet-
tered*, *leagues*, *laggard*, *boscage*, *foray*. And perhaps most interesting of
all, the very instrument of Reason, the falcon, is a medieval, and
hence Romantic, object.'[2] The conflict and the balance consist
mostly in the use of alternately ancient and common words, and the
thought is essentially a poetical thought. The rejection of analytical
thought is carried further in short poems without verb ('Giovanni di
Paolo') or in a 'surrealist' joke like 'Melville'. Consciously or not,
however, the poet is always applying his ideas to his poems; most of
his images reflect his idea of the design of life:

> I sit and watch
> the eye-iris water move
> like muscles over stones
> smooth'd by this ageless action.[3]

It is not necessary that this kind of image should be the instrument of
thought or that the poet should project his feelings or his ideas upon
it, for they are thoughts by themselves if they are precise and convincing enough. Read's lyricism is transfused into his images. The
images come sometimes like an illumination which supersedes the
darkness of the world:

> But stay! the light is cancelled there
> the dark eyes cease
> to stare at suns
> and light breaks in behind the brain.[4]

This attitude of the poet leads to a negation of death, death being
exactly the absence of being: like the ethic mind, death is an abstraction which cannot be seen. This thought is given poetic expres-

[1] ibid., p. 129.
[2] *Herbert Read, an Introduction to his Work by Various Hands*, p. 22; from Treece's
'Introduction'.
[3] 'The Ivy and the Ash', *Collected Poems*, p. 147.
[4] 'Logos', ibid., p. 145.

sion in 'Emblem', where the poet gives as an example of death-like abstraction the Arab who 'made the rose a rosette'. Beauty is something living and something which can be seen; what cannot be seen does not exist or is miraculous:

> Beauty has no other reason
>   than the eye can indicate;
> Only the miraculous conception
>   is immaculate.[1]

In this survey of Read's 'Lyrical Poems' we have left aside some poems, not because they are devoid of any thought, but because they need no elucidation.

(e) *The Struggle for Balance: 'Longer Poems' (1920–34)*

Unlike the other poems by Read, 'John Donne Declines a Benefice'[2] is built on the scheme of a logical deliberation. It is the poem of renunciation. In order to understand the poem it is necessary to know something about Donne's life, and especially the fact that for a certain time he acted as literary agent to his friend the Rev. Thomas Moreton, afterwards Bishop of Durham. His main task was to write controversial pieces against his old friends the Jesuits. Donne believed no more in his arguments than in those of the Jesuits,[3] but writing controversies enabled him to use all his faculties. For that reason he refused to take Anglican orders. Read uses this deliberation as a means to convey his conception of balance in nature:

>   '   Now Morton takes my hand
> And all too impressively points a way
> For this mind amorous of conflict.

The John Donne imagined by Read expresses views which can be found in Read's philosophy:

> The ego sings an individual praise,
> Graceful enough to God—whose mind is mine;
> Who is the supple flesh and bone
> Aggrandised in aeriness, eaten by no worms
> Of dutiful doubt.

[1] ibid., p. 151.   [2] ibid., p. 150–64.

[3] This information is taken from *John Donne and Baroque Doubt*, by Kathleen Raine (*Horizon*, June 1945).

Man is made of soul and body, and death is the end of the body; wisdom is a balance between spiritualism and materialism:

> Yet doubt dissembles all—there's aid
> In equilibrium alone

and:

> There's some divine amalgam
> Of flesh and spirit, an alloy
> Which I must find—must make my God
> Invisibly from spit and clay.

Donne refuses to indulge in a settled faith under the shelter of an established institution; he must make truth out of his own life and participate in the building of a faith which will outlast his own life:

> Such monuments will wane
> Many men's lives; or even
> Petrify to indestructible stone.

Donne's choice is dictated by his desire for freedom and his sense of reality; he wants to be free to express himself and to give himself up to reality:

> I must complete the dizzy tower;
> Rectify Babel's shame and Job's despair,
> And in the fullness of one made all
> Pour this hydroptic flesh and aery soul,
> Death emptying the vessel quite.

Read's ideas of balance between reason and emotion, of anarchism and of the final surrender of the self appear in this early poem. His idea of balance is particularly emphasized; he insists that life is not an alternative: either to be a pure soul,

> To make a logic on a scroll

or to live according to the flesh, like the young Donne. The worst Donne could choose now that he is no longer young would be a hieratic occupation which would keep him apart from life and make him resemble

> a palsied doge,
> His city built into the sea of lust
> On rotting piles.

'The Analysis of Love'[1] presents us with one more alternative, which the poet would like to transform into a synthesis. It is the alternative between finite perception and total apprehension. Love, as far as it has mechanical lust for its spring, is incomplete, but on the other hand, perfect love is impossible, for there is always a struggle between reason and emotion. The solution of this conflict is not to be found on this earth, and the poet hopes that in another world we may attain perfect understanding and communion. The idea of the brokenness and imperfection of earthly life is already hinted at by the epigraph of the poem: 'Else a great Prince in prison lies (John Donne).' Such is, roughly outlined, the substance of the poem. A closer analysis of the poem would reveal in each of the ten sections one aspect of the conflict.

The first section is an affirmation of the poet's aspiration towards perfection, and at the same time the poet realizes that there is no life without imperfections: to express one's vision of the world would halt the world.

The second section reveals two antitheses: between intuition and reason, symbolized respectively by the uncertain outline of things during the night and the intensity of the stars; between lust and reason, symbolized by sleep and the morning.

The main theme of the next five stanzas is the failure of attaining perfect unity of being and of solving the conflict of the passionless, reasonable mind with finite, unfulfilled emotion. Reason is submerged by a flood of emotion and both are defeated, for their origin and their end are outside the scope of human experience.

The eighth and ninth sections express the poet's striving towards unity of vision and perfection;[2] he finds, however, that perfection is not to be attained in life and that human life is as it were apart from the rest of nature; the mind cannot perceive the totality of the universe and through the imagination only can we build a perfect world, but that world vanishes:

> We'll be insensate when the whirl
> Of circumstance is past.

Love is a finite thing and as such is mortal; our passions are vain

---

[1] ibid., pp. 165–9.

[2] Read may have been influenced here by Bradley's idea that the self should find complete attainment in becoming a member of the immanent and infinite All.

and we are unable to build our life in 'the scheme of things', so that death is a disintegration of our mind as well as of our body, and the poet complains that he has failed in establishing a balance between love and nature:

> This mental ecstasy all spent
> In disuniting death;
> And the years that spread
> Oblivion on our zest.

The vision of perfect beauty which cannot be attained in this life, the pure exaltation of the soul, and the creation of a superreal or supernatural world are the theme of 'Beata l'Alma'.[1] That the protagonist of the poem is Michael Angelo, the creator of godlike figures, suits perfectly the poem, which is a vision of ideal beauty, and a revolt against time and finiteness.

The first section of the poem illustrates the idea that time and eternity are irreconcilable, that the mind which perceives eternity cannot find a consistent and real form in time, and that the mind which is plunged into time cannot find an issue towards eternity. The soul and the world are apart. The soul despises the world, for the world is not a place for the soul to dwell in. Man, 'a cynic race', destiny, and the horror of war are a torture to the soul which is their witness and yet cannot stay with them. The first stanzas of the poem contrast the opacity of the world with the crystal limpidity of the soul. The soul cannot redeem the darkness, the agony and the 'bleak ecstasies' of life: beauty escapes the world, and the seven sleepers (cf. the poem with that title) when waking find only desolation and barrenness on the earth ('a solitude on land and sea'):

> Time ends when vision sees its lapse in
> liberty. The seven
> sleepers quit their den and wild
> lament-
> ations fill out voiceless bodies. Echoes only are.

The purposely disjointed verses and the violent storm of emotions and of high-relief forms make of 'Beata l'Alma' perhaps the most beautiful of Read's poems. Moreover, this burst of revolt leads to the calmness of the second section, like an explosion of the imperfect

[1] ibid., pp. 170–2.

world ending in a vision of order. The second part of the poem is important for the understanding of Read's attitude. It contains explicit statements, although they are expressed as usual in the most economical manner: (1) the soul must bear fruit, immortal fruit, in this life, it must communicate with the beyond, it must create:

> New children must be born of gods in
> a deathless land,

(2) the soul banishes love and words; we must create a new, perfect beauty which invents new objects instead of recreating worn-out images. (3) Art fails because it is corrupted by communication; the individual understanding is justified by itself:

> Art ends;
> the individual world alone is valid

(4) the world, when considered by a pure soul, is perfect; passions and torments die: serenity alone is eternal.

'Beata l'Alma' is one of the poems in which intuitions and emotions overpower reason: it is not a product of the intellectual, discursive mind. The idea, implied by the poem, that nature in its unity and perfection is transcendental, and the aspiration towards a beauty which lies beyond immediate perception, and yet is felt by the senses, are connected with Read's interest in the surrealist movement, the technique of which is applied to some images:

> and the hissing darkness healed the wide wound of light.

and:

> . . . In the sky the unsullied sun lake.

These images lead us far from the quiet perceptions of the design of life, which is blurred here by the violence of the contrasts, and yet there is no contradiction in those two manners, for Read proposes in both an ideal beauty. 'Beata l'Alma', however, differs from the other poems by the fact that it expounds and solves a problem which does not preoccupy Read anywhere else: the problem of the independence and of the innocence of the soul. The soul must be kept pure from earthly contact in order to create an immortal beauty which is nevertheless the beauty of nature beyond finite perception.

'The Retreat',[1] like 'John Donne Declines a Benefice', develops the idea that life is a prison and, like 'Beata l'Alma', is an affirmation of

[1] ibid., pp. 173–5.

a transcendental beauty. The retreat is the moment of rest and leisure in which life appears *sub specie aeternitatis*, the moment of retirement in which the poet looks back at his life and discerns the real design of life, after many years of unconsciousness and passivity, symbolized by a screen, in which he lived

> Like the clean movement of a wheel
> Flying on so fair an axle that the eye
> Can hardly make its motion.

Eliot uses in the *Four Quartets* the symbol of the wheel in a very similar manner. But whereas Eliot relates the movement of the wheel to the stillness of the centre, Read shows the contrast between the passivity—the movement—of unconscious life and the stillness of the creative mind. Both poets, however, take the unapparent movement of the wheel as a symbol of blindness. For Eliot the movement ends when the mind surrenders to a superior intelligence: for Read when the mind harmonizes with nature.

A great part of 'The Retreat' is philosophical poetry. The symbol of the wheel implies that Read distinguishes two periods in life (or two modes of living), a period of receptivity in which the mind is passive, and a period of activity in which the mind holds the world within its scope as if the world were not moving:

> But now, the world is real and calm:
> The body lives, a limp container
> Of this bounding mind;
> And the mind notes the visible world—
> How it moves with mechanic evenness,
> Dismissing hope and hasty exaltations.

It is better to use the words 'activity of the mind' instead of 'creativity', for the mind is not the principle of a world apart; it is not an abstraction: it is a living thing, a part of the scheme of things. The reality of the mind is not less certain than the reality of the earth; the mind is the principle of life, 'the base of things':

> Not mind and matter, co-distinct
> In man alone, or alone in living things,
> But a tympanum for the rhythms of ether,
> An element
> Incarnate in everything.

Life cannot be taken as a thing in itself without relation to the mind, and as a manifestation of the spirit of order and harmony, life is of little importance: it is but a temporary disorder. Life

> Is but one mechanism more to manifest the force
> Active even in the gulfs of uncreated space.

Read has a tendency of explaining evil merely as the absence of good: this is the doctrine of Plotinus. There is an emptiness in human life which provides for the display of vain passions, and to that emptiness corresponds the emptiness of space:

> These echo faintly in the corridors
> Carved cavernously wherever the mind
> Looks down into the waste of stars.

Evil, or 'agonies', however, are real in the immediate world, and the mind is wounded by the imperfection of the present life; there is no thought without pain, for joy is a synonym of forgetfulness: happiness is a folly sheltered and authorized by a kind of providence, but as soon as we begin to think we feel pain. 'The ultimate harmony of the world' is nevertheless accessible to the mind, but it can be wholly perceived only after death, when the mind has reached a state of complete stillness. Plenitude alone is real, and the perception of finite things leads necessarily to death, for finite things are like a hole in the universe. Because it is imperfect human life is unreal and filled only with longing and sickness; besides, the past is lost, and in order to see reality the mind has to look through life:

> Some state of high serenity
> Exists beyond the range
> Of fevered sense.

The ending of 'Beata l'Alma' implies that the creation of godlike figures is a bridge between finite and eternal life. There is no such possibility in 'The Retreat': the mind is imprisoned in imperfection and can hardly have a glimpse of beauty, which remains on the whole invisible. Life is full of unfulfilled desires until death frees us from imperfection:

> unto the dark return
> Of the world's harmony.

185

THE PHILOSOPHICAL POETRY OF HERBERT READ

In philosophical poetry there is the danger of replacing the feeling by the notion or even the notion by words which have, as in philosophy, only an instrumental value.[1] That danger becomes apparent in the repetition of words like 'the world's harmony' in Read's works, or 'pattern' in Eliot's works. The difference between philosophical thought and poetical thought is one of substance rather than of vocabulary. The same words with the same meaning can be repeated many times in philosophy, provided they conform to a pre-established and clear definition. It is not so in poetry, where a new and fresh meaning has to be created whenever a word is used,[2] so that an even intensity may be preserved throughout the poem. A philosophical poet, like any other poet, uses vivid images or confers a deep resonance to abstract words. The same words, used in philosophy, have an instrumental and purely logical function; they usually lose their poetic flavour when they are repeated.

The thought of 'Mutations of the Phoenix'[3] is to be analysed with reference to precise ideas, and it seems that the word 'mutations' should be connected with a passage from Santayana's *Reason in Religion*,[4] quoted in *Annals of Innocence and Experience*:[5] 'By becoming the spectator and confessor of his own death and of universal mutation, he will have identified himself with what is spiritual in all spirits and masterful in all apprehension; and so conceiving himself, he may truly feel and know that he is eternal.' Santayana, like Read, postulates immortality of the mind, not personal immortality. The idea of the survival of the mind is based upon the conception of a perfect nature in which there is no flaw, no stopping, no void, and which is governed by the spirit of harmony; the mind, however, survives only as far as it is assimilated, beyond death, to the spirit of harmony; that is, only as far as it transcends the emptiness of temporal human life. That was the main theme of 'The Retreat'.

The 'Mutations of the Phoenix' are an allusion to the temporal shapes taken by the spirit. Each moment of life and all the shapes of inanimate things are burnt away and replaced by the flames of the spirit, of the Phoenix, but the human mind lives instant after instant

---

[1] This passage should be considered as a digression dealing very briefl with an important problem in all philosophical poetry. This is not the place to insist on a danger which Read skilfully avoids.

[2] 'In Poetry the words are born or re-born in the act of thinking.' (*English Prose Style*, London, Bell, 1934, p. x).

[3] ibid., pp. 176–81.   [4] 1905, pp. 272–3.   [5] pp. 2 4–5.

and sees shape after shape: the eternal light is hidden from us. When, at the end of the poem, Read asks the Phoenix to extinguish the flames which devour our life, he expresses our wish that we may be spared the vision of change and imperfection, but he knows that eternity reveals itself only after death. Beauty is ideal and ashes are the best emblem we can find for it on earth; this explains the choice of the epigram:

> Beauty, truth and rarity,
> Grace in all simplicity,
> Here enclosed in cinders lie.

The poem becomes simple once the general idea is understood. The scenery of the poem is the sea-coast: the endless breaking of the waves provides the poet with a suitable simile of change. The symbols of the first section are impressive and remarkably well chosen: the crumbling sand, symbol of passivity, the waves, symbol of change and struggle, and the white flame, hidden behind the white surf, which the poet would like to see, but the surf comes back and prevents him from having 'beauty settled in his mind', for beauty participates in a world in which there is no change, in which the flame appears through the waves:

> At Aphrodite's birth
> were the waters in white flame?

These symbols of the first section are used as a frame in which Read draws a picture of life. Blood has a movement similar to the movement of waves and is also a symbol of change. The impress of our limbs into the sand is blurred and flattened by the tide; similarly, the flame reduces all finite things 'to its innate intensity' and annihilates all particularities through change.

The light of the flame is beyond the reach of the human mind and that is why, in the second section, the poet turns from the contemplation of endless change:

> Why should I dwell in individual ecstasy?
> It is a hollow quarry of the mind
> rill'd with rock drippings, smooth'd with silt;
> and only the whorlminded Hamlet walks there
> musing in the gutters.

Instead of looking in vain for the invisible flame, the poet makes an effort, as in 'The Retreat', to see the real design of life as it is manifested in finite things. The third section is a meditation on the mind whose activity, as we have already seen, is part of the scheme of things; the mind is a spark of the flame of the Phoenix and as such it has the power to dominate and ordain life, and to survive change:

> Mind wins deciduously,
> hibernating through many years.

In the fourth section the poet adds to the idea that life must be subordinated to conscience the idea that there is nothing but what exists in the mind, and that lust, frenzies and evil in general are false features of the external world to which the mind gives a semblance of reality. Existence implies conscience:

> Yet how persuade a mind that the thing seen
> is inhabitant of the cerebral cave
> and has elsewhere no materiality?

The sun is the symbol of reason, reason which is unable to eradicate the phantoms created by lust, symbolized by the moon. The phantoms, however, are driven away by a clear perception which restores reality to reason:

> There silhouettes are etched
>   not phantomly
> but in living areas of the mind.

Then, in the fifth section, Read illustrates the antithesis between the Phoenix (conscience) and the visible or the finite world by the image of the limit between sea and land on the shore. Sea and land end where they meet:

> So time breaks in spume and fret
> of intensified worlds.

The mind sees both, sees the end of both and consequently spans, measures, and outlives finite, mortal things. The world is finite only when related to the infinite in which it dissolves. Time exists and ends in the mind and man cannot escape death and eternity. Similarly, the waves cannot escape the flame:

See where that curl'd surf clashes
in a wreath, in a running crest,
in a fan of white flame!

This passage marks a progression of the poem, for the poet sees the
meeting of the finite with the infinite, and the finite appears as a
perpetual death: only the flame, only eternity is real; life is reduced
to a limit, to a line without substance:

All existence
past, present and to be
is in this sea fringe.
There is no other temporal scene.

The sixth section develops the symbol of the shore and applies it to
considerations on the relations between the mind and the world. The
existence of the Phoenix is undeniable and nevertheless it is not
wholly perceived because we see it always at the moment of birth as
well as we see temporal existence at the moment of death. The
Phoenix is outside things and beings, but we can see its reflection on
them, a reflection which burns them. Similarly, we know the finite
only because we consume it. We are the last witnesses of the finite,
and we do not see what is beyond. To see is to destroy: 'vision is fire.'

The end of the sixth section is somewhat contradicted by the next,
which implies the statement that what is beyond life is sometimes
seen, that the Phoenix appears in a disguised form on the earth, and
that there are revelations of a superior light either in nature or in man:

when the night is black
settle in the bleak headlands.

Utter shrill warnings in the cold dawn sky;
let them descend
into the shuttered minds below you.
Inhabit our wither'd nerves.

In the last section the world appears as transmuted by the Phoenix.
The spirit reigns over an earth of silence and desolation. This is expressed by an apocalyptic vision of a profound night:

The sun is sunken in a deep abyss
her dying life transpires.

Each bar and boss
of rallied cloud the fire receives.

Till the ashen sky dissolves.

Only the stars are left to the ecstasy of the mind:

Yet still the stars—
intense remnants of time.

The poem ends with the invocation which we have already explained:

O phoenix,
O merciful bird of fire,
Extinguish your white
hungry flames.

Although time is redeemed only after death, we can hear on this changing earth a premonition of infinite stillness:

The river carries in its slaty bed
an echo from the sea.

These premonitions cannot be analysed, like the other images in which the thought is naked.

Much less philosophical is 'The Lament of Saint Denis', a narrative and allegorical poem which can be read for music's sake without paying much attention to its meaning. The images are grouped in episodes which lead to a crisis. St. Denis does not appear in the poem; he simply tells a tale illustrating man's dark destiny. We shall try to elucidate the general outline of the poem.

The first two sections of the poem are a prelude which can give rise to at least two different interpretations. The scenery of the poem is set in a moonlit landscape. The moon can be interpreted either as a symbol of the temporal, indirect light, the sun being the eternal light (in other words, the flame of the Phoenix), or as the world after the death of Christ, who is symbolized by the sun; this meaning is implied in the second section, whereas in the first section the moon is likened to a pagan deity:

I, said the moon, who have been a maiden
worshipp'd of man
am now but a burnished emblem
of the sun's span.

THE POETIC EXPRESSION OF READ'S IDEAS

Read's ideas on destiny and imperfection recur in these symbols: the moon is

> a fitful symbol in the broken sky.

In this moonlit earth appears 'a rheumy host of men' climbing in the darkness. They are the symbol of the past. The summit to which they climb is death, in which they hope to find some rest. Instead of rest, they encounter enemies, naked children (the future). There is a storm when they meet, and a figure carrying its head

> Like a lantern in one hand

appears to them; it is eternity in one moment, at the meeting of past and future:

> These two streams cross in me,
> Past and future are but two lines
> Intersecting at a point: in me.
> From this point of time I survey eternity,
> I am master of all nature and knowledge
> And all that exists in time
> Moves through me: these fair children
> Pass into life, these old bones disintegrate.
> And I, in a moment of time,
> Include them all;

The analogy between this figure and the symbol of the shore in 'Mutations of the Phoenix' is obvious. Moreover, this figure may be interpreted as Christ, for it is the incarnation of eternity in the storm, in time. All evil, lust and war, are contained in eternity which appears as a disfigured and debased creature:

> Uncrowned, ungrac'd, devoid.

Later, the chaos, evil, lust, sufferance will be without, will be chased, excluded, and the figure will appear in all its glory, having vanquished evil. But now evil and good, time and eternity co-exist, and there is no escape from death and woe:

> Rocks
> rain
> riven rocks
> eroded plains

191

> Pain
> anguish'd eyes
> hands and lips
> entreat in vain

The full meaning of the poem cannot be extracted in the form of philosophical statements: it is a poetical meaning, which prose is unable to express. Read's belief in the ultimate harmony of nature and his rejection of hasty hopes are nevertheless apparent in the poem.

'The Nuncio',[1] unlike 'The Lament of Saint Denis', proposes a 'modern' imagery and, in a way, appeals to modern readers; the theme, although treated ironically, is optimistic: it involves the belief in a brighter future. The poem is full of wit and satire. We are introduced to an assembly of modern clerks, or intellectuals listening to a modern prophet, or utopist, called Starr, a man of our time looking at the future and making projects:

> He spoke immediately
> into the ear of the microphone

What Starr says might be termed a disguised and an entertaining sermon. Instead of elucidating all the particular allusions, which are numerous, it is better to confine our study to the general ideas of the poem. Starr exposes the faith of anarchists, of those enemies of tyrants who want to build a world of freedom:

> Against tyrants there is only one weapon
> anciently the pen now the microphone.

He deplores the disorder of our time:

> Any demagogue can raise a wind
> to break the logic of the mind.

The masses do not listen to logic: we must use emotion to persuade them. Read's ideas on education through art recur in this poem:

> We must design with brighter colour
> borrowing harmonies from children at school

Read's interpretation of our time[2] (a time of servitude and stagna-

---

[1] ibid., pp. 189–94.
[2] cf. the epigraph of the poem:

> So our virtues
> Lie in the interpretation of the time. (*Coriolanus*, IV, 7.)

tion) is as important in this poem as his projects for the future. Starr's projects are compared to the building of a modern house in which the lift is the symbol of a society without tight classes. Like all utopias, Starr's society takes peace and union for its mottoes. Starr, however, treats humanity ironically; men are accustomed to power: we must provide them with a semblance of authority, and our strategy must be to catch them in a transparent net:

> But we must reduce the area of glass:
> we have avoided darkness
> our structures are transparent—
> only the skeleton visible and adamant
> lies like a net embedded criss-cross.

It is obvious that Starr is speaking to those who believe that human life could be improved upon or at least should be changed and his vision is that of a world in which men, although wanting faith and hope, might live freely, led by those who have a solid faith and an active reason:

> Reason like a lily
> fed by sense and feeling
> blooming eternally
> ruling
> all the flowers of the field.

Starr adopts, needless to say, Read's theory of the self: 'the individual is the pivot of our plan,' so that union and peace must be founded on individual reflection rather than on general agreement.

III. THE POETRY OF ANARCHISM

An analysis of Read's poems shows the consistency of his thought. A comparison of his prose works with his poems leads to the conclusion that Read's ideas are more independently and profoundly developed in his poems although they are applied to a greater variety of subjects in his prose works. To conclude that poetry is a better medium for thought than prose would be a hasty judgment, and yet it is true that poetry is the best medium for a certain kind of thought.

The philosophy of Herbert Read is simple: it is not systematized, but it is coherent enough to deserve to be called philosophy. The nature of Read's ideas, however, is different from what we usually call philosophy, that is, a doctrine divided into a theory of knowledge, ethics, and aesthetics. The clue to that difference may be found in Read's statement that 'My profoundest experiences have been not religious nor moral, but aesthetic'.[1] In other words, Read's ideas are not derived from an analysis of thought, dogmas or sensations, of experience, but from the application of his own faculties, from the practice of both reason and imagination and above all from his innate and intense sense of harmony. Read's philosophy is made, in a way, of ideas transformed into action: 'the highest manifestation of the immanent will of the universe is the work of art.'[2]

We have discussed Read's ideas on aesthetics, but it is more important to read and enjoy the works for themselves,[3] for the thought integrated in a poem is richer and more musical (provoking an infinite number of resonances in the mind) than the purely analytical and discursive (each element being one link in a static chain) thought expressed in prose. Eliot's opinion that metaphysical poets have the essential quality 'of transmuting ideas into sensations' might be applied to Read, but only to a certain extent, for the starting point of Read's images is already a sensation, a perception of truth and beauty, so that Read's ideas are necessarily poetical ideas, or ideal values created by an act of conscience and not arbitrarily imposed upon and determining the poet's perceptions.

The source of his ideas, and the source of his pantheism, is his lyricism; he is exalted when he is one with his images, when he feels part of the universe, immersed in the 'pattern' or scheme of things, in other words, when he participates in the beauty of nature.

He is not satisfied, however, with this sense of communion; he has also an intellectual passion which urges him to analyse his lyrical impulse and to test it before the eye of the mind. This attitude of detachment allows him to build a coherent vision of the world and to create his own world of beauty. He reflects upon nature and finds that life and death alike are ruled by the same laws, which dwell in his mind,[4]

[1] *Annals of Innocence and Experience*, p. 226.

[2] ibid.

[3] 'We still treat art as an aid to thought, instead of as a mode of thought in itself.' (*Art and Society*, London, Faber and Faber, 1946, p. 134.)

[4] This attitude calls to the memory the motto adopted by Kant: 'The starry heaven above me, the moral law in me.'

and upon which it is possible to build a future world of peace and order. This utopia is based upon a belief in the perfectibility of mankind; the more man is conscious of the harmony of the world the better he may apply the principles reflected in his mind to his life. Being able to think and to feel, he is endowed with an independent power which brings him into relation with the principles of the universe, even if these principles are but the Spencerian 'first principles' of matter. But this utopia is far from our eyes and the best we can do is to draw our resources from the well of all being, and to create a beauty controlled by reason and nourished by intuition.

CHAPTER V

THE PHILOSOPHICAL ELEMENT IN
C. DAY LEWIS'S POETRY

I. LEWIS'S AIM

BORN in 1904, Cecil Day Lewis belongs to a generation of writers and, among them, to a small group of poets (Auden, Spender, and MacNeice) who, after the Great War, without accepting the state of corruption and distress of society, tried to re-establish the communication between poets and readers, and conceived of a regenerate man within an ideal society.

Beside his social preoccupations, Lewis displays great intellectual abilities, so that two elements can be distinguished in his work: a constantly alert thought, and a desire to face the problems of his time. His poetry is an effort to unite these two tendencies, although he is not always successful in doing so because the first one predominates, and for this reason Lewis is more relevant to our study than his friends.

His poetry does not always correspond to what he proclaims in his critical essays. When, for example, he rejects surrealism, he does so on the ground that the doctrine of André Breton is a form of escapism which deprives words of their social connotations, but what estranges him most from surrealism is the absence, in that school, of analytical thought. His reaction against the Dada Manifesto is shown in the following passage: 'Every conscious human activity is to some extent a social activity and in consequence must be judged by social criteria.'[1] These criteria, however, could not be applied to the activities referred to, which are supposed to be unconscious. It would be more convenient to accuse the surrealists of working against the laws of the human mind, which are apparently not observed by a blind and indifferent society. Lewis's desire to be 'contemporary', to address his

[1] *A Hope for Poetry*, Oxford, Basil Blackwell, 1936; Postscript, 1936, p. 88.

readers directly, and his anxiety concerning the survival of poetry in a scientific era, are symptoms of a disintegration of society which compels him to serve two gods. It may be presumed that most poets, if they are anxious about the future, do not question the survival of poetry. The assimilation of modern knowledge, upon which Lewis insists so much, is not of vital importance to poetry. Fortunately Lewis, especially in his early poetry, is less expansive than he claims.

In emphasizing the thought which underlies Lewis's poetry, we have to neglect two important characteristics of his work: the rhetorical element of his speech which answers his need of communication with the reader, and the satire directed against 'a world so inimical apparently both to poetry and to the social ideals which living poets affirm'.[1]

Lewis's poetry is a compromise between abstract thought and pure poetry, on one side, satire and rhetoric on the other. We shall lay more emphasis on the first aspect, at the risk of being partial, and blind to the social value and to the directness of his poems.

This complexity is the result of the dual aim assigned by Lewis to his poetry, a social aim and a metaphysical one. The first is best stated in the following passage: 'We shall not begin to understand post-war poetry until we realize that the poet is appealing above all for the creation of a society in which the real and living contact between man and man may again become possible. That is why, speaking from the living unit of himself and his friends, he appeals for the contraction of the social group to a size at which human contact may again be established and demands the destruction of all impediments to love.'[2]

It is difficult to grasp how the poets of our time might assume the task of social reformers through their work, but the second task assigned by Lewis to poets seems to be more congenial to bards:

'It is the nature of the poetic vision to perceive those invisible truths which are like elektrons the basis of reality; the nature of the poetic imagination to become aware of the cryptic links that bind our universe together, to find similarity in difference and to make coherence out of contradiction. If the poet is not clairvoyant, he is nothing. And this clairvoyancy is particularly directed towards discovering the 'supernatural' in nature and the "superhuman" in humanity. There can be no such thing as realist poetry.'[3]

[1] ibid., chap. VII, p. 40.   [2] ibid., p. 38.   [3] ibid., p. 75.

Lewis's dual aim accounts for the uneven quality of his verse, which is, in his own words, 'a constant alternation of lyricism and flatness'.

More attention is paid to the aesthetic problem in *The Poetic Image*.[1] Lewis has done, and perhaps was supposed to do, something very different from a classification and an evaluation of the poetic images, for which the title prepares the reader. The volume contains a series of academic lectures which occasionally allow personal opinions, but the reader would like to have either an impersonal study or a resolute affirmation of Lewis's ideas and observations. The professional critic will find nothing new in the book, whereas the common reader will like it, for Lewis writes: 'I have given the ordinary reader an introduction.' He divides his field into disconnected chapters without engaging in thorough research. The first three chapters are mainly concerned with the aesthetic problem, and illustrate the well-known ideas that pleasure and truth are the substance of the image, that the freshness and intensity of the image charm and convince, and that the structure of an image or a group of images is made by wholeness and consistency of impression, from the point of view of the creative process, and by a concord between image and theme, from the point of view of the finished poem. The three last chapters consider the problem in relation to the present time. Lewis examines the extent to which all images are poetical, refutes the theory of poetry for poetry's sake, and insists on communal experience and collective emotion. He gives this advice to future poets: 'May you have the power and the luck to give your own generation images of virtue—natural, consoling, heartening.'[2] Then he explains his definition of virtue: '. . . the virtues which unite mankind in families and societies are themselves variations of that single theme which also unifies your disjointed memories and warring modes to make a poem.'[3]

Lewis advocates what he calls 'personal poetry': 'This kind of personal poetry is the antithesis of that to which we are most accustomed nowadays—the poetry which looks inwards to find images valid for the outward world and powerful enough to illuminate its anfractuous ways.'[4] And he goes on to explain this attitude: '. . . should not there be a poetry to-day which looks outward, which keeps its eyes firmly focused upon the object in the external world and, brooding passion-

[1] *The Poetic Image*, London, Jonathan Cape, 1947.   [2] ibid., p. 156.
[3] ibid., p. 157.   [4] ibid., p. 153.

ately over that object, perceiving at last its value, its necessary part in the scheme of things, may disinterestedly reflect upon it an image of human virtue?

If poetry is still to do its civilizing work, that kind of poetry is needed.'[1]

From his study, Lewis has chosen two principles for future poets: first, to face the external world, secondly to project on it the sympathy which has its source in creative imagination and its proof in facts, so that the poets may shape and recreate reality, instead of losing themselves in the ethereal kingdoms of the interior mind.

These principles inform the poetry written by Lewis since the approach of World War Two. He is more and more trying to face the external world, to communicate with it directly and, in sympathizing with it, to find again some sort of unity. It is a new path to the 'magnetic mountain', more indirect perhaps than the one of the first period—spiritual progression—but more congenial to Lewis.

II. 'TRANSITIONAL POEM'

Lewis writes, in his first period, poems of sustained unity, but with an analytical structure. Because of his discursive manner of composing, we have to respect the chronological order and to avoid a general discussion which would prevent us from taking any of the three poems as a whole.

The first of the long poems is *Transitional Poem*.[2] *Notes to Transitional Poem*, written in January 1929, may serve as an introduction to the poem. Their first part indicates Lewis's purpose: 'The central theme of this poem is the single mind. The poem is divided into four parts, which essentially represent four phases of personal experience in the pursuit of single-mindedness: it will be seen that a transition is intended from one part to the next such as implies a certain spiritual progress and a consequent shifting of aspect. As far as any definitions can be attached to these aspects, they may be termed (1) metaphysical, (2) ethical, (3) psychological; while (4) is an attempt to relate the poetic impulse with the experience as a whole. Formally, the parts fall with fair accuracy into the divisions of a theorem in geometry, i.e. general enunciation, proof, corollaries.'

[1] ibid., p. 154.   [2] *Collected Poems*, Volume One: 1929 to 1933, p. 9.

In the 'enunciation' of Part One, the mind is presented as the source of order. The allusion to Spinoza[1] is significant, for it shows that what is considered is the abstract mind, pure reason, of which the best manifestation is geometry:

> It is certain we shall attain
> No life till we stamp on all
> Life the tetragonal
> Pure symmetry of brain.

It shows also that the poet is not satisfied with uncertainties and vagueness, and wants to free his thought from all that does not obey logic.

This leads him to justify his scorn for banalities, prejudice, and uncontrolled statements. He knows that his obscurity is based upon solid logic, and he does not care for the opinion of those who do not see where this leads. The atmosphere of metaphysics is rarefied, but it is clear, without shade, without defects, and precisely because it is rarefied, almost inaccessible and changeless, it is unshaken: it is impassive and indestructible:

> Let figs from thistles fall
> Or stars from their pedestals,
> This architecture will stand.

The second section develops the same idea, namely, that we must find an absolute, an unshakable basis for our thoughts, and that we must refer to it constantly, instead of being driven from opposite to opposite:

> For the mind must cope with
> All elements or none—
> Bask in dust along with weevils,
> Or criticize the sun.

The mind has to remain undivided, and calm as a kite in the wind:

> A boy's kite sits as calm as Minos.
> If the string be sound:

---

[1] Spinoza, *Letters:* 'I would warn you that I do not attribute to nature either beauty or deformity, order or confusion. Only in relation to our imagination can things be called beautiful or ugly, well-ordered or confused.'

We have to reach a point of fixity. This point of transcendental calmness or constancy, or the ability to think *sub specie aeternitatis*, is symbolized in the third section by the Sphinx, whose light prevails over the varying, uncertain light of the day:

> But finding all things my strenuous sense included
> Ciphers new-copied by the indefinite sunlight,
> I fell once more under the shadow of my Sphinx.

That the Sphinx is a creation of the human mind is shown by the aimlessness of nature: finality is considered by Lewis as an absurdity. But, at the same time, the Sphinx is a necessary projection of the mind, it cannot be avoided:

> The aimlessness of buttercup and beetle
> So pestered me, I would have cried surrender
> To the fossil certitudes of Tom, Dick, and Harry,
> Had I known how or believed that such a surrender
> Could fashion aught but a dead Sphinx from the
> > live Sphinx.

Consciousness (the Sphinx) survives even death and darkness:

> > > yet was I lord of
> Something: for, seeing the fall of a burnt-out faggot
> Make all the night sag down, I became lord of
> Light's interplay—stoker of an old parable.

Lewis considers, in the fourth section, particular illustrations of his thought. First, material and spiritual life. Time does not impress the metaphysical mind, a moment is worth a long life: there is no advantage in becoming as old as Methuselah. Man lives in time and in eternity, has a material and a spiritual life:

> I have a lover of flesh
> And a lover that is a sprite:

But these two lives are united in the metaphysical mind:

> Twin poles energic, they
> Stand fast and generate
> This spark that crackles in the void
> As between fate and fate.

Love is essential, not accidental (if we follow Spinoza's termin-ology), to destroy it would be to destroy the whole of creation:

> Time, we allow, destroys
> All aërial toys:
> But to assail love's heart
> He has no strategy,
> Unless he suck up the sea
> And pull the earth apart.

Another particular illustration is to be found in nature. Nature, which psycho-analysts would identify with the symbol of the mother,[1] attracts Lewis because of its complete humility and obedience. Nature is the proof of a supernatural power, and has a language; it is sublime and transparent. The mind feels at ease in it and finds a place where nothing can disturb or contradict the metaphysical mind. This justifies the poet's recourse to nature:

> Dismayed by the monstrous credibility
> Of all antinomies, I climbed the fells
> To Easedale Tarn.
>   . . . (So the dog
> Returns to his vomit, you protest. Well only
> The dog can tell what virtue lies in his vomit.)

This section (the sixth) is more poetical than the others, perhaps because the thought is less abstract, less rigid and, above all, more direct. The vision surges immediately, without intermediacy, and reaches a cosmic feeling:

> How can I wear the clouds, who feel each mountain
> Yearn from its flinty marrow to abdicate
> Sublimity and globe-trot with the world?

Both the language of nature and the language of the poet ex-press eternity:

> Prophetic earth, you need no lumber of logic
> Who point your arguments alike with a primrose

[1] cf.:
> Could I be child again
> And grip those skirts of cloud the matriarch sky
> Draggled on mere and hillside? . . .

And a sick sheep coughing among the stones:
And I have only words; yet must they both
Outsoar the mountain and lap up the wind.

The seventh and last section of Part One deals with aesthetics. 'Abstract art' is an impossibility, Cassandra and Helen are symbols of a material reality. Yet these symbols are but a cover, like the body's clothes, with the difference that, if the mind's covering becomes old-fashioned, the substance it covers is an indirect expression of eternity:

> While that other (i.e. thought) may
> Reverberate all along
> Man's craggy circumstance—
> Naked enough to keep its dignity
> Though it eye God askance.

This last section is very elaborate, and perhaps might equally be expressed in rhetorical prose. Moreover, the transition from the beginning, which postulates either abstract thought or pure poetry, to the denial of non-representative art, is not clear. In this passage, as well as in others, Lewis does not follow his thought to the end. The distinction between his two lovers is an easy one.

Parts Two and Three deal with the ethical and psychological aspects of the single mind. They are conceived, to a certain extent, like a treatise, and they are too often prosaic and indirect.

Part Two, however, is not simply a treatise on original sin. In the opening, after paying his tribute to tradition, Lewis considers the problem of the poet in modern times. Poetic tradition in relation to modern poetry plays a part similar to the Garden of Eden in relation to the moral life of to-day. What the poet says of poetic tradition:

> So cheat I memory that works in gilt
> And stucco to restore a fallen day.

the modern man may say of Eden:

> Adam must subdue
> The indestructible serpent,
> Outstaring it: content
> If he can transplant
> One slip from paradise
> Into his own eyes.

The basic theme of *Transitional Poem* is the effort of the poet to come to terms with the world. Lewis expresses the 'self-disgust of the introvert content to brood over his own subjective "chaos" ':[1]

> Then there came disgust
> Of the former loon who could
> Elbow a bridge and brood
> From Chaos to last Trump
> Over the imbecile pomp
> Of waters dribbling past.

'This village idiocy', which 'it is high time to renounce', is deplored in *The Poetic Image*: 'Can he', writes Lewis, speaking of the poet, 'survive in the modern world except as a kind of village idiot, tolerated but ignored, talking to himself, hanging round the pub and the petrol pumps, his head awhirl with broken images, mimicking the movements of a life in which he has no part?' The passage of the village idiot leads us far from the theme of Part Two, so subtle and elusive are the threads of Lewis's composition. He achieves communication at the expense of concentration.

The three principal steps of the part might be singled out in the following manner:

1. Man is far from Eden, separation is everywhere:

> Can the mole take
> A census of the stars?
> Our firmament will never
> Give him headache.

2. Damnation is over mankind:

> I see the constellations
> But by their gaps.

3. Unity of the personality is achieved in the moral conscience:

> So from this ark, this closet of the brain,
> The dove emerges and flies back again
> With a Messiah sprig of certitude—
> Promise of ground below the sprawling flood.

[1] This interpretation has been suggested by Lewis in a letter to the author of the present essay (6 May 1949).

Part Three is a search for the integrity of the soul:

> For I had been a modern moth and hurled
> Myself on many a flaming world,
> To find its globe was glass.

There are some ironical, satirical, and humorous touches through which Lewis sometimes tries to cover the dryness of his subject. The unity of the soul is achieved only after death:

> Passion dies from the heart
> But to infect the marrow;
> Hold dream and act apart
> Till the man discard his narrow
>
> Sapience and folly
> Here, where the graves slumber
> In a green melancholy
> Of overblown summer.

The beginning of Part Four, like the end of T. S. Eliot's *The Hollow Men*, is interspersed with biblical sentences. According to the *Notes to Transitional Poem*, this part 'is an attempt to relate the poetic impulse with the experience as a whole'.

The origin of the Word is the origin of the world:

> In the beginning was the Word.

Before the Fall, there is no separation between the Creator and His creation, and the creation is the word:

> For him rise up the litanies of leaves
> From the tormented wood, and semi-breves
> Of birds accompany the simple dawn.

Then Lewis recalls the origin of sin:

> Green fields were my slippers,
> Sky was my hat,
> But curiosity
> Killed the cat.

It is interesting to note how Lewis avoids Milton's epic manner and treats his subject with a familiarity which may seem out of place. The parodies and disguises are sometimes unjustified, especially when Lewis is dealing with a definite subject which becomes almost unrecognizable. When imprisoned in a subject, Lewis compensates for his servitude by his wit, as if wanting to preserve an apparent freedom. He is at his best, however, when he abandons himself to thought:

> Nevertheless you are well out of Eden:
> For there is no wonder where all things are new,
> No dream where all is sleep; no vision where
> Seer and seen are one; nor prophecy
> Where only echo waits upon the tongue.

Now that man is separated from God, nature is no longer a living symbol, and the immediacy of emotion and words is lost. (This might justify Lewis's preoccupation with the social meaning of his works.) Man needs a language of his own to relate himself to God, and that relation is re-established only through the intermediacy of visions and miracles:

> Now he has come to a country of stone walls,
> Breathes a precarious air.
> Frontiers of adamant declare
> A cold autonomy. There echo starves;
> And the mountain ash bleeds stoically there
> Above the muscular stream.
> What cairn will show the way he went?
> A harrow rusting on defeated bones?
> Or will he leave a luckier testament—
> Rock deeply rent,
> Fountains of spring playing upon the air?

The three last lines express the thought that even the glory of great civilizations is a witness of man's perdition. This first section of Part Four might be compared with the exposition of a theorem in geometry. The rest might be compared with the proofs and corollaries of the same theorem.

First, Lewis develops, this time in poetical terms, the idea that ecstasy, or the vision of the absolute, is only a part of man's experience, and occurs only at rare moments of poetical felicity:

> Those Himalayas of the mind
> Are not so easily possessed:
> There's more than precipice and storm
> Between you and your Everest.
>
> You who declare the peak of peaks
> Alone will satisfy your want,
> Can you distil a grain of snow?
> Can you digest an adamant?

Man must be satisfied with relative truths (symbolized here by the household cock and the sea-gull) which expire on the shore of the absolute.

> 'What are these rocks impede our pomp?'
> Gesticulating to the sun
> The waves part ranks, sidle and fume,
> They linger grovelling; where assault
> Has failed, attrition may tell.
>
> The bird sees nothing to the point;
> Shrugs an indifferent wing; proceeds
> From rock to rock in the mid-ocean
> Peering for barnacles and weeds.

Section 30 is a corollary of the preceding section (the proof), and expresses man's inability to reach the absolute. Beauty is but a shadow of the mind without immediate relation with the external world (Spinoza). There is a separation between fact and idea, and each has a necessity of their own, either the external world:

> Now that the crust has cooled
>   The floods are kept in pen,
> Mountains have got their mould
>   And air its regimen.

or the mind:

> And show that beauty is
>   A motion of the mind
> By its own dark caprice
>   Directed or confined.

The last idea, recalling the passage of Spinoza quoted on page 6, shows clearly the profound separation between fact and idea, between the categories of the mind and those of nature. Nature is neither sad nor beautiful nor hostile: the mind makes it so. Lewis insists rather on the separation than on the power of the mind.

While section 31 is an allegory opposing antiquity to the Christian era, section 32 comes back to the idea that human knowledge, however relative it may be, is a sufficient measure of the universe; the same idea recurs in the next two sections, where the central image is that of the crow:

> . . . A crow
>
> Sees more than meets the eye—
> What marrow in fleshless bones may lie.

The symbol of the crow means that the human mind, although limited, is universal and prophetic. Lewis has a rather clumsy way of announcing a prophecy:

> Put down the tripod here.

But if the crow is the symbol of human experience as a whole, the hawk, as in the beginning, is the symbol of the metaphysical mind. The crow feeds on bones, but the hawk looks at his prey from afar, and, when the prey is taken, returns to his height (where one can consider the world *sub specie aeternitatis*), confirming the separation of truth and reality:

> Then trod the air, content
> With contemplation till
> The truth of valley and hill
> Should be self-evident.[1]

The poet imitates the hawk, or, better, the lark

> Who veins the sky with song,

and who, after he has sung all day, returns to the tree where he is hidden for the night:

> And the famed singer ends
> In anonymity.

A closer analysis of *Transitional Poem* would disclose many intricacies of thought and a general complexity which is not far from dispersion. The structure is not apparent and the links between the various parts are only suggested. Nevertheless, they exist. It could be ob-

[1] Section 34, p. 54.

jected to such a scheme, however, that it is not fit for poetry. It is logically coherent, but it is not a progression and even less a duration, precisely because it is construed like a series of static theorems, and not like a musical composition, in which the parts are involved in one another and participate in a flowing, moving duration. There is not much progression from Part One to Part Three. The first three phases of personal experience are conceived as separate themes occupying a fixed place and the attempt to reconcile the world of pure ideas with the world of reality has failed.[1]

Lewis tried to mark a progression in *From Feathers to Iron*, and fulfilled this desire better in *The Magnetic Mountain*.

Lewis's failure in this respect might be explained from the fact that he considered *Transitional Poem* less as a progression of his own mind than as the development of a settled subject which was imposed upon him. His poetry has a didactic turn which is still evident in *From Feathers to Iron*, but which is nourished by conviction and inspiration in *The Magnetic Mountain* where his lyricism yields its place to satire. Many of his similes are not truly similes: they are examples.

III. 'FROM FEATHERS TO IRON'

The poem[2] is preceded by two mottoes indicating its purpose:

Do thoughts grow like feathers, the dead end of life?

(W. H. Auden)

We take but three steps from feathers to iron.

(John Keats)

The transition from feathers to iron is similar to the transition from dreams to reality in *Transitional Poem*. The beginning is full of hope. Life comes to an end, but has its place in the divine order: life is positive, and death does not diminish it; we are not living in eternity, but life is a certainty:

Love's proved in its creation, not eternity:
Like leaf or linnet the true heart's affection
Is born, dies later, asks no reassurance.

[1] This problem is clearly stated in the 'Appendix' to *Coleridge as Critic*, by Read.
[2] *Collected Poems*, Volume One, 1929–33, p. 63.

Then, from life, the poet turns to his thought. He abandons the artificial town and proceeds to the shore, where he compares his swift thought with the always moving winds, whereas the other men are, like the tides, moving to and fro:

> You are the tides running for ever
> Along their ancient groove:
> Such winds am I, pause not for breath
> And to fresh shores will move.

It is not necessary to insist on the beauty of the last line.

Then, the poet turns to the seasons, to the countryside, at last to the idea of the return of the seasons, linked with the idea of the perpetuation of the human race. It is useful to recall here the circumstances with which the poem is connected. Lewis explains them in *A Hope for Poetry* (Chapter Six, p. 38): 'A year or two ago I wrote a sequence called "From Feathers to Iron" which for me expressed simply my thoughts and feelings during the nine months before the birth of my first child: the critics, almost to a man, took it for a political allegory; the simple, personal meaning evaded them.'

The vision of the poet is a vision of light; life, renewed every spring, is for him the day's affirmation, and the thought of the poet is proceeding forward in trust:

> Here's no meaning but of morning.
> Naught soon of night but stars remaining,
> Sink lower, fade, as dark womb
> Recedes creation will step clear.

Section 8 is a dialogue between He and She, two characters alone on an island, who prepare themselves to meet the future alone:

> . . . We've a stout boat
> Provisioned for some years: we need endure
> No further ill than to be still alone.

These two characters are the symbol of man's condition, who has to fulfil his needs without external help. Then, the vision is enlarged and purified. It is no longer the vision of the senses, but the vision of the mind:

> Waning now is the sensual eye
> Allowed no flaw upon the skin
> And burnt away wrinkle and feature,
> Fed with pure spirit from within.

This vision is compared with the earth embraced in a single sight at moonlight:

> Nesciently that vision works.
> Just so the pure night-eye, the moon,
> Labours, a monumental mason,
> To gloss over a world of stone.

Life appears as a solid whole (the feathers become iron), and the vision becomes complex and complete:

> Shadow takes depth and shape turns solid:
> Far-ranging, the creative eye
> Sees arable, marsh, enclosed and common,
> Assents to multiplicity.

The vision is then universalized, the seed of 'the creative eye' takes shape and promises fruit everywhere; the poet includes in his vision the complete circle of life and death, life perpetually doing what death is undoing, and the inevitable consequence of that tension— human suffering:

> Nothing we can do
> Will sweeten the real rue,
> That we begin, and end, with groans.

The poem goes on, for there is something beyond the circle of life and death. Although that circle is an inevitable necessity, it is not all, it does not satisfy the thought of the poet. At this point, Lewis's image of life might be compared with Plato's Cavern. Man is imprisoned and seeks an opening to freedom and light, works obscurely for a change and tends towards a mysterious goal which is hidden from him.

Man's condition resembles the situation of somebody who is taken between the coming tide and the cliffs, and for whom there is no escape:

> Nightmare nags at his elbow and narrows
> Horizon to pinpoint, hope to hand's breadth.

His whole being lives to find an opening:

> But we seek a new world through old workings,
> Whose hope lies like seed in the loins of earth,
> Whose dawn draws gold from the roots of darkness.

So the development of Lewis's thought brings him closer to the idea of finality and of human progress:

> Not shy of light nor shrinking from shadow
> Like Jesuits in jungle we journey
> Deliberately bearing to brutish tribes
> Christ's assurance, arts of agriculture.

The idea of finality is further developed in section 13, where Lewis emphasizes the contradiction of human nature: man is situated between actual life and future life, and this torture is imposed upon him by love and pain:

> Those absolute dictators will enchain
> The low, exile the princely parts:
> They close a door between the closest hearts:

Love is a sickness, pain an exile, and we can neither recover nor find the happy land on this earth, for this earth is a place of contradiction and confusion which can be solved only after death by a separation of light from darkness:

> Contact the means, but travellers report
> The ends are poles apart.

Section 13 is an example of Lewis's natural type of composition: first an exposition (first stanza), then a development of the two elements contained in the exposition (passion and pain, second and third stanza), then a conclusion leading to the next section. This is typical of an analytical, intellectual composition.

The transition between section 13 and section 14 is perfectly logical. Section 13 already conveyed the image of a blind struggle towards light, and section 12 developed that theme and hinted the possibility of a solution. The solution, as might be guessed, is resurrection, symbolized by the evocation of spring and the birth of the child.

Lewis's vision goes on developing itself on another plane. We leave the order of nature and enter the order of grace or, better, we reach the limit where a creative vision is substituted for a speculative vision. In a way, we pass from the thought to the application of the thought. This moment is marked in the poem by a pause and a glance towards the future:

> I have come so far upon my journey.
> This is the frontier, this is where I change,
> And wait between two worlds to take refreshment.

That change is symbolized by the transition between winter and summer, and suggests the coming of a new aeon:

> So, waiting here between winter and summer,
> Conception and fruition, I
> Take what refreshment may be had from skies
> Uncertain as the wind, prepare
> For a new route, a change of constitution.

The new era or, if we may call it so, the order of grace, is envisaged here in historical terms. A symbolical interpretation of the poem should perhaps be abandoned here, for it would be ridiculous to mistake a belief in a terrestrial paradise for a belief in resurrection. Lewis undoubtedly believes in human progress and betterment. The difficulty might be solved by saying that Lewis believes in a progress such as that indicated by Berdiaeff in *Dialectique existentielle du Divin et de l'Humain*,[1] in the actual accomplishment of God's will through man on the earth. If we consider the past in the light of that belief, it appears to us as a succession of trials and errors in a striving towards peace:

> Some change of constitution, where
> Has been for years an indeterminate quarrel
> Between a fevered head and a cold heart;
> Rulers who cannot rule, rebels who will not
> Rebel; an age divided
> Between to-morrow's wink, yesterday's warning.

Strangely enough, Lewis introduces here a conception which Berdiaeff thought essential to belief in a progress in time: man contains in himself something greater than himself:

[1] Paris, Janin, 1947.

And yet this self, contains
Tides continents and stars—a myriad selves,
Is small and solitary as one grass-blade
Passed over by the wind

The future is therefore full of promise. To-day's struggles will come to an end, to-day's problems will be solved, and our sons will inherit whatever we have achieved towards that end:

You in there, my son, my daughter,
Will you become dictator, resolve the factions?
Will you be my ambassador
And make my peace with the adjacent empires?

It is obvious that, in these lines, the personal meaning prevails over the symbolical one, but it would be a mistake to underestimate the philosophical implications which underlie the passage. According to Lewis, human progress in time is sustained by tradition, and tradition here means the gradual regeneration of man, so that there is a transcendental force at work in history, which gives a meaning to the successive generations. Our sons, future men, are our heirs, and improve what we have done. We live in them until the completion of human destiny.

In section 16, that historical process is compared with an artesian well. The men of to-day, the ancestors, are symbolized by the 'living water', our sons by the 'metal', history by 'the impermeable clay and rock', and the completion of human destiny by 'the arable land':

More than else might you,
My son, my daughter,
Be metal to bore through
The impermeable clay
And rock that overlay
The living water.

Through that artesian well
My self may out,
Finding its own level.
This way the waste land turns
To arable, and towns are rid of drought.

The last lines might be an allusion to Eliot's *Waste Land*.
Lewis proceeds along three parallel lines: the spiritual line drawn

by the progress of the human soul, the allegorical line, which is an evocation of summer, or the time of gestation, and the personal meaning, the expectation of a child. It is a pity that this simple meaning is sometimes the least apparent of the three, or that it should exist at all. As in *Transitional Poem*, Lewis is caught in the net of a theme which he tries to amplify and to diversify, and which prevents his thoughts from being anything but episodic and fragmentary.[1] If we consider them together, however, we find that, in spite of their complexity, they are united. The idea of constancy in change, of permanence in spite of interruption recurs in every symbol:

> That golden grace must all be shed
> To fill granaries, to make bread.

and:

> Child shall recreate the mother.

As the prevailing symbol in section 20 was that of procreation, Lewis proceeds further and introduces the theme of childhood. Human life appears here as a transition from deceptions to contentment in humility.

Section 22 is the counterpart of the two preceding sections. Life and history appear in them as a progress, and procreation as the vehicle of betterment. Now the poet meditates upon the vanity of life and the necessity of death. This is no time to procreate, to look at the future, it is time to look at the unchanging sky, for there are two realities: eternity and history. The future is dark and our sons will inherit 'our dead follies' and our suffering:

> Beget and breed a life—what's this
> But to perpetuate
> Man's labour, to enlarge a rank estate?

If there is no promise in the future, it is good to rely upon some sort of constancy:

> Yet I look up at the sky's billowing,
> Surprised to find so little change there,
> Though in that ample ring
> Heaven knows what power lies coiled ready to spring.

[1] 'My method in the first three volumes was to move round an experience in a sequence of poems, approaching it thus at a number of different angles, and trying to discover, from the facets it offered, what truth lay beneath.' (Letter of 6 May 1949, to the author of the present essay.)

However vain they may be, human undertakings and love find their achievement beyond mortality. The idea of finality appears here under another form. It is no longer an historical progress, but an absolute completion of human destiny in eternity. These two conceptions of finality are not necessarily contradictory (it has been seen that Lewis denies the first one in the beginning of *Transitional Poem*), they may be regarded as the same phenomenon examined successively in the categories of time and eternity. In the second case, there is a gap between man and God: what happens on earth is not decisive:

> Speak then of constancy. Thin eyelids weakly thus
> Batted to beauty, lips that reject her, is not this,
> Nor lust of eye (Christ said it) denied the final kiss.

Human destiny finding its end beyond the earth is symbolized by a river:

> Happy this river reach sleeps with the sun at noon,
> Takes dews and rain to her wide bed, refusing none
> That ful-filled peace, yet constant to one sea will run.

Love is the bond between earth and heaven, and this makes love so immediate and at the same time so inaccessible:

> So melt we down small toys to make each other rich,
> Although no getting or spending can extend our reach
> Whose poles are love, nor close who closer lie than leech.

The poet is able to answer, in section 25, the questions he asked in section 22: we may have some hopes for the future. We may hope that our sons, who will inherit both our defects and our virtues, and the result of both, will inherit the benefits of our practical wisdom, for our dreams bring no sure advantage.

Opposing nature to civilization, and obeying his natural trend, Lewis, after an exposition in speculative terms, illustrates his thought with material symbols. He connects his hope of the future with technical progress, which, according to him, coincides with the birth of a new era:

> Beauty breaks ground, O, in strange places.
> Seen after cloudburst down the bone-dry watercourses,
> In Texas a great gusher, a grain-
> Elevator in the Ukraine plain.
> To a new generation turns new faces.

Then, in section 27, the poet thinks of the last hours of the earth. Death is symbolized by men who, under a threatening sky, creep in the towns, and salvation by mountaineers who climb the summit:

> The climbers from the highest camp set out
> Saying good-bye to comrades on the glacier,
> A day of rock between them and the summit
> That will require their record or their bones.

Finally, resurrection is hinted here by the blank space left by earth's destruction. What we loved still exists after death, but in another place (Lewis, in this passage is inspired by the fear that his wife might die):

> Shells begin to drop in the capital.
> So I, indoors for long enough remembering
> The round house on the cliff, the springy slopes,
> The well in the wood, nor doubting to revisit
> *But if* to see new sunlight on old haunts
> Swallows and men come back *but if* come back
> From lands *but if* beyond our view *but if*
> *She dies?* Why, then, here is a space to let,
> The owner gone abroad, never returning.

The poet, however, overcomes his fear (section 28), for there is no separation between earth and heaven. Love is everywhere and death cannot break it:

> Though bodies are apart
> The dark hours so confine
> And fuse our hearts, sure, death
> Will find no way between.

Finally, the poet expresses his joy at the birth of his son; the new man is born, the dead arise from the tomb, the air-men 'write a new sky-sign',

> The nine tramp steamers rusting in the estuary
> Get up full pressure for a trade revival,

the light and the spirit spring from the dark exhausted earth.

It may be deduced from this cursory analysis that *From Feathers to Iron* is the embodiment of a spiritual progress from the belief in the goodness of life to the belief in resurrection, and yet ideas are only casual and secondary.

We may wonder how it is possible to conciliate occasional inspirations with a long poem. The continuous shifting of theme, and the changing meaning of the various symbols make the poem hard to read. One would like to cling to a central symbol, and it seems that the progression of Lewis's thought lacks a unifying link between the successive sections.

IV. 'THE MAGNETIC MOUNTAIN'

There is both a progression and a central symbol, around which the poem is crystallized, in *The Magnetic Mountain*,[1] which is the symbol of the future, of beauty and of social welfare. The structure of the poem depends on the gradual pursuit and discovery of the magnetic mountain by the poet. There is, however, an ambiguity of meaning which is derived from the fact that the poem has both a social and a metaphysical significance. The conflict which, at that time, pre-occupied the poet, is expressed in a passage which helps to situate the poem:

'The "First Hymn to Lenin" (by Hugh MacDiarmid) was followed by a rush of poetry sympathetic to Communism or influenced by it. "New Signatures" (1932) showed the beginning of this trend; "New Country" (1933) contained definitely Communist forms by Auden, Charles Madge, R. E. Warner and others: Spender's "Poems" and my own "Magnetic Mountain", both published in 1933, continued the movement.'[2] And: 'In most poets there is an intermittent conflict between the poetic self and the rest of the man; and it is by reconciling the two, not by eliminating the one, that they can reach their full stature.'[3]

Part One expresses the hope to reach the magnetic mountain and the resolution to leave the earth, although there may be found some beauty on it. Parts Two and Three are the trial of those who avoid the magnetic mountain; two causes are pleaded, the bad cause, or that of the established world, and the good cause, or that of moral and social progress symbolized by the journey to the mountain, or by Noah's Ark.

[1] ibid., p. 107.   [2] *A Hope for Poetry*, p. 53.   [3] ibid., p. 54.

Part Four is both a satire of the modern world, especially of England, and a vision of humanity in the future, living on the magnetic mountain, of a new world which appears as a resurrection of the present one.

Auden's *For the Time Being*[1] resembles, in some respects, *The Magnetic Mountain*. Auden's work is a series of pictures, more complex and less explicit; but there are in it both satire and a vision of a new era.

The plan of *The Magnetic Mountain* is clearer than that of the two preceding poems; its structure is more evident.

Part One

The poem begins with an evocation of joy, symbolized by the kestrel

> Whose beat is wind-wide, whose perch a split-second.

But joy is solitary and avoids the earth. The poet wishes joy to rejoin earth:

> Void are the valleys, in town no trace,
> And dumb the sky-dividing hills:
> Swift outrider of lumbering earth
> Oh hasten hither my kestrel joy!

For earth is darkened by two shadows: fear and pain. There exists, however, outside the ordinary ways a mountain which exerts an irrational attraction:

> Somewhere beyond the railheads
> Of reason, south or north,
> Lies a magnetic mountain
> Riveting sky to earth.

There are men without spiritual aspirations, and millions of men who failed to fulfil their aspirations, who lived outside the attraction exerted by the magnetic field:

> No line is laid so far.
> Ties rusting in a stack
> And sleepers—dead men's bones—
> Mark a defeated track.

[1] London, Faber and Faber, 1945.

It is as if nobody could ever disentangle himself from the earth, and yet there are certain signs which indicate the way to the magnetic mountain:

> Kestrel who yearly changes
> His tenement of space
> At the last hovering
> May signify that place.

These signs are:

> Iron in the soul,
> Spirit steeled in fire,
> Needle trembling on truth—
> These shall draw me there.

The magnetic mountain is universal and eternal, like the gaol of dialectical materialism, which is a negation of itself, since the struggle of classes ends in a classless society:

> Near that miraculous mountain
> Compass and clock must fail,
> For space stands on its head there
> And time chases its tail.

Then, Lewis proceeds to expose the problem of death: we have to make plans for life after death, for there is no coming back to earth, no reparation of mistakes. As at the end of *From Feathers to Iron*, the poet uses modern, comic images:

> Make no mistake, this is where you get off,
> Sue with her suckling, Cyril with his cough,

and:

> Positively this is the end of the track;
> It's rather late and there's no train back.

The poet laughs at those who doubt of the life after death, or of a better future:

> 'Is it mountain there or mirage across the sand?'
> That's Terra Incognita, Bogey-Man's-Land:

and at those who, doubting, don't worry:

> . . . 'No, no, that's going rather
> Too far; besides, the whole thing may just be a sell.'

Man cannot live without hope: life would be unbearable. Before he leaves for the mountain, that is, before he starts his journey towards perfection, the poet casts a last glance at the beauty of the countryside.

Part Two

The poet imagines that he has left earth and that he comes to the trial of those who believed only in the present, earthly life, of those who were not attracted by the magnetic mountain. He wonders at their being beguiled by life, since life has nothing to offer us but a worn-out delusion which can easily be unmasked. The delusion is symbolized by the sirens:

> Nearing again the legendary isle
> Where sirens sang and mariners were skinned,
> We wonder now what was there to beguile
> That such stout fellows left their bones behind.

Then he hears four defendants who argue in favour of earthly life. The first defendant is a mother who has lost her child;[1] to her grief, the answer of the poet is:

> Let love be like a natural day
> That folds her work and takes to bed;
> Ploughland and tree stand out in black,
> Enough memorial for the dead,

Earthly love must have an earthly end and is without reward. The second defendant[2] is the glory of those who,

> Facing the Adversary with a clean collar,
> Justified the system.

They are those who work for established society, as if society were the only good to strive for:

> Here we inoculate with dead ideas
> Against blood-epidemics, against
> The infection of faith and the excess of life.

[1] Section 7 was published in *New Signatures* (Hogarth Press, 1932) under the title '*The Mother Speaks*'.
[2] Section 9 is entitled '*The Schoolmaster Speaks*'.

They deny the existence of mystery, there is no problem of conscience for them but to live well in the present time, beyond which they care not to look:

> Our methods are up to date; we teach
> Through head and not by heart,
> Language with gramophones and sex with charts,
> Prophecy by deduction, prayer by numbers.

They ignore that there is a struggle between the world and the City of God, and that we have to make our choice. To those who fight for the established, present world, the answer of the poet is full of familiar irony, interspersed with expressions taken from newspaper advertisements and political propaganda, and it is summarized in the two following lines:

> Can you sing at your work? Enforce discipline
> Without insignia? Then you've still a chance to win!

The third defendant[1] is established religion, or the priest who deplores that religion should not be allied to the rulers of the earth:

> I am a man apart
> Who sits in the dark professing a revelation:
> Exploiting the Word with the letter I turn
> Joy into sacraments, the Holy Ghost to a formula.

For him religion is a sacerdotal garment, the only use of which is to endow earthly power with dignity:

> I have called down thunders on the side of authority,
> Lightnings to galvanize the law;

This man will have no place in heaven, and will be condemned.

The fourth defendant is the epicurean, who wants to enjoy his life and accept few responsibilities. He is also the superficial artist who follows the fashion of the day. To-day the artist who praises life and easiness and who is an enemy to effort has to become a hypocrite:

> I was the body slave, am now the spirit's.
> Come, let me contemplate my own
> Mysteries, a dark glass may save my face.

[1] Section 13 was entitled 'The Wife Speaks'.

For the world has become civilized and artificial:

> But he made bricks of earth, iron from fire,
> Turned waves to power, winds to communication;
> Setting up Art against chaos, subjecting
> My flux to the synthetic frost of reason.

Part Two ends[1] with a meditation on those who live only in the present time (the four defendants):

> Consider. These are they
> Who have a stake in earth
> But risk no wing on air,
> Walk not a planet path.

And the conclusion is that man must strive for perfection and approach the magnetic mountain:

> The tree grips soil, the bird
> Knows how to use the wind;
> But the full man must live
> Rooted yet unconfined.

Part Three

Part Three has for its motto: 'Never yield before the barren' (D. H. Lawrence). It is based on the antithesis between cynicism and idealism, or those who live according to the flesh, and the poet who condemns them.

Lewis dedicates the introduction of Part Three (section 16) to his friend Auden, and invites him to ponder over the sadness of modern life:

> No wing-room for Wystan, no joke for kestrel-joy.

Philosophy is reduced to an abstract, unreal commonplace:

> While comfy in captive balloons easily brought down
> Sit frail philosophers, gravity gone to the head.

The only salvation possible in our stifling life is to come from the elevation of the soul, in a widening of the horizon and in an escape

---

[1] Section 15 is entitled '*The Observer Speaks*'.

from common opinions; the poets must warn their time of the danger:

> Gain altitude, Auden, then let the base beware!
> Migrate, chaste my kestrel, you need a change of air!

There are four enemies of the spirit. The first is sensual love which is an earthly appetite without hope and ends in hate:

> Reach for the powder-puff, I have sinned greatly.
> *I suppose you hate me, now.*

Love should not be confined by lust, its roots are deeper, its goal is farther:

> My wells, my rooted good
> Go deeper than you dare:
> Seek not my sun and moon,
> They are centred elsewhere.

The second enemy is conformism, satisfaction in the present social conditions, and official wisdom (a typical Audenesque theme):

> I'll have no long faces on this ship while I'm captain.
> And you know what happens to mutineers.
>
> .   .   .   .   .   .
>
> Smile! All together! You'll soon be better.
> Have you got a grouch? Do you feel an itch?
> There, there! Sit down and write uncle a letter.

It is not surprising that the answer to the speech of the conformists should be satire:

> They tell you all's well with our lovely England
> And God's in our capital. . . .

Exploitation and servitude reign over England:

> That young inventor—you all know his name—
> They used the plans and he died of their fame.
> Careful, climber, they're getting at your nerve!
> Leader, that's a bribe, they'd like you to serve!

Old John Bull is dead and Bimbo has ceased to be funny; the state has no tolerance.

The third enemy is modern science, when taken for an absolute, for a sufficient rule of conduct and explanation of the world, and for a substitute for religion and spiritual activities. It leads to intellectualism, which reduces everything to rational knowledge:

> God is a proposition,
> And we that prove him are his priests, his chosen.
> From bare hypothesis
> Of strata and wind, of stars and tides, watch me
> Construct his universe,
> A working model of my majestic notions,
> A sum done in the head.
> Last week I measured the light, his little finger;
> The rest is a matter of time.

The disguise of religious belief in scientific terms is still more emphasized in the next stanza, where algebra and its applications are deified:

> God is an electrician,
> And they that worship him must worship him
> In ampere and in volt.
> Scrap sun and moon, your twilight of false gods.
> X. is not here or there;
> Whose lightning scrawls brief cryptograms on sky,
> Easy for us to solve;
> Whose motions fit our formulae, whose temple
> Is a pure apparatus.

Statistics is the next victim:

> God is a statistician:
> Offer him all the data; tell him your dreams.

Medicine replaces morality:

> God is a Good Physician,
> Gives fruit for hygiene, crops for calories.
> Don't touch that dirty man,
> Don't drink from the same cup, sleep in one bed:
> You know He would not like it.
> Young men, cut out those visions, they're bad for the eyes:
> I'll show you face to face
> Eugenics, Eupeptics and Euthanasia,
> The clinic Trinity.

Science is unable to grasp the ultimate reality, a telescope or equations will not bring us nearer to God:

> Analyst, you've missed him. Or worse and worst
> You've got him inside? You must feel fit to burst.
> Here, there, everywhere
> Or nowhere. At least you know where. And how much do
> you care?

God is hidden, but his presence is certain, in nature and in the human soul:

> In the moment before the bombardment, poised at peace
> He hides. And whoever sees
> The cloud on the sky-line, the end of grief,
> Dust in the distance that spells a relief,
> Has found. Shall have his share
> Who naked emerges on the far side of despair.

In other words, God is revealed in the poetic vision. All of us experience the presence of God, in various ways, under various circumstances, and some will find Him very near.

The fourth enemy is the escapist, the man or the poet who leaves the earth and its sorrows in order to take refuge in unreal dreams of ephemeral beauty, and whose two main defects are irresponsibility and evasiveness.

The poet rejects the temptation of escape: he has to face reality and not to abandon the other men.

What he has to say is not pleasant: he chooses the difficult way, the right way which leads to a goal. Work and patience is what he proposes, but it is the only way leading to salvation:

> And if our blood alone
> Will melt this iron earth,
> Take it. It is well spent
> Easing a saviour's birth.

Then, the poet resumes his accusations against the four enemies of the right path, who are enemies of both the world and the city of God, and who, whether they are sensuous people, conformists, intellectualists or escapists (all mainly rich people), guide men into a blind alley. They are greedy, egoistic and sterile; the only thing they can breed is destruction.

And Part Three ends in a resolute warning:

> Drug nor isolation will cure this cancer:
> It is now or never, the hour of the knife,
> The break with the past, the major operation.

Part Four

Lewis's purpose is indicated by the motto:

> He comes with work to do, he does not come to coo.
>> (Gerard Manley Hopkins)

The beginning of Part Four marks a turning point in the development of the poem, in the journey towards the magnetic mountain. It is the point where the poet bids good-bye to those who are stationary, far from the magnetic mountain and who have chosen to leave things as they are which is, by 1930, in the ruins of war and of economic crisis:

> A world behind us the west is in flames,
> Devastated areas, works at a standstill;
> No seed awakes, wary is no hunter,
> The tame are ruined and the wild have fled.

It is time to build a new world with new ideas:

>> An untrodden territory
> Promises no coolness, invites but the brave.

This new world is not a utopia, there are signs which indicate it: it is drawn towards the magnetic mountain; it is a world in which earth and heaven are reconciled.

Neither life nor death can disturb from their journey those who are on the way to the magnetic mountain:

> Wystan, Rex, all of you that have not fled,
> This is our world, this is where we have grown
> Together in flesh and live; though each alone
> Shall join the enclosed order of the dead,
> Enter the silent brotherhood of bone.

The new life is a changed life, a life of work and of construction which, however short it may be, is a contribution to eternity:

> All you that have a cool head and safe hands
> Awaken early, there is much to do;
> Hedges to raze, channels to clear, a true
> Reckoning to find. The other side commands
> Eternity. We have an hour or two.

The first thing to do is to disavow the old masters, fear and pain. They are the real disturbers, and prevent any brotherhood or progress. The poet leaves definitely the 'defendants' and the 'enemies' and disembarks on the new land: he rediscovers earth. The spiritual journey is symbolized by material symbols, like the daffodils, symbols of innocence:

> They from earth's centre take their time
> And from the sun what love they need:
> The proud flower burns away its prime,
> Eternity lies in the seed.

the kestrel, symbol of elevation:

> Follow the kestrel, south or north;
> Strict eye, spontaneous wing can tell
> A secret. Where he comes to earth
> Is the heart's treasure. Mark it well.

and of certitude:

> Here he hovers. You're on the scent;
> Magnetic mountain is not far,
> Across no gulf or continent,
> Not where you think but where you are.

Faith, humility and elevation walk along that path and are creative:

> Out of that dark a new world flowers.
> There in the womb, in the rich veins
> Are tools, dynamos, bridges, towers,
> Your tractors and your travelling-cranes.

The present time is, as in *From Feathers to Iron*, symbolized by winter; the future, or the approach of the magnetic mountain, by summer. Although the mountain is in sight, winter is still there, and before we can reach the mountain, symbolized here by Mount Ararat, we have to undergo the floods (the deluge) and to prepare the Ark, or the Argo, that is, the faith which may save us from a dying world. Only those who have faith and hope, 'the true, the tested', may enter the Ark, may approach the magnetic mountain (symbol of resurrection), where they will live a new life.

Then, the poet warns all those who stand at the Ark's entrance of what they are going to lose:

> An assured income, the will
> In your favour and the feel
> Of firmness underfoot.

They will have to lose all their habits, and to possess the sacred flame, if they do not believe in a change.

As a prelude to the voyage, the poet evokes a vision of the future, when joy will correspond to reality, progress to the Second Coming:

> In happier times
> When the heart is whole and the exile king returned
> We may sing shock of opposing teams
> And electric storms of love again.
>
> Our voices may be tuned
> To solo flight, to record-breaking plane;
> Looking down from hill
> We may follow with fresh felicities
> Wilful the light, the wayward motion of trees,
> In happier times when the heart is whole.

In the future, both world and vision will be definitively settled and perfect. Then, to bring his prelude to an end, the poet invokes, not the Muses, but the spirit, 'the wind' which will save humanity from catastrophe:

> Make us a wind
> To shake the world out of this sleepy sickness
> Where flesh has dwindled and brightness waned!

Then the poet directly addresses the English people and, among them, those who love England as it is and do not suffer a change:

> Listen. Can you not hear the entrance of a new theme?

That love is hopeless, and those who still cling to what they are accustomed to loving cling to a corpse. There is, however, a remedy:

> We can tell you a secret, offer a tonic; only
> Submit to the visiting angel, the strange new healer.

The modern Noah enters the Ark and refuses those who have loved corruption. This is a pretext for a violent satire against Lewis's contemporaries. Very few people are spared by the satire, but those who are most attacked are people of the liberal professions: 'politicians, prelates and pressmen' and more especially the esoteric aesthetes, the archaeologists and the philologists, or those among them who might be called 'escapists'. If we add to them the middle-class people and the vulgar, very few are left.

Now the poet turns from the old world and sets forth a vision of resurrection which is, in a way, similar to Herbert Read's vision in *The Nuncio*. Lewis asks 'that we may be given the chance to be men'.

The magnetic mountain is near, but the poet's vision is not a fairyland: it is a probable utopia proclaimed through a loudspeaker:

> Publish the vision, broadcast and screen it,
> Of a world where the will of all shall be raised to highest power,
> Village or factory shall form the unit.
> Control shall be from the centres, quick brain, warm heart,
> And the bearings bathed in a pure
> Fluid of sympathy. There possessions no more shall be part
> Of the man, where riches and sacrifice
> Are of flesh and blood, sex, muscles, limbs and eyes.
> Each shall give of his best. It shall seem proper
> For all to share what all produced.
> Men shall be glad of company, love shall be more than a guest
> And the bond no more of paper.

The passage above is perhaps one of the weakest in the poem; the reader was waiting for a more attractive mountain. Besides, such a vision resembles the goal of ideal communism, but not if we relate it to the scheme, which is based upon a spiritual progress. This progress, however, develops itself also in history, and the final stage, man's happiness, will be reached through successive periods of misfortune:

> They remember the ancestors that gave them ease,

Then, the poet evokes once more the symbols of resurrection: spring, summer, and

> Love that was sleeping, not extinct,

and finally greets the new era of peace, when humanity will be dwelling on the magnetic mountain:

> Beckon O beacon, and O Sun be soon!
> Hollo, bells, over a melting earth!
> Let man be many and his sons all sane,
> Fearless with fellows, handsome by the hearth.
> Break from your trance: start dancing now in town,
> And, fences down, the ploughing match with mate.
> This is your day: so turn, my comrades, turn
> Like infants' eyes like sunflowers to the light.

Some passages of *The Magnetic Mountain* are rhetorical. This is due to the structure: Parts Two and Three are the exposition of four causes. But the unity of the whole is maintained by the central symbol. Moreover, there is a progression from one part to the other.

Some passages are not properly symbolical of a spiritual reality, but the whole is related to a metaphysical vision which cannot be easily reconciled with dialectical materialism. Obeying his natural trend and the influence of his left-wing friends, Lewis expresses his ideas in images of social and moral life (the tone is, indeed, sometimes didactic and moralizing). These images seem more 'real' than in the two preceding poems, which are rather indirect and intricate. None of the symbols looks like a riddle, whereas, in *Transitional Poem* especially, they are so elaborate that it is difficult to relate them to one another and to interpret them. On the whole, *Transitional Poem* is addressed to a small group of readers, whereas *The Magnetic Mountain* appeals to a wider public, and is sometimes boisterous.

Lewis, however, is more than a social reformer. The critics who follow him as far as *The Magnetic Mountain* are tempted to neglect his lyricism: those who go past that stumbling-block realize that he was looking for his own way, and that the philosophical element of his poetry was accidental. Dilys Powell,[1] comparing Lewis with Auden, writes: 'The work of Mr. Day Lewis shows a talent less self-willed, less boisterous, less robust; a talent which, left to itself, might even

---

[1] *Descent from Parnassus*, London, Cresset Press, 1934.

have kept aloof from politics.'[1] The same critic considers Lewis's development as a transition from 'adolescent egotism' to 'contemporary expression', and lays much stress on the influence of Auden: 'In "The Magnetic Mountain" Mr. Day Lewis has made a complete surrender. The themes are pure Auden: warnings against the Enemy, threats of disaster, promises of salvation through "the attacking movement".'[2] 'Poetry becomes the last message of the saved to the lost.'[3] And: 'Technical virtuosity becomes a matter of mere bravado—or of advertisement. It is the drum beaten outside the gospeller's tent.'[4]

Auden's influence is perhaps over-emphasized, but it is true that Lewis was misled by his political preoccupations. Moreover, the words 'adolescent egotism' cannot be applied to a poet who was already twenty-five when he wrote *Transitional Poem* and whose 'attempt to relate the poetic impulse with the experience as a whole' is continued in his later work, especially during the war years, where he 'looks inwards to find images valid for the outward world and powerful enough to illuminate its anfractuous ways'.[5] The improvement of his poetry is proportional to his giving up imposed ideas and acquired mannerisms, and he develops his lyrical powers at the expense of his tendency to fake his contemporaries.

V. LATER POEMS

The high hopes proclaimed in *The Magnetic Mountain* are abandoned in *A Time to Dance*,[6] where the poet writes 'A Warning to those who Live on Mountains'[7] and marks his resolution to face the tragic limitations and shortcomings of life. And yet he has a message for future men, which still favours theoretical developments in his poetry. Rather than in an indefinite bettering of man he believes in a new beginning which is suggested in *Noah and the Waters*.[8] The doctrinal element, however, is less and less obtrusive, and it is obvious that his poetical thought is at its best when it is free of any political or didactic implications.

[1] ibid., p. 195.   [2] ibid., p. 203.   [3] ibid., p. 207.   [4] ibid.
[5] *The Poetic Image*, p. 153.
[6] *Collected Poems, 1929–1936*, pp. 157–203; London, Hogarth Press, 1948.
[7] ibid., p. 169.
[8] cf. *Prologue and Two Choruses from Noah and the Waters*, ibid., pp. 204–15.

LATER POEMS

(a) Overtures to Death[1]

The warning uttered in *Noah and the Waters*, confirmed by the imminent catastrophe, recurs in *Overtures to Death and Other Poems*. The volume contains poems inspired mainly by contemporary circumstances, and may serve as an introduction to *Word Over All*.[2] The atmosphere of fear which pervades the collection does not prevent the reader from getting an impression of pity, serenity, and even hope, for the poet accepts the terrible doom, which is to fall on Europe, as an act of justice. He is less rhetorical than in *The Magnetic Mountain*, and his collected calmness is a step towards the serenity of *Word Over All*. Whereas, in *Word Over All*, he tries to outstare the catastrophe, in *Overtures to Death* he is still waiting and interpreting:

> Stay away, Spring!
> Since death is on the wing
> To blast our seed and poison every thing.[3]

> O light's abandon and the fire-crest sky
> Speak in me now for all who are to die![4]

>   . . . those rocking bells
> Buoy up the sunken light, or mark
> What rots unfathomed in the dark.[5]

In an attempt to familiarize himself with death, the poet evokes with remarkable strength, in the title-poem,[6] the multiple images which tell him that death is the master on earth. There is no need, however, for fear or affliction; it is better to look beyond death:

> Built from their bone, I see a power-house stand
> To warm men's hearts again and light the land.[7]

It is better also to show unflinching resolution, for

> Nothing is innocent now but to act for life's sake.[8]

[1] *Overtures to Death and Other Poems*, London, Jonathan Cape, 1938.
[2] London, Jonathan Cape, 1943.
[3] *Overtures to Death*, February 1936, p. 14.
[4] ibid., 'Maple and Sumach', p. 13.   [5] ibid., 'The Bells that Signed', p. 24.
[6] ibid., 'Overtures to Death,' pp. 26–35. (Sections 4 and 5 were published in *The London Mercury*, September 1938.)
[7] ibid., 'When they have Lost', p. 36.
[8] ibid., 'In the Heart of Contemplation', p. 37.

Those who die for liberty are praised in a long narrative poem, 'The Nabara'.[1] Lewis once more attacks the escapists, who are for ever solitary:

> He's one more ghost, engaged to keep
> Eternity's long hours and mewed
> Up in live flesh with no escape
> From solitude.

Finally, in 'Self-Criticism and Answer',[2] the poet calls for a voice which will be heard above the chaos:

> When madmen play the piper
> And knaves call the tune,
> Honesty's a right passion—
> She must call to her own.
> Let yours be the start and stir
> Of a flooding indignation
> That channels the dry heart deeper
> And sings through the dry bone.

(b) Word Over All

The title is explained by a passage from Walt Whitman's *Reconciliation*:

> Word over all, beautiful as the sky,
> Beautiful that war and all its deeds of carnage
> must in time be utterly lost,
> That the hands of the sisters Death and Night
> incessantly softly wash again, and ever
> again, this soiled world. . . .

These poems were written and published during the war, some of them already in 1940 under the title of *Poems in Wartime*. They all contain more or less direct allusions to World War Two, and they bring a message of hope, not of worldly hope, but of the hope implied by Whitman's poem: it is a recurrence, under another form, of the leading ideas of *The Magnetic Mountain*. War engenders hatred and confusion, all the mighty deeds of war have no fruit, but over the desolation flies the bright word of purity and innocence. The task of

[1] ibid., pp. 41–52. [2] ibid., p. 61.

the poet is to be watchful and to keep in sight, through the ruins and the confusion, the eternal victory of the spirit. Now that the catastrophe has not been prevented, there is no need to weep and to fall in irretrievable distress: now that the world is dark, the flame of the Word is brighter.

The first part of the collection opens with 'The Lighted House', which is the symbol of the poet's watch during the period of darkness and confusion which preceded the war. It might illustrate Wordsworth's definition of poetry: 'emotion recollected in tranquillity'. More exactly, it expresses the conjuring of fear:

> Peeling off fear after fear, . . .

It is significant, however, that the poem could not be described as philosophical: it is a lyrical poem written in praise of a woman. A passage recalls Botticelli's spring:

> One night they saw the big house, some time untenanted
> But for its hand-to-mouth recluse, room after room
> Light up, as when Primavera herself has spirited
> A procession of crocuses out of their winter tomb.

The anguish of departure is expressed in the five stanzas of 'Departure in the Dark'.[1] The fourth is an allusion to the nomadic life of the Jews and to their present tribulations. That anguish, which is one of the fundamental emotions of life, has a double aspect: departure means at the same time separation and freedom:

> At this blind hour the heart is informed of nature's
> Ruling that man
> Should be nowhere a more tenacious settler than
> Among wry thorns and ruins, yet nurture
> A seed of discontent in his ripest ease.
> There's a kind of release
> And a kind of torment in every good-bye for every man—
> And will be, even to the last of his dark departures.

The starting point of this poem has probably been a profound emotion, which has found its embodiment in incoherent, ebbing statements imitating chaotic throbs set in the frame of a few firm

[1] *Word Over All*, p. 11.

lines (usually the first and the last line of each section). Such a poem would be said by Herbert Read to be inspired by the 'innocent eye': it is the recapture of a primitive feeling, and even the word 'recapture' would be inaccurate, for the emotion is the direct source of the images. The poem achieves the unity of effect extolled by Poe; emotion and its objects are one.

This poem, and the following one, 'Cornet Solo',[1] mark a more comprehensive, more creative vision than *Transitional Poem*. In the latter, the mind is alone, and considered apart from everything else: in 'Cornet Solo', the emotion has an echo and the fresh impressions are a revival of the impressions of childhood; the inspiration resolves itself in sonorous images, is no longer repressed and controlled, widens and overflows in its process of creation:

> Plaintive its melody rose or waned
> Like an autumn wind
> Blowing the rain on beds of aster.

A return to simplicity and genuineness is advocated:

> Last night, when I heard a cornet's strain,
> It seemed a refrain
> Wafted from thirty years back—so remote an
> Echo it bore: but I felt again
> The prophetic mood of a child, too long forgotten,
> Too lightly forgotten.

Another tribute to childhood is paid in 'O Dreams, O Destinations',[2] a series of nine compact and rich sonnets. There, the thought is no longer explicit, but involved in a continuous stream of images. The sequence follows the order of man's transformation from childhood to old age, from dreams to destinations. Lewis's return to the theme of childhood and to the past is a sign of his desire to go back to the source of inner experience.

Part Two opens with the title-poem. The first four stanzas are a picture of the beginning of the war, and are dominated by the question: where is the rescue, what is the answer to suffering and destruction? Worldly wisdom is a lure:

[1] ibid., p. 13.   [2] ibid., p. 15.

Busy the preachers, the politicians weaving
Voluble charms around
This ordeal, conjuring a harvest that shall spring from
Our hearts' all-harrowed ground.

There is no help from outside, but the words that tell of the present distress tell also of the end of distress:

Yet words there must be, wept on the cratered present,
To gleam beyond it:

.   .   .   .   .   .

See wavelets and wind-blown shadows of leaves on a stream
How they ripple together,
As life and death inter-married—you cannot tell
One from another.

Words cannot save us from the disaster:

Our words like poppies love the maturing field,
But form no harvest:

But they confer immortality upon events:

Dark over all, absolving all, is hung
Death's vaulted patience:
Words are to set man's joy and suffering there
In constellations.

The epochs of mankind leave no trace and lead nowhere, eternity alone is there, and men die in order to attest the presence of eternity.

The end of the poem is not very clear. There is a discrepancy between the intended subject, namely, that times express eternity in an obscure way:

We speak of what we know, but what we have spoken
Truly we know not—

and the last development of the subject:

The Cause shales off, the Humankind stands forth
A mightier presence,
Flooded by dawn's pale courage, rapt in eve's
Rich acquiescence.

If we relate this to the main theme, it means that the Word transfigures man's suffering, but hides its meaning, and God's judgment.

A more adequate interpretation of Whitman's lines is given in 'The Image',[1] where Lewis has recourse to the allegory of Perseus fighting the monster: 'We should remember the legend of Perseus and the Medusa—how Athene gave Perseus, amongst other things, a shield, bidding him focus in it the image of Medusa, whom no one could look at face to face and live; and by this primitive radar device he was able to attack her without setting eyes upon her.'[2]

In the poem, as soon as Perseus strikes the Medusa, the sky is illuminated and purified. The monster, if this interpretation is right, is the symbol of the world at war, and the sky is the symbol of eternity. The first symbol, when transmuted into poetry, becomes the image of evil, which shields us because we know that behind that image is eternity. Here the relation between the presence of God and the words is explicit and illustrates, in an original manner, Lewis's conception of catharsis: the image of evil and misfortune is the sign of the divine presence, there are words 'gleaming beyond the cratered present'. The poet himself presents us with an interpretation of the tercets. There, the sky is the symbol of imagination: 'Reality to-day presents an even more "immense, moving, confused spectacle" to the poet than it did to Matthew Arnold. More and more, therefore, lest he be petrified by it, he uses the image as a shield in which he may focus reality for the sword-thrust of his imagination: that is the point of my own lines,'[3]

> Now, in a day of monsters, a desert of abject stone
> Whose outward terrors paralyze the will,
> Look at that gleaming circle until it has revealed you
>
> The glare of death transmuted to your own
> Measure, scaled-down to a possible figure the sum of ill.
> Let the shield take that image, the image shield you.

The poem is further elucidated in the following lines: 'This last point bears out what I was saying in my reference to the Perseus legend, that the image, as surely to-day as in the primitive times, is a method of asserting or reasserting spiritual control over the material.'[4]

[1] ibid., p. 22.   [2] *The Poetic Image*, p. 99   [3] ibid.   [4] ibid., p. 104.

The thought in the poem is strong, but we are far from the genuineness of 'Cornet Solo'. What perhaps most puzzles the reader in this sonnet is the laborious development of the allegory. This allegory is not self-explanatory and its meaning seems to be disembodied: Perseus is forgotten in the tercets.

The same theme is developed in 'The Poet',[1] together with the theme of serenity expressed in The 'Lighted House':

> For me there is no dismay
> Though ills enough impend.

Poetry is the shield which promises eternity:

> Death's cordon narrows: but vainly,
> If I've slipped the carrier word.

'The Lighted House' already implied that hope includes despair; 'The Assertion'[2] implies that love embraces cruelty:

> Therefore be wise in the dark hour to admit
> The logic of the gunman's trigger,
> Embrace the explosive element, learn the need
> Of tiger for antelope and antelope for tiger.

There is in these lines a loosening of the poetic strength.

Among other poems expressing the horror of war, 'The Stand-To'[3] and 'Lidice'[4] evoke the theme of martyrdom. 'Lidice' borrows its motto again from Walt Whitman:

> Not a grave of the murdered for freedom but grows
> seed for freedom.

The innocents will not die in vain, there is a reward:

> The pangs we felt from your atrocious hurt
> Promise a time when even the killer shall see
> His sword is aimed at his own naked heart.

The idea of collective guilt appears in the war poems together with a strong, eloquent fear ('Ode to Fear')[5]:

> To-day, I can but record
> In truth and patience

---

[1] *Word Over All*, p. 23.   [2] ibid., p. 26   [3] ibid., p.28.   [4] ibid., p. 33.
[5] ibid., p. 34.

This high delirium of nations
And hold to it the reflecting, fragile word.
Come to my heart, then, Fear,
With all your linked humiliations,
As wild geese flight and settle on a submissive mere.

This fear is no doubt inspired by the horrors of war, and it is at the same time the fear of judgment.

What is remarkable in these war poems is that none of them expresses a renunciation of the poetic faith, not even dejection, perhaps because dejection is an essentially individual state. Poems like 'The Dead'[1] and 'Reconciliation'[2] are impersonal. But the disgust at what is happening and at what the post-war period will bring is resolutely expressed:

Shall it be so again?
Call not upon the glorious dead
To be your witnesses then.
The living alone can nail to their promise the ones who said
It shall not be so again.

(c) Poems (1943–47)[3]

There is no set of ideas behind the poems of this volume: Lewis turns more and more from philosophical to lyrical poetry. Among poems of an autobiographical nature there are some of a wider scope. 'A Failure'[4] is in praise of perseverance:

But it's useless to argue the why and wherefore.
When a crop is so thin,
There's nothing to do but to set the teeth
And plough it in.

The Sitting[5] is a figuration of the creative process. Lewis finds that his person is split in two: the man and the artist. The man is compared with a mute god who has no secret:

And the god asks, 'What have I for you
But the lichenous shadow of thought veiling my temple,
The runnels a million time-drops have chased on my cheek?

[1] ibid., p. 36.   [2] ibid., p. 37.
[3] London, Jonathan Cape, 1948.   [4] ibid., p. 33.   [5] ibid., p. 37.

The artist is ever endeavouring to model his work on the stony god, on man, but the god is impenetrable, and thinks:

> Let him make, if he will, the crypt of my holy mountain
> His own: let even the light
> That bathes my temple become as it were an active
> Property of his sight.

The artist imitates an illusion, for the god is a shadow:

> I know the curious hands are shaping, reshaping the image
> Of what is only an image of things impalpable

and the artist is creating an aimless work without object: he has only the illusion of a model, and what he makes must be taken from himself:

> O man, O innocent artist
> Who paint me with green of your fields, with amber or yellow
> Of love's hair, red of the heart's blood, eyebright blue,
> Conjuring forms and rainbows out of an empty mist—
> Your hand is upon me, as even now you follow
> Up the immortal clue
> Threading my veins of emerald, topaz, amethyst,
> And know not it ends in you.

'The Sitting' marks the introduction of a new element in Lewis's thought. This may be due to the influence of Valéry, from whom Lewis translates, at the end of the volume, *Les Pas* and *Le Cimetière Marin*.

The satirical element has completely disappeared from Lewis's poetry, as well as his utopian dreams. Although he expresses, in some war poems, the feeling of communion he experienced in the Home Guard, his interest in politics has been changed into disillusionment,[1] his concern is for problems of a personal (cf. Heart and Mind, p. 31), philosophical (cf. Two Travellers, p. 78) or aesthetic (cf. Statuette: Late Minoan, p. 39) nature. His pity for the oppressed masses shifts to individuals, for the tyrant is no longer a group of men, but a

---

[1] Read remarks on the Left-Wing school: 'Leur attitude de "sympathisants" s'est changée depuis en désillusion, et la poésie est restée à ces poètes comme *moyen de consolation*. Mais la poésie entre leurs mains est devenue artificielle: c'est un jeu de haute habileté pour Auden et Day Lewis. . . .' (*Présence*, avril 1946, *Révolte et réaction dans la Poésie Anglaise Moderne*, par Herbert Read, traduit de l'anglais.)

natural, anonymous, and irremediable force which makes men seem ridiculous, and yet the poet is deeply moved by these insignificant beings. Lewis's concern for 'The Neurotic'[1] is similar in a way to Baudelaire's pity for old women:

> Who would suppose, seeing him walk the meadows,
> He walks a treadmill there, grinding himself
> To powder, dust to greyer dust, or treads
> An invisible causeway lipped by chuckling shadows?
> Take his arm if you like, you'll not come near him.
> His mouth is an ill-stitched wound opening: hear him.

The failure of that man obsesses and moves the poet:

> Death mask of a genius unborn:
> Tragic prince of a rejected play:
> Soul of suffering that bequeathed no myth:
> A dark tower and a never-sounded horn.—
> Call him what we will, words cannot ennoble
> This Atlas who fell down under a bubble.

Lewis describes, in 'The Misfit',[2] a shepherd who is enrolled for the army:

> He wore a long black cutaway coat
> Which should have been walking by blackthorn-fleeced
> Hedges to church; . . .

It is difficult to say whether the injustice that this man should be killed is a social or a natural one; in any case the poet praises 'the rude rightness of instinct' of the shepherd 'along the Calvary road'.

Moreover, Lewis, as can be judged from 'Seen from the Train',[3] is turned less towards the future and all that it represents: a break with tradition, industrialism, and modern imagery. He casts a nostalgic glance at the past:

> . . . The whole
>
> Stood up, antique and clear
> As a cameo, from the vale. . . .

[1] *Poems 1943–1947*, ibid., p. 76. [2] ibid., p. 84. [3] ibid., p. 80.

He regrets the years of blind excitement:

> What came between to unsight me? . . .
> There was a time when men
> Would have called it a vision, said that sin
> Had blinded me since to a heavenly fact.
> Well, I have neither invoked nor faked
> Any church in the air,
> And little I care
> Whether or no I shall see it again.
> But blindly my heart is racked
>
> When I think how, not twice or thrice,
> But year after year in another's eyes
> I have caught the look that I missed to-day
> Of the church, the knoll, the cedars—a ray
> Of the faith, too, they stood for,
> The hope they were food for,
> The love they prayed for, facts beyond price—
> And turned my eyes away.

There are beautiful passages in 'Sketches for a Portrait',[1] as in all the autobiographical poems, but it is enough if we have suggested where Lewis, who is still full of promises, is going.

There is a real progress in Lewis's later poetry, which is emotional rather than intellectual, and in which the similes are no longer mere examples. His early poems have their source in the mind, and their limits are those of the mind in all their various aspects, whether it is the source of order, moral conscience, integrity of soul and poetic impulse, as in *Transitional Poem*, a progress from conception to creation, as in *From Feathers to Iron*; a journey towards a future reality (*The Magnetic Mountain*); or a discovery of the Word through present events as in the later poetry (*Word Over All*). It may be objected to this interpretation that it does not take account of the social meaning of Lewis's poems; but the present study shows that his materialism is a disguised idealism and that, if the community for which Lewis hoped has not been established, the value of the poems does not depend upon theories and events.

[1] ibid., p. 17.

243

VI. LEWIS AS A THINKER

To bring together the statements contained in Lewis's poems and to group them in a doctrine would be to breed a monster. There is a multiplicity of stray thoughts in his work, and they are inconsistent as a whole. For those who are interested in his ideas, however, it is convenient to distinguish two periods in his work, a first one in which, on the ground of his belief in the power of the human mind, he hopes that the human condition will improve in the future, and a second period in which the disillusionment brought by the war, and the collapse of his political ideal, lead him to distrust the future and to assert less indirectly the prevalence of the spirit over matter. In both periods his attitude is contradictory, in the first he implicitly believes in the existence of a transcendental reality but is concerned only with immediate reality, in the second he often expresses a religious feeling and implicitly believes in the future. What is perhaps more important than his thought is the disappearance of his ideas until he finds his medium in short, lyrical poems with only discreet philosophical implications. The thought contained in the first three volumes analysed here is incoherent, even in *The Magnetic Mountain*, where it is systematized. There is an absurdity in his utopia, for he conceives it at the same time as an immediate and as a transcendental change, as a material reality 'riveting sky to earth', so that he wavers between Communism and Christianity. He is far from Communism, first because his starting point is alien to the method of dialectical materialism, secondly because he believes in a radical change of human nature rather than in a change of the conditions of life. Besides, he proposes no coherent economic, social or theological system. His schemes for the future are vague:

> You who would come with us,
> Think what you stand to lose—
> An assured income, the will
> In your favour and the feel
> Of firmness underfoot.[1]

He is rather concerned to write a satire against the established institutions and opinions than to foresee the future.

[1] *The Magnetic Mountain*, p. 147.

244

Lewis's thought as a critic is characterized by the same inconsisten-
cies as his poetical thought. His idea of a tradition is limited to the
near past: 'I have claimed Hopkins, Owen and Eliot as our immediate ancestors.'[1] Lewis's belief in an improvement of the human condition (a Communist belief) through love and spiritual progress (a
Christian belief) leads him to consider the modern poets as the in-
heritors of a light which the ancestors prophesied, but did not see:
'So it is with a poet's real ancestors. They disappear into the darkness
ahead, and he who follows finds that they are not merely the
geographers but in a sense the creators of his poetical world.'[2]

As a critic, Lewis is mainly preoccupied with the use of 'contemporary imagery'. In the field of aesthetics, he is a heretic. Lewis
writes of a poem by Auden: '. . . to the intrinsic energy of the poem
is added a social energy working through contemporary images so
integrated with the poem as to release into it the external life they
represent.'[3] This conception of poetry as a passive receptacle for external things is opposed to the following theory, quoted by Lewis's
friend, Michael Roberts, in his *Critique of Poetry*:[4] 'If a poet is anybody, he is somebody to whom things made matter very little—
somebody who is obsessed by Making.'[5] In his early poetry, Lewis
expresses the feeling that reason is an enemy, and shows that his hope
in the future is irrational. His attitude to science is that of the tamer
in front of the lion: 'Poetry has its roots in incantation; its effect has
always been to create a state of mind; but it may well despair of com-
peting with the incantation of Big Business; . . . it is possible for poetry
to steal the thunder of science, to absorb these trivial business incantations and turn them to its own uses.'[6] What is the aim of magic if
not to create strange, unreal objects, to produce instead of absorbing?
That poetry depends on the external world is another tenet of Lewis's
doctrine (a tenet which cannot be made consistent with his idea of
creation): 'We shall not begin to understand post-war poetry until
we realize that the poet is appealing above all for the creation
of society in which the real and living contact between man and
man may again become possible.'[7] This is the source of Lewis's
disillusion in the second period, for, if the poets have to wait for

---

[1] *A Hope for Poetry*, p. 3.   [2] ibid., p. 5.   [3] ibid., p. 27.
[4] London, J. Cape, 1934, p. 154.
[5] Foreword to *Is 5* (New York, Boni & Liveright, 1926), by E. E. Cummings.
[6] *A Hope for Poetry*, p. 30.   [7] ibid., p. 38.

a better world in order to express themselves, they have nothing to say.

Lewis believes also in the supernatural, unconscious influence of inspiration: 'Whence these visitors come the poet cannot say: whether out of the upper air, influences from the source of all light: or are daimons, the lords of energy, alive in all matter; or from the dark continent of his own mind where mankind's past is stored, an Atlantis lost beneath the waves of consciousness.'[1] This is the source of Lewis's resignation in the second period, for if poetry cannot find any support in the external world, it may still come from inside. Poetic inspiration, as Lewis sees it, should be aimed at building a new society; it breeds a moralizing poetry leading to action. The value of that poetry would be determined by the value of what it represents or advocates, it would have no value by itself.

The compromise achieved by Lewis between the external world and inspiration as the sources of poetry is still more evident in *The Poetic Image*, where he boldly declares that the truth of the heart and that of the world are the same, or that dreams correspond to realities: 'You will realize how Mr. Prufrock and that "hierarchy of the equal —the Kingdom of Earth" whom Mr. MacNeice celebrated, are each of them double images perfectly combined into a single image: they represent what a poet has seen looking outwards at humanity and what he has seen looking into his own heart, focused together to make a whole truth.'[2] It may be objected to this that only Mr. Prufrock is real in Lewis's point of view, whereas 'the Kingdom of Earth' does not represent reality; it induces the readers to imitation or to action, but it does not represent an external reality. The two notions of inspiration and representation, as they are used by Lewis, are contradictory. The first advocates a moralizing poetry, the second a didactic poetry. They tend to make of the poet either the legislator of a hypothetical society or an instrument for recording indifferent, passing events. We may agree with Lewis when he says that future poets should present us with 'images of virtue', and of Christian virtues, 'the disinterested movements of moral fervour and intellectual curiosity, the spontaneous springings of Mercy, Pity, Peace and Love', but we rather doubt if these images can be seen in the external world, or are to be sought there.

To this vague affirmation of Christian beliefs (which are not as

[1] ibid., p. 77.   [2] *The Poetic Image*, p. 156.

novel as the author is inclined to demonstrate), Lewis adds, in the conclusion of *The Poetic Image*, a belief in the power of 'the eternal spirit', a belief which is not connected with what he says in his book: '. . . all men and all their actions are playthings of

> The eternal spirit's eternal pastime—
> Shaping, reshaping.'[1]

The function of the spirit is to shape the external world, and not to represent it.

This survey of Lewis's ideas shows that they could not be grouped, like Muir's ideas, so as to constitute a coherent doctrine. Because of his education (Lewis was the son of an Anglican clergyman of Ballintubber, in Ireland), he is, consciously or not, influenced by Christian doctrine. In a deliberate effort to give all his attention to the temporal and contemporary aspect of life, however, he is engaged in a narrow strait which the war proves to be a desperate strait. This accounts for the change in Lewis's poetry after *The Magnetic Mountain*. His experiences in the Home Guard provide him with but a poor image of his utopian dreams of a community and, later, while his friend Auden leaves for America and turns to mysticism, Lewis can no longer find a support for his poetry in anything else than is suggested by the motto 'word over all'.

In *Overtures to Death, and Other Poems*, war is presented as a means of purification through death, and, in *Word Over All*, the purification is no longer in an external justice, but in the Word, so that Lewis is moving in a direction opposite to Communist philosophy, since Marxist doctrine rejects all transcendental values. Lewis's new attitude is more apparent in *Poems 1943 1947*, for instance in 'The Christmas Tree', where his latent religious feeling lurks through a frozen landscape:

> So feast your eyes now
> On mimic star and moon-cold bauble:
> Worlds may wither unseen,
> But the Christmas Tree is a tree of fable,
> A phoenix in evergreen,
> And the world cannot change or chill what its mysteries mean
> To your hearts and eyes now.

[1] ibid., p. 157.

The change is in his religious feeling, but in the disappearance of rhetoric, intellectualism and even satire from his work, and in the assertion of his lyrical gift. It is difficult to predict what will be Lewis's attitude to life in the future, for there is no logical conclusion to his development, as in Eliot's case. While asserting explicitly the existence of a transcendental reality, Lewis expresses, in all his works, his desire to meet the 'here and now', to represent the immediate reality, two tendencies which are not clearly defined and which are opposed to each other. The first is expressed in the 'Ode' of the 'New Year's Eve':[1]

> Bound by the curse of man—
> To live in his future, which is to live surely
> In his own death—we endure the embrace of the present
> But yearn for a being beyond us;

The second tendency appears in the 'Meditation' of the same poem:

> To live in the present, then, not to live for it—
> Let this be one of to-day's
> Resolutions; and the other, its corollary,
> To court the commonplace.[2]

Let us remark that we live in the present whether we want it or not, and that the corollary of 'not to live for it' would seem to be rather 'not to court the commonplace'. Lewis's resolution 'to look with the naked eye of the Now', or 'to witness the rare in the common' is vague until we come to its applications, such as 'The Misfit' or 'A Failure', portraying two characters overwhelmed by life. But they are rather exceptional characters, and we do not see how their tragic doom might be redeemed.

Some passages of Lewis's later poems, when brought together, do not harmonize. The variety of his poetical experience corresponds to a dispersion of his thought. If in his first period he fails to produce a work which survives the events, he presents us, in the second period, with a work in which the philosophical element is scattered and disconnected, but for the benefit of his lyricism. It is natural that his last attitude should be agnosticism:

[1] *Poems 1943–1947*, p. 50. The poem was broadcast on New Year's Eve, 1947.
[2] ibid., p. 54.

Call no man happy. . . . Our actions burst like spray
Upon a reef, nevertheless we must act . . .
Know yourself. . . . But knowing, do not presume
To swerve or sweeten what is foreordained . . .
For the heart, magnanimity; for the mind, good sense;
For the soul, a natural piety; for fate,
A stoic's bending steel. . . . Nothing too much.[1]

This attitude is secondary in a work which, after many philosophical experiments, celebrates the triumph of lyricism and proves
that didactic, discursive thought, unlike concentrated, musical
thought, finds no place in poetry.

[1] 'Sketches for a Portrait' (*Poems 1943–1947*, pp. 19 and 20).

CHAPTER VI

OTHER POETS

Astudy of the poetical thought in the work of other poets is a way of placing the attitude and thought of each of the poets to whom a chapter is devoted. Most poets of the twentieth century are isolated figures who do not belong to any recognizable school of poetry or of philosophy. They have all in common, however, the same questioning urge, the same doubt which compels them to find their own solution. All beliefs fall apart and destroy one another and, as men cannot help believing, each poet is looking for a beauty and a truth which may satisfy him. Each poet creates, not only a doctrine upon which he can rely, but also a beauty and a sense of beauty which may stand up against doubt and criticism, so that the readers are confronted with scattered, monolithic experiments which can hardly be compared with one another.

In spite of their isolation, many of them have a common feature which can be described as a tendency towards expressing their inward experience as opposed to an attitude of objectivity. Moreover, it is in their inward experience rather than in the facts of science that they expect to find the truth. Their aesthetic sense and their philosophy are intimately linked; this is perhaps most obvious in the case of Herbert Read.

We have chosen a few poets who are representative of the tendency to look for truth in beauty, for beauty in truth. Some of them have developed philosophical ideas in prose or in verse, and the less abstract the ideas the greater the poets, so far as we can judge from the poets we have chosen. Sometimes these ideas can only be expressed in myths, and although they may be reduced to philosophical conceptions, they have a richer meaning than abstractions are able to convey.

We have judged a certain number of poets by the quality of their thought. This is an arbitrary point of view, but the scope of this study does not allow for a complete survey of twentieth-century poetry, a task which would be outside our aim.

A.E. and W. J. Turner, whose thought is essentially poetical, may be grouped together. Two American poets, Jeffers and Robinson, find a place in this study, the first because his knowledge and experience as a scientist is recorded and interpreted in his poems, the second because a great intellectual tradition is represented in the core of his symbols. Apart from their interest in psycho-analysis, D. H. Lawrence and Robert Graves have in common a rejection of the modern world and of abstraction. Stephen Spender who, like Auden, was one of the chief poets of the 'thirties, has in common with C. Day Lewis a growing desire to face reality in his lyrical poems, whereas the careers of both Aldous Huxley and Auden are characterized by the growth of a religious thought after a period of scepticism in the case of Huxley, and of materialism in the case of Auden.

There are various reasons for confining our study to these poets, but this does not mean that they are isolated in their attempt to express a poetical thought. On the contrary, many others might be interpreted from our point of view. In Masefield's *Everlasting Mercy*, for example, a spiritual conflict is in the background of beautiful country scenes, and here and there in the Laureate's work one finds thought-provoking maxims, such as

Thought is but joy from murder that has been.[1]

But Masefield's idealism (in the platonic sense of the word) is conventional, and symptomatic of a discrepancy between traditional thought and poetry.

There is also a poetical thought in Walter de la Mare's poems, but his symbols cannot easily be translated into clear ideas. As to the aesthetic problems presented by Ezra Pound in his *Cantos*, they need an elaborate study; besides, his thought is so dispersed that an analysis of his works from our point of view would not be fruitful.

Perhaps the most isolated literary figure of the beginning of this century is A.E. (George William Russell).[2] A.E. does not, like Blake, create his own mythology, but his poetry is inspired by a tradition to

[1] 'Sonnets', LIX, *Collected Poems*, p. 438.

[2] The American poet Vachel Lindsay may be compared to A.E. in some respects: esoteric symbols, fantastic visions, and a mixture of religion and patriotism. But Lindsay is inspired by Swedenborg, A.E. by Celtic culture.

which modern western civilization is diametrically opposed: a combination of theosophy with Celtic mythology. Whereas Yeats was influenced by French symbolism and other literary movements, A.E. remained faithful to his essentially religious sources. His poetry does not reach the perfection achieved by Yeats, and he considered life to be much more important than poetry. It has been said that, among great Irishmen, Yeats was the poet, and A.E. the saint. A.E. dismisses Christianity as a belief which has been artificially grafted on the Irish soil while the cosmic consciousness was dwindling and replaced by individual perception. Christianity, according to A.E., is but a moral code, whereas three things are required of a religion: a cosmogony, a psychology and a moral code.[1] A.E.'s doctrine might be summed up by saying that he believed in the divinity of both Man and the Earth, and that the purpose of life is to re-unite with the Ancestral Self; for A.E. admits the Fall of man. His aim in his poems is to communicate with the divine beings who are still present in the Memory of Earth, and in this respect his poetry may be regarded as fervently religious: 'I believe that most of what was said of God was in reality said of that Spirit whose body is Earth.'[2]

An introduction to his poetry is provided by his letter of October 1934 to Seán O'Faoláin in which he explains the line into which, he claimed, he had put most meaning:

All our thoughts are throngs of living souls.

'I think with many others that the universe we see is made by the congregation of spirits which inhabit it as they again live and have their being in an incomprehensible Absolute. We have imagined ourselves into littleness, darkness, and ignorance, and we have to imagine ourselves back into light.'[3]

A.E.'s spiritualism prevented him from devoting all his efforts to poetry. Like Blake, he was a painter, and his poems were often accompanied by sketches: 'Painting is the only thing I have any real delight in doing. Nature intended me to be a painter.'[4] His spiritualism reflected itself in his practical activities and in his political pamphlets: 'The words "republic" or "empire" are opaque words to me. I cannot see through them any beauty or majesty to which they

[1] *A Memoir of A.E., George William Russell*, by John Eglington, London, Macmillan, 1937, p. 166.

[2] ibid., p. 130.   [3] ibid., p. 257.   [4] (From a letter to Pryse) ibid., p. 40.

inevitably lead. But I do believe in freedom. If the universe has any meaning at all it exists for the purposes of the soul, and men or nations denied essential freedom cannot fulfil their destiny, or illuminate earth with light or wisdom from that divinity without them, or mould external circumstance into the image of the Heaven they conceive in their hearts.'[1] In spite of all these different activities and interests, he knew all his poems by heart.

The first collection of poems in which his thought comes to maturity is *Homeward, Songs by the Way*.[2] The title is explained by a short preface in which the basic theme of his poetry, and at the same time his leading idea, is summed up: 'I moved among men and places, and in living I learned the truth at last. I know I am a spirit, and that I went forth in old time from the Self-ancestral to labours yet unaccomplished; but filled ever and again with home-sickness I made these songs by the way.' From his Celtic and Hindoo sources A.E. has taken a belief in metempsychosis which appears in his poems. Man is an exile on earth, accomplishing an obscure task, but he is soon to return to his home in heaven, to what he calls the Self-ancestral or the Mother, or in Emerson's phrase the Oversoul. Most of the poems in *Homeward* illustrate the journey of the soul. To A.E. heaven is more concrete than it is to a Christian: it can be seen and heard in nature, which is an image of eternity revealed through the motions of the stars.

Human suffering, according to A.E., derives from the fact that the earth is a place of exile where the vision of eternity is a release from pain. This is why his poems are so human and so touching (cf. the poem entitled 'Pain', p. 34). Moreover, they are full of a warm sympathy towards nature, for in his eyes nature is not impersonal but the very face of the spirit.

Almost all his poems express communion with the spirit of life which endows all things and beings with the halo of a magic presence, as if they reopened the dried-up source of primitive, myth-creating poetry. The world seems new and wonderful when the humblest things have a soul, and a scientific mind is bound to be startled by this transfigured world. This new appearance, together with the opposition between the physical reality and the reality of the soul, are described in 'The Vesture of the Soul':[3]

[1] *The Inner and the Outer Ireland*, the Talbot Press, Dublin, 1921.
[2] London, Lane, 1908.
[3] *Homeward, Songs by the Way*, p. 51.

I pitied one whose tattered dress
Was patched, and stained with dust and rain;
He smiled on me; I could not guess
The viewless spirit's wide domain.

He said, 'The royal robe I wear
Trails all along the fields of light:
Its silent blue and silver bear
For gems the starry dust of night.

'The breath of Joy unceasingly
Waves to and fro its folds starlit,
And far beyond earth's misery
I live and breathe the joy of it.'

The vividness with which A.E. perceives spiritual realities enables him to connect them with material things, for the spirit is over the whole of creation. The feeling of the unity of spirit and matter is expressed in 'Dust':[1]

I heard them in their sadness say
'The earth rebukes the thought of God;
We are but embers wrapped in clay
A little nobler than the sod.'

But I have touched the lips of clay
Mother, thy rudest sod to me
Is thrilled with fire of hidden day,
And haunted by all mystery.

Men are more and more blind to that spiritual reality; an age of darkness and materialism will come, in which men will only see ugliness and feel pain:

For earth's age of pain has come, and all her sister planets weep,
Thinking of her fires of morning into dreamless sleep.
In this cycle of great sorrow for the moments that we last
We too shall be linked by weeping to the greatness of her past:
But the coming race shall know not, and the fount of tears shall dry,
And the arid heart of man be arid as the desert sky.
So within my mind the darkness dawned and round me everywhere
Hope departed with the twilight, leaving only dumb despair.[2]

[1] ibid., p. 50.   [2] ibid., 'The Dawn of Darkness', p. 37.

The world of divine beings captured by the poet, however, has not completely disappeared, and is still recorded in the Memory of Earth. The poet overcomes despair and exalts his soul above both joy and sadness, pain and ease:

> We are men by anguish taught
> To distinguish false from true;
> Higher wisdom we have not;
> But a joy within guides you.[1]

This pure spiritualism leads the poet to a dualism where soul and body are not reconciled:

>   Until
> Body and spirit are apart
> The Everlasting works Its will.[2]

A.E.'s dualism, however, finds a solution in his doctrine of retribution. We have to expiate our sins and those of our former lives:

> Let the dragons of the past
>   In their caverns sleeping lie.
> I am dream-betrayed, and cast
>   Into that old agony.[3]

The soul which would escape into heaven and evade the expiation would find no peace there, for its sins have not been purified:

> Thou would'st ease in heaven thy pain,
>   Oh, thou fiery, bleeding thing!
> All thy wounds will wake again
>   At the heaving of a wing.[4]

If any doctrine can be learnt from A.E., it is a personal theosophy, a spiritualism which was rather strengthened than diminished by the years and which is expressed in a series of poems, each of them written from the same height but each expressing a new experience:

> You tell me of my songs you cannot fit
> Their thought together, so contrary the lights.
> I cannot help you to the sense of it.

[1] ibid., 'Childhood', p. 52.   [2] 'Continuity', 1918.
[3] and [4] 'Resurrection', 1925.

255

> We rise and fall, have many days and nights,
> Make songs in both; and when we are in our pit
> Gaze back in wonder at our own endless heights.[1]

Because of their esoteric sources, A.E.'s poems lack a universal appeal, but it is not fair to presume that his poetic experiments are derived from a specific science or religion: a profound anxiety, accompanied by doubt, lurks behind his faith, and in this he resembles his contemporaries:

> Were beauty only
> A day the same,
> We could know the Maker
> And name His name,
> We would know the substance
> Was holy flame.
>
> Is there an oasis
> Where Time stands still,
> Where fugitive beauty
> Stays as we will?
> Is there an oasis
> Where Time stands still?[2]

These lines add a tragic touch to the visions of pure ideas and dreams of the Everliving which fill A.E.'s poetry. His whole effort was to keep a fresh vision of peace while struggling against adversity. This vision was so deeply anchored in his nature that he had no difficulty in sacrificing what was unworthy of it; one may remember that he refused to be a Senator of the Irish Free State on the ground that he could not earn the money he would receive.

While A.E.'s work is focused on religious experience, W. J. Turner's poetry and musical criticism are focused on aesthetic experience. Turner's thought, like his, is opposed to materialism. In the preface to *The Oxford Book of Modern Verse*, Yeats pays tribute to Turner for rejecting at last the prevailing materialism and raising the cry: 'The flux is in my own mind.'

Turner's poems offer a greater variety than A.E.'s, and it is con-

[1] 'To One who Wanted a Philosophy from Me', 1934.   [2] 'Time', 1925.

venient to study here only those of his poems which are centred upon his unique philosophical experience.

Turner's thought, as it is expressed in the volumes which follow *The Dark Fire* (1918), can be simply explained by saying that nature is a product of the living imagination, and that we are living to the extent to which we possess this imagination. Abstract signs and musical notes are not artificial simplifications of reality, but creations of the imagination, and time is the first half of an equation, the second half of which is eternity; nature is transparent to our mind, which is present everywhere: these considerations are on the way to perfect solipsism.

This, however, is too easy a simplification. Among Turner's prose books, those devoted to music are the best introduction to his poetical thought. In the first chapter of *Orpheus*,[1] Turner asserts his belief in the spiritual basis of the universe: 'The world about us *seems* to be material, but exists in rhythm. It is a living world, and it is kept alive by a spiritual force which we can best describe as love. . . .' Not less important is Turner's conception of death, or the absence of creative imagination, a conception which is the source of his satirical verse: 'But this power of becoming *physical* (life taking on flesh, the spirit achieving form) or *material* (electricity becoming molecules of hydrogen, lead, etc.) is the process which I have described as death, and as that necessary and important death, death the complement of life. But . . . a third kind of death, other than the material and the physical, is that of *intellectual* structure—known variously as tradition, belief, dogma, logic, technique or, most comprehensively, as knowledge. Just as a multitude of deaths were necessary to the evolution of the eye and the ear so a multitude of deaths (an Encyclopaedia is a mental cemetery) are necessary to the evolution of the mind. The past experience which every trained musician possesses is such knowledge.'[2] In the Introduction to *Music and Life*,[3] Turner develops the idea that all human activities spring from abstract, that is, imaginative notions like the simple $2 + 2 = 4$, and in his essay on César Franck he insists that 'the revolution he accomplished in French music was a spiritual one.'[4] A piece of music which appeals exclusively to the aesthetic sense without arousing a spiritual emotion is of an inferior kind, and Turner writes in his essay on Debussy: '. . . it is the

[1] *Orpheus, or The Music of the Future*, London, Kegan Paul, 1943, p. 19.
[2] ibid., p. 39. [3] London, Methuen, 1921. [4] *Music and Life*, p. 125.

grandeur, the sublimity of the soul that makes the music of Beethoven and Bach so immeasurably greater than the music of Wagner and Debussy. There are many people, chiefly among professional musicians, who dislike and do not understand this judgment by spiritual values. They do not analyse the music they hear except harmonically —and harmonic originality is the passport to their favour.'[1] The same spiritual element should be present in poetry, where Turner emphasizes the part played by ideas or what is called poetical thought. Although

> With words not ideas is poetry made,

a word is nothing without an idea: it is the intellectual death which corresponds to the physical death of the skull:

> Wordless and riddle-hard the skull of man,
> It will not wash away, it tells us nothing,
> Nothing at all.
>
> .   .   .   .   .
>
> Landfall now here! Here where a Spirit sitting
> Takes up its skull, looks at its smitten teeth,
> Its barest meaning, here is poetry
> Here where there are no words, wash of flesh-confusion,
> Only the ultimate It, result of the Spirit's smiting
> Man-anvil, at last motionless, shell-like and without breath.[2]

This analysis of the aesthetic experience and of the springs of the imagination is typical of Turner, who looks inward through a transparent nature and 'in time like glass': 'Turner represents that type of expressionist artist whose inner experience is not characterized by baroque strain and violence but rather by its tendency towards aesthetic sublimation of strain.'[3] Many poems, such as 'In Time like Glass',[4] are so impersonal that they resemble the works of the French *Parnasse*, but the likeness is perhaps superficial, for Turner's impersonality originates in his conception of time, a time without duration, which is equal to eternity, the astronomer's time where all sights, like stars,

> . . . vanish but can never pass;

[1] ibid., p. 157.

[2] 'Words and Ideas' (*Fossils of a Future Time?* O.U.P., 1946, p. 38).

[3] *W. J. Turner, a Georgian Poet*, by H. W. Häusermann (*English Studies*, February 1943).

[4] *Selected Poems 1916–1936*, O.U.P., 1939, p. 64.

In this vision nature becomes transparent to the mind, every object
fades and gives way to a pure, eternal, and neutral essence:

> In Time like glass the stars are set,
> And seeming-fluttering butterflies
> Are fixèd fast in Time's glass net. . . .

The same atmosphere is created in 'Men Fade like Rocks':[1]

.   .   .   .   .

> Rock-like the souls of men
> Fade, fade in time;
> Smoother than river-rain
> Falls chime on chime.

Other titles in the same volume, such as 'Giraffe and Tree',[2] 'The
Lion',[3] 'The Ape',[4] 'The Forest Bird'[5] and 'Man with Girl',[6] suggest
again a comparison with poems of the *Parnasse*, but the likeness does
not go beyond the indifference or neutrality of the poet towards his
subject. Turner's impersonality does not denote the resignation or
the despair of the poet before an objective world which carries away
the soul in its flight and destruction, in other words, before the soulless
world discovered by science: it is rather a disguised mysticism, a
communion of the spirit with itself where all natural objects become
imperceptible and evanescent. This 'mystical' tendency manifests itself in 'The Forest Bird', where the poet develops the theme that 'the
loveliest things of earth' are not natural sights

> But in transparency of thought
>   Out of the branched, dark-foliaged word
> There flits a strange, soft-glimmering light,
>   Shy as a forest bird.
> Most lovely and most shy it comes
>   From realm of sense unknown,
>   And sings of earthly doom,
> Of an immortal happiness
>   In the soul's deepening gloom.

The disappearance of external objects in the poet's contemplation
prevents 'Landscape of Cytherea' from being a collection of love-

---

[1] ibid., p. 65.   [2] ibid., p. 68.   [3] ibid., p. 68.   [4] ibid., p. 70.
[5] ibid., p. 72.   [6] ibid., p. 73.

poems: the image of the beloved becomes also transparent, and the burden of 'Journey to Cytherea'[1] is:

Lonely, lonely, lonely, lonely am I!

Turner's Cytherea is a still island where Love walks blind, blind because all mortal sights have disappeared and give way to the mysterious transparency in which Turner's poetical experience of that period is crystallized:

Dense stillness molybdenean
  Is Aphrodite
  (Crystal of the sea
That is rolling, rolling, rolling)
  Far from this migration
  This flow pythagorean
Life scenes from her essence unscrolling.[2]

Turner's mystical experience takes a new shape in *The Seven Days of the Sun*,[3] and attempts to explain creation or the imagination, for Turner's genesis is essentially aesthetic. The Sun is the Creator, and the poet is his prophet, who proclaims the seven days of creation. The sequence of poems, however, is far from following a coherent scheme and seems to mark a transition in Turner's development. But his solipsism is nowhere else so acutely manifested and, although better controlled in the next volumes, has a growth which is not disorderly.

The first day, 'Monday', is a day of pure light; everything is immaterial and incandescent, the spirit has not yet awakened, and the human sense has not yet 'drunk the soul of Virginity'.

'Tuesday' is the beginning of human consciousness, and it is an absolute beginning: there is no independent object, everything exists in, and comes from, the mind; even animals are ideas of the human mind and nothing can be conceived apart from the mind which conceives:

I do not believe that the earth rotates
Or circles the Sun,
Or that there are myriads of solar systems:
These are ideas like chastity—
The goddess Diana
Or the Virgin Mary![4]

---

[1] ibid., p. 90.   [2] 'Mystery', ibid., p. 118.
[3] London, Chatto and Windus, 1925.   [4] ibid., p. 6.

Everything is closed in the human mind as in a vicious circle, and included in our self:

> Now to conceive the idea chastity
> Is to be chaste.
> You cannot be chaste and not know it.
> Therefore to be chaste is to conceive.
> But only philosophers can conceive and be chaste;
> Only scientists can rotate on their axes
> And go round the Sun in three hundred and sixty-five and
> > one quarter days.
> The Sun and the Earth know nothing of such performances
> Being merely ourselves in remarkable attitudes.
> We are self-gazers. [1]

The differentiation of objects is but a complexity of our mind:

> Since we know nothing but our own ideas
> Why should one idea be incompatible with another?

and cosmic distances are but extensions of our mind, in which everything is immediately present:

> I roar with laughter when I hear that the Sun
> Is nearly ninety-three million miles from the earth.

The most ridiculous idea in Turner's eyes is that of a finite world which can be represented as independent from thought:

> Let us have another funny story!

> Let us listen to the astronomers
> While they tell us
> How the still shapelessness of cold
> Rolls itself up into hot balls.
> Perhaps they will say it is because the world is finite
> And there is pressure at the extremities.

> All creation is due to pressure at the extremities. [2]

There is perhaps no reason why Turner should not have written the preceding lines in prose. The tone is ironical, the style conversational. Turner probably believed that the thought was poetical in itself, and did not care much about the form and the images; he was

---

[1] ibid., p. 7.   [2] ibid., p. 9.

only engaged in refuting ideas and theories. He discards such well-established sciences as astronomy and biology, and especially the evolutionary theory:

> No doubt women are all descended from cats
> Psychologically![1]

and the idea of progress:

> The idea of progress
> Is vertical—
> In geological strata.
>
> It is a geometric illusion.[2]

Turner reviews the ideas and theories he acquired at the University and realizes that science is a 'Great Mythic System', and that human knowledge is dry and fragmentary (the notion of intellectual death recurs here). Even Christians are vain because there is no other God than the self:

> Martyred upon this pyre—
> Inwardly burning—all other senses die,
> And *Christian* souls turn to aethereal prayer;
> To whom? Their bones in water or in clay beds lie
> Strange tracings! Vanished their wind-blown hair![3]

'Wednesday' is inspired by the same satirical mood and brings nothing new to Turner's solipsism:

> I drank from the mirror of my imagination.[4]

The beautiful passages are scattered among unnecessary outbursts in this overcharged, loose, and unequal poem, for Turner is excited by his revolt against accepted ideas. After the passionate satire of 'Wednesday', however, the poet calms himself, and the feeling of transparency which is communicated with restraint in the preceding volumes reappears. The world is again sleeping, harmless and calm, and this stillness is linked with a new assertion of Turner's solipsism:

> I had watched the ascension and decline of the Moon
> And did not realize that it moved only in my own mind.[5]

[1] ibid., p. 10.   [2] ibid., p. 11.   [3] ibid., p. 16.   [4] ibid., p. 17.
[5] ibid., p. 27.

But now I know that the solar system and the constellations
                                                    of stars
Are contained within me.
Nothing exists outside me.
Outside me everything is the same but I do not exist.[1]

The last line is a conceit which means: outside me everything is just as if I or anything did not exist, in other words 'nothing exists outside me'. The repetition of the same fundamental idea throughout the poem is a proof that the poet has not yet mastered, and consequently not yet felt his thought: it is not a poetical thought, and the language is that of philosophy. Turner's poetry is informed by the idea that everything is imagination or thought, the idea of an idealist, Berkeley's '*esse est percipi*' and Gentile's absolute subjectivism. Turner asserts the primacy of the poetic imagination, maintains that all things are fragments of the imagination and that the world is an ineffable poem. This poetical idea perhaps induces the poet to mistake the idea itself for poetry, and prompts his preference of the abstract, the pure and the spiritual over the concrete, the complex and the real:

In the innumerable curves of the Universe
I have found the peace that passeth all understanding,
In the curves of music
And all the modulations of numbers.

When I look upon a beautiful body
And rapidly make an *Abstract*
I tingle with pleasure at the deviations and aberrations
Of the *Real*.
I become alive through a series of shocks.

My heart thunders as I race along this asymptote
                                        everlasting
Which is my life among other bodies.[2]

Much of Turner's poetical thought is inspired by the language of philosophy and geometry. The last two lines are again an assertion of his solipsism; they mean that the self tends to unite with everything and, at last, hypothetically does so. Another consequence of Turner's

[1] ibid., p. 28.   [2] ibid., p. 29.

solipsism is the absolute negation of death. As there is nothing outside
the self, the otherness of things or beings is an illusion:

> Every moment is an increasing peril,
> Then every moment is a forlorn leave-taking,
> A farewell to someone you have never known.[1]

The words 'leave-taking' and 'farewell' are connected with the image
of the asymptote which, in the finite, visible curves, means separation;
while the infinite, invisible straight lines of the asymptote mean unity.

The two following sections of the poem do not mark a progress of
Turner's idea. In 'Friday' he applies his idea to love and refutes the
theory that there is a difference between fleshly and ideal love. The
Dark Lady of Shakespeare's sonnets, even the real being, if we assume
she is a woman, can be nothing but imagination:

> If I could have analysed my sensation
> 'The Dark Lady' would have disappeared.
> And I would have got up from the bed
> Seeing nothing there.[2]

> Let me tell of the Dark Lady
> With whom I lay down in a corner of my brain![3]

The last section of the poem, 'Sunday', summarizes the poet's experience in an apocalyptic vision of the universe, which may be
called the Sun as well as the self or eternity:

> And there was no high nor low,
> Neither loud nor soft,
> Nor *time*.
> But the music was still music
>
> And it was me and I was in it.
>
> . . . . .
>
> And there was but one *Beam*
>
> And the *Beam* was still.[4]

The culmination of Turner's experience is a moment of communion
where all opacity vanishes, where the spirit is still and all-including,
and where music is silent: 'The numerous passages where music is

---

[1] ibid., p. 29. [2] ibid., p. 33. [3] ibid., p. 34. [4] ibid., p. 55.

described as being silent point to the same idea: the eternal flux being caught and made transparent like a mathematical equation.'[1]

The volumes which follow *The Seven Days of the Sun* are characterized by a deeper investigation into the meaning of Turner's ideas. After a boisterous exhibition of his discovery the poet feels the need for a trial of his *Weltanschauung* in *New Poems*.[2] The most significant poem in this respect is 'The Morning Star',[3] which is based upon the distinction between unity and plurality, oneness and separation. Whereas unity is boldly proclaimed in *The Seven Days of the Sun*, the idea is opposed to its contrary and sharply delineated in 'The Morning Star'. The poet must admit the existence of multiplicity but he is in revolt, and his protagonist is Prometheus, or the morning star, who rebels against the law of God. The poet complains of being expelled from the peace of Paradise and condemned to wander like a solitary star:

> Thou rope of white smoke, flameless ring of God
> Absorb me quick, I burn, I freeze in fire,
> I am a thing apart, I shriek with pain,
> Torn from perfection am a wandering star
> That sleeps upon no orbit; burns and burns
> Thousands of evenings in an empty sky
> Vainly consumed.[4]

In the world of separation, love and death are for ever opposed to each other. In order to palliate this everlasting struggle, Lucifer creates a world of space and abstract shapes which express symbolically a perfect unity, so that death becomes 'the necessary complement of life', as Turner suggests in *Orpheus*, and these abstractions, pure creations of the imagination, are a bridge between spirit and flesh:

> A world which is but *Figures*, Shapes and Things
> But where some mystery guiding them to Thee
> Bends and perplexes all to subtleties
> In which my grief of separation hides
> In arabesques so strange, so lovely strange
> Boundaries dissolve, I tremble, dream of Thee
> And that I am within thy bosom again.[5]

---

[1] H. W. Häusermann, op. cit., p. 6.
[2] London, Chatto and Windus, 1928.   [3] Ibid., p. 21.   [4] ibid.   [5] ibid., p. 23.

More directly symbolical of unity is poetry:

Vast metaphors of severed Unity.

Time is but a dispersion of eternity, and the finite world, when reflected in Lucifer's mind, expresses a longing for eternity. Lucifer and God are face to face, like the asymptote rejoining the straight line in infinity:

> In Time and Space must I forever dwell
> Exiled from Thee and, burning, lean nightlong,
> Darken huge mountains, brighten into streams
> And fill that landscape with a myriad masks
> That seek Thy face when gazing into mine.[1]

Turner's ethics are overshadowed by his aesthetics. While Lucifer accepts time, the poet goes a step further in 'The Rotten State of Denmark'[2] and accepts evil, not with resignation, as if evil were a just punishment, but with joy, because evil is the source of good. The poet wonders at the mood of pessimism which characterizes the literature of our time, as if writers were surprised that evil should exist, and answers:

Evil is no more than the manure from which springs the Flower,
It has its own virtue and is the root of all Heavenly Power.[3]

Turner goes even as far as saying that he prefers sincere evil to disguised and false goodness. 'Ballad of an Idealist'[4] is a satire of hypocrisy: the poet prefers the darkness of pure, ideal Hell, to the false earthly light where love and hatred are a pretence and idealists are always cheated and vanquished:

> There is no pretence of love here, of art, of poetry, or of music;
> There is nothing but silence here, silence and darkness;
> It is quite black here, there is no false light.[5]

Some poems in *Songs and Incantations* show a weakening of Turner's vision, and clichés such as 'starry skies' and 'starry solitude' are used repeatedly. As Turner's thought comes always back to itself, he is bound to repeat the same themes, and a whole sequence of poems,

---

[1] ibid., p. 24.
[2] *Songs and Incantations*, London, Dent, 1936, p. 72   [3] ibid.   [4] ibid., p. 5.
    ibid.. p. 6.

The Pursuit of Psyche, has that return to the self for its theme. It is an extension of his solipsism:

> The human spirit is not a spirit behind fleshly bars
> But is the chrysalis of its own cocoon
> Like the image of space in things geometrical.[1]

In his last volume of poetry, *Fossils of a Future Time?*[2] Turner affirms the same conception. Quotations could be multiplied. It is not a repetition, but a discovery of new facets of the same vision, as in 'Poetry and Science':

> There is no positive truth:
> 'There is no other truth than purest fiction.'[3]

This crystallized vision is so well established in Turner's mind that he may face war and strife with serenity:

> Calm shines down from the stars
> Despite their cosmic wars
> Combustion multitudinous man's spirit never jars.[4]

The mind is the principle of stability, but this ideal eternity is attained through a series of conquests. The spirit is perpetually facing and defeating the nothingness of meaningless matter. 'The Signs of the Zodiac'[5] are the symbol of man's power to endow material, blank things with a meaning. It is significant that the blue sky which, for other poets, is a symbol of exaltation becomes a symbol of nothingness in Turner's poetry:

> The sky was emptied with my heart,
> Mere data of my brain,
> O Scorpio stab me with thy dart
> That I may feel again!

This conquest is without defeat, for the struggle is only apparent, and all antinomies meet and find their solution in the human mind:

> All that has been I am, all that shall be is I.[6]

---

[1] *Selected Poems*, p. 180.   [2] O.U.P., 1946.   [3] ibid., p. 34.
[4] ibid., 'Death, Lines on the War, 1939–1945', p. 38.   [5] ibid., pp. 46–8.
[6] ibid., 'How we Advance', pp. 115–16.

In 'Nature and Mind'[1] Turner presents another facet of his solipsism; this sonnet is based upon an interpretation of the word 'self-preservation'. There is another self-preservation than the biological, racial one, for the real self is the spirit, where everything is deathless. Nature and mind are one and the same, for:

> Unvalued words, true flowerings of the mind
> Are natural as the very earth and air.

One should remember that for Turner knowledge and the physical substance are death itself, but this death is constantly contradicted and renewed by the active spirit which is life. Death cannot be understood and cannot exist without life. By endowing nature with a meaning the mind is preserved from death:

> Thus having carved into a sign its breath—
> That all else crumbling is effaced in death.

Turner's work is unique in contemporary literature in its constant affirmation and illustration of the reality of the spirit. This belief is intermittent in the works of other poets, it is secondary in A.E.'s poems, and Yeats is preoccupied with this problem chiefly in his correspondence with Thomas Sturge Moore. With Turner it is not an affirmation, it is an axiom and a source of inspiration. The world is a poem and cannot be explained without reference to the invisible forces working in the mind: it is as if everything comes from the mind and dies outside the mind, but keeps an immortal shape in the secret recesses of the mind. Only death and nothingness exist outside the mind, where the primacy belongs to the imagination.

The fundamental theme of 'In Time Like Glass' is the vanishing of all objects before the searching mind, and this aesthetic sublimation of the physical world endows the poems with charm and mystery. *The Seven Days of the Sun*, however, presents Turner's solipsism in its most naked and abstract form, so that the sequence is at times too philosophical in spite of the bursts of revolt and the touches of irony which rather increase by contrast the dryness of abstract statements. In *New Poems, Pursuit of Psyche, Songs and Incantations*, and *Fossils of a Future Time*, Turner's mind is shown in a state of conflict, and the tension between the antinomies of self and death transforms his otherwise philosophical thought into poetical thought. Turner deserves a

[1] ibid., p. 116.

place in the history of English literature through his significant attempt to find an essentially poetical thought.

Among the philosophers who tried to express their doctrine in poetry, Ralph Waldo Emerson may be regarded as the initiator of the American tradition, of which the best representatives are Edwin Arlington Robinson and Robinson Jeffers. Whereas Emerson's themes are definitely philosophical, E. A. Robinson's poems are chiefly lyrical and, for the most part, narrative. This is not the place to analyse Robinson's work, but one of his narratives, *Merlin*,[1] may be taken as an example of his thought. Robinson's source is Sir Thomas Malory's *Morte d'Arthur*, a condensed version of the Arthurian romances of the later French versifiers. Unlike Swinburne's and Tennyson's versions, Robinson's Merlin is at the same time an enchanter and a seer, and an unfortunate one. His lady, Vivian, instead of being an ideal fairy, becomes a beautiful woman who cannot hear of evil and mortality. A reason why Robinson took both Merlin and Arthur as symbols of failure is that the poem was written in the beginning of the First World War: the fall of Arthur's kingdom corresponds to the destructions of modern warfare. But the most important event in Robinson's *Merlin* is not the fall of Arthur's kingdom, but the failure of Merlin; that is, the failure of the mind. Robinson endows the theme with a modern symbolism which compels him to follow two different actions: Vivian is the symbol of beauty, pure and undisturbed; Arthur is the symbol of misfortune which, in Merlin's eyes, is considered as a 'speck' in beauty. Merlin is the human mind torn in two pieces between beauty and reality, and overcome by Time and Fate which are the two dominant abstractions of this narrative poem, even while seeing them clearly. Another new element in Robinson's Merlin is the self-consciousness of the four main characters: Merlin, Arthur, Vivian and Dagonet. Merlin foresees the whole tragedy, and although in his 'living tomb' he loses his beard and his senility, and forgets for a while Arthur and Camelot, he is tormented even there by his knowledge of the future and leaves Broceliande as an old man deprived of his former power. Arthur is self-conscious in his despair: since Lancelot has fled with Guinevere, Arthur has lost

---

[1] *Collected Poems*, New York, Macmillan, 1924, p. 233. cf. also: *E. A. Robinson and the Arthurian Legends*, by Lucius Beebe, Cambridge, Mass., 1927; and *E. A. Robinson*, by Ivor Winters, Norfolk, Conn., 1946.

the hope of the Grail and considers his brilliant life to have been vain. Although Merlin promises to return, Vivian knows that her love was only a dream and that she has lost Merlin forever. As to Dagonet, although he plays with his madness he is well aware of its cause.

All the characters and events in *Merlin* converge in the symbolism of the poem. This symbolism has very little to do with the idealism, the brilliance or the mysticism of the original versions, and proves that Robinson was able to transform a mighty theme so as to make it his own. Because many characters in other poems than *Merlin* are human failures, and because sadness and disgust are the dominant notes in Robinson's poetry, it should not be inferred that he is a pessimist. He is rather an idealist whose ideal beauty is intimately linked with the darkest aspects of living.

Another representative of American poetry, John Robinson Jeffers, may be described as a pessimist, but his pessimism is of a peculiar kind, opposed to any belief in the fundamental goodness of nature. Jeffers takes from his scientific and medical training, and from his reading of Freud and Jung, the conviction that the only antidote to vices and deformations (one of his favourite themes) is a return to nature and to unconsciousness. This unconsciousness is the only relief from evil, from pain, and from that new invention of the scientific mind—modern warfare; for the world is now governed by the scientific mind which is without love, and war has no songs. If there is any spirit, it is for Jeffers the spirit of nature which is alive in inanimate things; hence a poem such as 'Life from the Lifeless':[1]

> Spirits and illusions have died,
> The naked mind lives
> In the beauty of inanimate things.
>
> Flowers wither, grass fades, trees wilt,
> The forest is burnt;
> The rock is not burnt.
>
> The deer starve, the winter birds
> Die on their twigs and lie
> In the blue dawns in the snow.

[1] *Chief Modern Poets of England and America*, selected by Sanders and Nelson; New York, Macmillan, 1946, p. 757. cf. *The Selected Poems of Robinson Jeffers*, New York, Random House, 1938.

Men suffer want and become
Curiously ignoble; as prosperity
Made them curiously vile.

But look how noble the world is,
The lonely-flowing waters, the secret–
Keeping stones, the flowing sky.

This praise of unconsciousness is exceptional in modern poetry,
which is rather characterized by a desperate effort to regain self-
control. Jeffers's unconsciousness, however, should not be interpreted as an abdication of the human mind, but rather as a belief in
the ideal perfection which is hidden behind reality:

Misery and riches, civilization and squalid savagery,
Mass war and the odor of unmanly peace:
Tragic flourishes above and below the normal of life.

.   .   .   .   .   .

From here for normal one sees both ways,
And listens to the splendor of God, the exact poet, the sonorous
Antistrophe of desolation to the strophe multitude.[1]

The third line of this quotation might well serve as an introduction
to Jeffers's long narrative poems, where a picture of tragic excesses
and abnormalities is balanced by a serene pantheism which presents
nature as essentially quiet and impassible, whereas suffering and evil
originate in knowledge.

A similar rejection of modern thought and more generally of
modern ways of life is to be found in David Herbert Lawrence's
work. But whereas Robinson Jeffers finds an answer to his anxiety in
the solitude of nature, Lawrence proposes a reform of human relations. Lawrence's denial of the conscious life of reason and will and
his emphasis on the contact of the sexes seem to inspire anything but
thought in his poetry, but his deepest desire is metaphysical.[2] His
praise of the Unconscious, and the recurrence of expressions such as
'depth of life', 'unity of perception', 'instinct', and 'intuition' in his

---

[1] ibid., 'Still the Mind Smiles', 1933, p. 756.
[2] cf. Clifford Collins: 'The Letters of D. H. Lawrence' (*Politics and Letters,*
Summer 1947, p. 8).

letters suggest a desire to reopen an unknown source of life. 'Men are free', he says, 'when they belong to a living, organic, *believing* community, active in fulfilling some unfulfilled, perhaps unrealized purpose.'[1] There is, however, no social doctrine in Lawrence's poems, but a religion of natural love and a cult of instinct (cf. 'New Heaven and Earth').[2] The theme of a long series of poems entitled 'Look! We Have Come Through!' is the flight from our mechanical world where love has no place. Lawrence's 'heaven' is not an ideal place, for the poet rejects all absolutes and claims that his poems are the fruit of experience: 'So one would like to ask the reader of "Look! We Have Come Through!" to fill in the background of the poems, as far as possible, with the place, the time, the circumstance.'[3] Most of Lawrence's lyrical poems are autobiographical, but the descriptive poems of 'Birds, Beasts and Flowers' are impersonal.

Whatever the circumstances which inspired the poems may be, there is a constant emphasis on the facts of generation; two stanzas from a poem entitled 'Mystery'[4] may be chosen as typical of Lawrence's love poetry:

> Ah, drink me up
> That I may be
> Within your cup
> Like a mystery,
> Like wine that is still
> In ecstasy.
> Glimmering still
> In ecstasy
>
> Commingled wines
> Of you and me
> In one fulfil
> The mystery.

The fulfilment of love, however, is possible only through a flight from the present civilization and a return to the less intellectual and more instinctive life of the past:

> For oh, I know, in the dust where we have buried
> The silenced races and all their abominations,
> We have buried so much of the delicate magic of life.

[1] ibid., p. 10. [2] *Collected Poems*, London, Secker, 1932, p. 325.
[3] ibid., 'Note' (1928). [4] ibid., p. 108.

The whole course of history appears to Lawrence as a gradual desiccation of life and a growth of artificiality:

> Evil, what is evil?
> There is only one evil, to deny life
> As Rome denied Etruria
> And mechanical America Montezuma still.[1]

Whereas Robinson Jeffers sees in knowledge the source of suffering, Lawrence goes further and considers all abstract activities of the mind as evil and unnatural. The most unnatural of these activities, in Lawrence's eyes, is religion, and a sequence of poems, 'The Evangelistic Beasts', is a satire on Christianity. The most significant passages of this satire are perhaps to be found in 'St. John',[2] whose symbol, the eagle, is the paragon of what Lawrence deprecates most:

> In the beginning was the Word, of course.
> And the word was the first offspring of the almighty
> Johannine mind,
> Chick of the intellectual eagle.

Religion is not only unnatural, but also decadent:

> For the almighty eagle of the fore-ordained Mind
> Is looking rather shabby and island-bound these days:
> Moulting and rather naked about the rump, and down in
> the beak,
> Rather dirty, on dung-whitened Patmos.

Lawrence is an enemy of spiritual values, and if there is any philosophy in his poems, it implies a denial of philosophy.

A similar rejection of the modern world is to be found in the poetry of Robert Graves; Graves's solution is not a return to a primitive stage of life, but a liberation of the will through poetry. Graves's work, like that of D. H. Lawrence, is connected with the birth of psycho-analysis; but instead of emphasizing the problem of sex, Graves insists on the irrational elements of the human mind, on what he calls 'poetic unreality' or 'poetic unreason'. Poetry, according to Graves, is the result of a struggle for the primacy of 'poetic unreality'

[1] ibid., 'Cypresses', p. 375.   [2] ibid., p. 417.

over human reality, corresponding to Herbert Read's distinction between 'personality' and 'character'. This conception of poetry as the solution of an unconscious conflict results in the affirmation of a supra-logical element in poetry. Graves's purpose in his critical books is to analyse what is behind the rational elements of poetry, and his method consists in apprehending what is symbolical in terms of symptomatic materials; in other words, in interpreting symbols as signs of a deeper reality: 'All poetry written under emotional stress, although its manifest statement suggests a form of mental disintegration, has a latent meaning which the reader of emotional sympathy will be able subsequently to grasp and to present intellectually as a history of conflict.'[1]

Graves's interest in psycho-analysis was checked by the influence of Laura Riding, whom Graves met in 1925. He became then the champion of 'modernist poetry', which proclaims the independence of the poem 'comparable with the new sense in modern times of the independence of the child'.[2] Graves attacks the classical prosody and the intrusion of theoretical knowledge in poetry, a defect which is apparent in Tennyson's *In Memoriam*: 'Deprive the poem of its sectional division; deprive it of its metrical regularity; and it will appear the loose and ill-assorted bundle of lost ideas it really is. Such feeble and false material would certainly not be tolerated in a poem which, like *The Waste Land*, had to invent its metrical changes as it went along.'[3] Many well-known contemporaries make the same mistake: 'Alfred Noyes, although neither mature nor serious, has written a long narrative poem, *The Torch Bearers*, to celebrate the progress of science from its beginnings to the present days. Patronizing of modern musical theory appears in the poetry of W. J. Turner, of modern painting theory in that of Edith Sitwell and Sacheverell Sitwell, of psychological theory in that of Herbert Read and Archibald MacLeish, of modern sex-engrossment in that of D. H. Lawrence, of philosophical theory in that of Conrad Aiken and T. S. Eliot, of encyclopedic learning in that of Marianne Moore, T. S. Eliot—and so on and so on.'[4]

[1] *Poetic Unreason and Other Studies*, London, Palmer, 1925. cf. also H. W. Häusermann: *Studien zur Englischen Literarkritik, 1910–1930*, Bochum-Langendreer, Pöppinghaus, 1938, p. 201.
[2] *A Survey of Modernist Poetry*, by Laura Riding and Robert Graves; London, Heinemann, 1929, p. 124.
[3] ibid., p. 55.   [4] ibid., p. 167.

This rejection of psychology and philosophy does not impair Graves's belief in the irrational element in poetry. In his retrospective 'Foreword' to his *Collected Poems*,[1] he sees his poetry as an attempt to free the poetic self from the bonds of reason. His whole poetical production appears to him as a struggle for the independence of the poem, either through a flight into 'romance' (first stage), through conflict or through 'a more immediate sense of poetic liberation' (fifth stage). In this 'Foreword' written in 1938 he realises that all his poems written since 1925 are 'unpleasant' poems: instead of escaping into a world of fiction, the poet faces the 'world in gloom which is before his eyes: 'To manifest poetic faith by a close and energetic study of the disgusting, the contemptible and the evil is not very far in the direction of poetic serenity.'[2] If any philosophy may be attributed to Graves, it is a philosophy of disillusionment:

> Nature is always so: you find
> That all it has of mind
> Is wind.[3]

Most of his poems are occasional pieces made of impressionistic touches, and his general purpose is aesthetic. His general development from romantic enthusiasm to a controlled realism enables him to choose apparently indifferent subjects in order to express his poetic faith. His reluctance for grand themes:

> No new ghost can appear. Their poor cause
> Was that time freezes, and time thaws;
> But here only such loves can last
> As do not ride upon the weathers of the past.[4]

is the manifesto of an impressionistic manner which gives up psychological investigations and places the poetic world in direct relation with the emotions and with the immediate perceptions of the senses. The creative act, according to Graves, is fortuitous, and cannot be related to any absolute.[5] It is a happy, unforeseen moment which escapes analysis. Graves's dislike of abstraction is founded on the same considerations as Lawrence's, betrays the influence of psychoanalysis and advocates a return to a primitive state of mind; the his-

[1] London, Cassell, 1938.　　　　　　[2] ibid., XXIV.
[3] ibid., '*Nature's Lineaments*', p. 134.　　[4] ibid., 'No More Ghosts', p. 189.
[5] cf. Häusermann, op. cit., p. 217.

tory of the Word is to Graves the history of the gradual sophistication
of the human mind:

> In the beginning, then, the Word alone,
> But now the various tongue-tied Lexicon. . . .[1]

As a result, the mind is blinded by knowledge and lives in an
artificial, closed world. Logic is merely a spider's web which con-
fines the philosopher in absolute solitude:

> Truth captured without increment of flies—
> Spinning till the cell became
> A spacious other head
>
> In which the emancipated reason might
> Learn in due time to walk at greater length
> And more unanswerably.[2]

This description recalls Herbert Read's 'a + b + c = x', where
thought 'accelerating in the void' is the symbol of nonentity.

More preoccupied with philosophical problems than Graves is
Stephen Spender. There are tentative ideas in most of his poems,
and in *Poems of Dedication*,[3] he becomes definitely philosophical. The
third part of the volume, entitled 'Spiritual Explorations', is the
climax of Spender's poetical thought. In a prologue to the eight sections of 'Spiritual Explorations', the poet evokes a cosmic peace
which is heard as a choir of 'frozen tongues', and which resembles
Pythagoras' harmony of the spheres:

> In a dome of extinct life, far far far from our wars.

The opening sonnet of the sequence is the expression of a pantheistic feeling: the self is overwhelmed and penetrated by the Universe. What Spender emphasizes is rather the disappearance of the
self than its union with the Universe, so that the artificial world
built by men is but a link between life and death, time and eternity:

> The tower we build soars like an arrow
> From the world's rim toward the sky's,
> Upwards and downwards in a dazzling pond

---

[1] 'History of the Word', *Collected Poems*, p. 141.
[2] ibid., 'The Philosopher', p. 136.
[3] London, Faber and Faber, 1947.

Climbing and diving from our world, to narrow
The gap between the world shut in the eyes
And the receding world of light beyond.

Spender's 'Spiritual Explorations' lead to the discovery that the human will is completely submerged by destiny, and the human spirit dependent on the material energies of nature. This conception resembles the point of view of the Stoics, and the exhortation which closes this sequence of sonnets can be identified with the ethics of the Stoics and of Seneca: make of the will of the Universe your will. The difference between a writer like Spender and La Boëtie's is that La Boëtie's stoicism is associated with the Christian faith, whereas Spender thinks as if many centuries of Christian thought were non-existent. The only reminder of Christianity in the preceding quotation is the tower which soars like an arrow (in French: *la flèche*). Spender's vocabulary is often poor, and his thought commonplace:

You were born; must die; were loved; must love;

In the fourth sonnet he expresses the well-known idea that man is a microcosm, but this poem is a series of abstract statements and enumerations.

The theme of the fifth sonnet is the struggle between what is universal in man (the spirit) and what is individual; which is also the conflict between charity and egotism. A similar dualism is stated in the next sonnet: the perception of the universe (the pantheistic feeling) is the immortal figuration of a mortal being, so that man is split into two selves: a witness of the whole universe and a solitary mortal being.

The last sonnet exemplifies the narrowness of destiny, the inescapable repetition of the same acts, and the law of heredity. The universe appears as one single being in whom individuality and liberty die away:

The Universe, the dead, humanity, fill
Each world-wide generation with the sigh
Which breathes the music of their will.

The didactic sequence ends in a moralizing section which advocates a stoical virtue, since Spender does not admit liberty:

Strike to the womb the unborn with new power
Speak to the boy back from the sword-bright war

. . . . .

> Tell him he does inhabit
> Himself yourself, his spirit your spirit,
> And let your purposes his purposes
> Unfold through buds of him their flowers.

This exhortation could be reduced to a simple statement: let be what will be, and even, were it not for the idea of the oneness of humanity, such preposterous maxims as: do what you are bound to do and be what you are. The thought in 'Spiritual Explorations' might perhaps be expressed better in prose, where the commonplaces could be more originally presented. This lack of originality in the thought has a corresponding influence upon the images, which are often neither precise nor convincing.

Similar exhortations are contained in *The Edge of Being*,[1] where many poems are concerned with the struggle between life and death:

> Here on our edge of clamant inexperience
> We use for murder our creating powers,
> And, building, destroy spiritual towers.
> Yet under blood and mire upon our hands
> The dead move through us into ordered lands.[2]

The only idea which stands out is that of the microcosm, which reappears in 'Midsummer':

> Man is that prison where his will
>   Has shut without pity
> In a clock eternity,
>   In his fist, rose of infinity.[3]

Spender is more preoccupied with social and political problems, with which he deals at length in his prose works, and the philosophy contained in 'Spiritual Explorations' is a shifting of interest from mere actualities to vaster, cosmic considerations. His imaginative insight into sociological problems and in the psychology of the war[4] is much profounder than his philosophy.

Aldous Huxley also offers the example of a writer who, in certain respects, is more successful in his prose-writing than in his poems.

[1] London, Faber and Faber, 1949.
[2] 'Speaking to the Dead in the Language of the Dead,' p. 53.
[3] ibid., p. 52.   [4] cf. *European Witness*, London, Hamilton 1946.

The difference is even greater with Huxley, since Spender is primarily a poet, whereas Huxley's poetical output is slight compared with his prose. From the philosophical point of view, Huxley marks an evolution from materialism to idealism, but this development is more noticeable in his novels than in his poetry,[1] and the last stage of his thought is fully explained in such essays as *Ends and Means*[2] and *The Perennial Philosophy*. Huxley's thought in this last stage is focused upon a religion without dogma which is nearer to Hindoo philosophy and religion than to Christianity. His doctrine of non-attachment contains an affirmation of the absolute values which have been proposed by most philosophers and believers: 'It is difficult to find a single word that will adequately describe the ideal man of the free philosophers, the mystics, the founders of religions. 'Non-attached' is perhaps the best. The ideal man is the non-attached man. Non-attached to his bodily sensations and lusts. Non-attached to his craving for power and possessions. Non-attached to the objects of these various desires. Non-attached to his anger and hatred; non-attached to his exclusive loves. Non-attached to wealth, fame, social position. Non-attached even to science, art, speculation, philanthropy. . . . Non-attachment to self and to what are called 'the things of this world' has always been associated in the teachings of the philosophers and the founders of religions with attachment to an ultimate reality greater and more significant than the self. Greater and more significant than even the best things that this world has to offer.'[3] From this point of view Huxley evolves a complete social, political, educational, ethical, and religious doctrine which, however, does not appear in his poems.

A similar conversion takes place in Wystan Hugh Auden's development, although much later, for it is only in 1938 that Auden retires to America and turns to mystical experience. One of the leaders of the left-wing movement of the nineteen-thirties, Auden displays a personal, indirect, and witty style which marks him as an outstanding poet. His achievement, however, is chiefly satirical and lyrical.

The change is already apparent in the poetry written in 1941, where the poet is eagerly in search of an absolute:

[1] cf. *Verses and a Comedy*, London, Chatto and Windus, 1946.
[2] London, Chatto and Windus, 1946.   [3] ibid., p. 4.

O sudden Wind that blows unbidden,
Parting the quiet reeds, O Voice
Within the labyrinth of choice
Only the passive listener hears,
O Clock and Keeper of the years,
O source of equity and rest,
Quando non fuerit, non est,[1]
It without image, paradigm
Of matter, motion, number, time,
The grinning gap of Hell, the hill
Of Venus and the stairs of Will, . . .[2]

Thought, however, is not the mainspring of Auden's poetry: it is dispersed, incidental, and connected with too many other elements. It continually refers to a multiplicity of aspects of modern life, and its thread is loosened in a superior kind of newspaper reporter's verbal facility, as in the following passage, which is a small part of a longer list:

. . . Flood, fire,

The desiccation of grasslands, restraint of princes,
Piracy on the high seas, physical pain and fiscal grief,
These after all are our familiar tribulations,[3]

It may be wondered that this passage is taken from 'a Christmas Oratorio', that is, a work which is supposed to deal with religious experience, and follows another, more enumerative, passage which shows that Auden's poetical thought is made of rough statements rather than of thought:

If, on account of the political situation,
There are quite a number of homes without roofs, and men
Lying in the countryside neither drunk nor asleep,
If all sailings have been cancelled till further notice,
If it's unwise now to say much in letters, and if,
Under the subnormal temperatures prevailing,
The two sexes are at present the weak and the strong,
That is not at all unusual for this time of the year.[4]

[1] Since it never was, it doesn't exist (see Origen—*author's note*).
[2] *New Year Letter*, London, Faber and Faber, 1941, III. *The Double Man*, lines 1662–72.
[3] *For the Time Being*, London, Faber and Faber, 1945, p. 63. [4] ibid.

Instead of the attitude of a detached thinker, Auden has that of a doctor who leans over the present time and utters a diagnosis:

> They will come, all right, don't worry; probably in a form
> That we do not expect, and certainly with a force
> More dreadful than we can imagine. In the meantime
> There are bills to be paid, machines to keep in repair,
> Irregular verbs to learn, the Time Being to redeem
> From insignificance. The happy morning is over,
> The night of agony still to come; the time is noon:
> When the Spirit must practise his scales of rejoicing
> God will cheat no one, not even the world of its triumph.[1]

Besides, Auden has the attitude of an actor who makes a performance before a big audience, in turn religious and profane, and this accounts for his use in *The Sea and the Mirror* and in *For the Time Being* of several characters (cf. 'Caliban to the Audience' and 'The Stage Manager to the Critics') and for the following lines:

> Let us therefore be contrite but without anxiety,
> For Powers and Times are not gods but mortal gifts from God;
> Let us acknowledge our defeat but without despair,
> For all societies and epochs are transient details,
> Transmitting an everlasting opportunity
> That the Kingdom of Heaven may come, not in our Present
> And not in our Future, but in the Fullness of Time.
> Let us pray.[2]

Neither the thought nor the use of the words is original. All these features make Auden's poetry a brilliant exhibition of fluency and wit, and leave little room for lasting poetical effect or for a consistent philosophy. Auden is not superficial, but he is not a thinker, for his thought is an echo of common opinions amplified by references to actuality. The style of his last poems is that of a preacher who was once a Marxist. In *For the Time Being*, whether we are in the desert or in Jerusalem does not matter: the atmosphere is that of a public entertainment.

[1] ibid., p. 124.   [2] ibid., pp. 90 and 91.

The foregoing survey is not exhaustive; some poets, such as Lascelles Abercrombie and William Empson, have been omitted. The few poets whose work has been characterized, however, stand out so clearly that they help to reconstitute the main features of their epoch. They have not been grouped according to their chronological order, for their work is seen from two points of view: their philosophical tendencies, and the quality of their poetical thought. The divergence of philosophical tendencies may estrange the poets from one another, and helps to classify them. When, for example, Stephen Spender writes that: 'Yeats has found, as yet, no subject of moral significance in the social life of his time',[1] he is looking for what does not exist in Yeats's work. This misunderstanding is caused by Spender's inability to share Yeats's view and perhaps prevents the younger poet from appreciating fully Yeats's poetry. Even pure poetry and art for art's sake have a purpose and a meaning and are considerably influenced by the poet's opinions. Spender's world is a material world governed by fate, but Yeats's world is more comprehensive and enshrined in a system of platonic ideas which catch history in a single glance and reduce contemporary politics almost to insignificance. This does not mean that Yeats's ideas are more acceptable to the historians or the philosophers than Spender's, but that they are perhaps more poetical. A criterion for the distinction between poetical and prosaic ideas is the success with which they are introduced into poetry. Like that of T. S. Eliot, the careers of Huxley and Auden are marked by a profound change in their philosophical outlook. If, among these three poets, Eliot is the only one who succeeds in turning his religious experience into good poetry, it is perhaps because his earlier poetry is not philosophical at all and allows a new manner to develop without endangering the poet's personality and the unity of his work. Huxley and Auden are perhaps too much interested in explaining and communicating their thought, whereas Eliot is content to feel it and to express its emotional qualities rather than its intellectual contents. What distinguishes Eliot from the other two poets is not so much his philosophical or religious tendency as the quality of his thought. There are some ideas, how-

[1] *The Criterion*, October 1934, *W. B. Yeats as a Realist*, by Stephen Spender.

ever, which belong to prose. The examples of C. Day Lewis and Stephen Spender will illustrate this point. The ideal Communism of *The Magnetic Mountain* mars Lewis's poetry, and the author admits, too modestly, that this poem is 'the worst of his failures'.[1] The thought in *Word Over All*, on the other hand, is implicit, has nothing rhetorical about it, and heightens the value of the poems. The same can be said of Spender's social and political considerations: they belong to prose, and even his fatalism, when elevated to a cosmic plane, encroaches on his poetry. It is not enough that, as I. A. Richards assumes, the thought introduced into a poem should be concerned with fundamental problems: thought must also be emotionally felt, as in Eliot's case, or must be grasped in a state of conflict. The poems of Edwin Muir illustrate the latter part of the alternative. The conflict between time and eternity in most of Muir's poems produces a poetical tension, and the conflict between platonic ideas like truth and beauty in the few philosophical poems by Masefield results in a similar tension.

The development of psychology and psycho-analysis in the twentieth century has influenced the poets as well as the novelists and the philosophers, not to speak of the surrealists, and has promoted another type of conflict: the conflict between reason and imagination (cf. 'The Falcon and the Dove' by Herbert Read), science and ignorance (Robinson Jeffers), reality and 'poetic unreality' (Robert Graves), and between modern life and unconscious life (D. H. Lawrence). These four writers are reacting in different ways against the artificiality of an over-specialized life, and advocate a return to the deeper resources of nature. The position of Herbert Read is different in this respect, since the influence of psycho-analysis marks a rather short period of his development. Read's 'Longer Poems', which have their starting point in his prose works and in his aesthetic feeling and conceptions, are definitely 'philosophical', and so are some of Jeffers's poems in which the author's studies in natural sciences and psychology bear fruit. Neither Graves nor Lawrence, however, who reject all kinds of 'intellectualism', have written 'philosophical' poetry because instead of expressing a tension between two orders of values they discard intellectual values and expel them from their poetry.

---

[1] In a private letter of 16 May 1949, to the author of this essay, Lewis writes: 'In none of my poems, except *The Magnetic Mountain* which was based on a romantic Communism and is the worst failure—I think—of all my works, have I ever imposed a philosophy upon the poetry. . . .'

The solution of the conflict between ideal values upon the one hand, facts and matter upon the other, is to be found in the works of the poets who tend to identify all phenomena with manifestations of the spirit. When asked if he believed in the actual existence of the fixed historical cycles of his system, Yeats replied: 'They have helped me to hold in a single thought reality and justice.'[1] The poetry of A.E., Yeats, and W. J. Turner does not originate in a tension between conflicting ideas, but in the very quality of their ideas. More than any others, their ideas are poetical, that is, they can be chosen, not simply as an auxiliary element of their poetry, but as their theme. This cannot be done with other ideas, and it is not difficult to understand why 'philosophical' poetry is considered by many critics as an impossibility. Tennyson's *In Memoriam* and Robert Bridges' *Testament of Beauty* offer some examples of unsuccessful attempts at expounding ideas in poetry. The reason why Yeats's, A.E.'s, and Turner's ideas can be introduced without infringing upon the beauty of their poetry is perhaps that they are more comprehensive or more absolute than any others: to these poets the world is included in their thought, to feel the world is to feel their thought, and to feel the beauty of the world is to feel their ideas. These ideas cannot be completely rationalized, and consequently cannot be examined with complete objectivity: they must be felt and experienced. When the poet ceases to live in them and expresses them as he would expound naked fact, he becomes dry and didactic; this is what happens with some passages of Turner's *The Seven Days of The Sun*: the poet is so triumphantly certain of his ideas that he stops putting them to a test, so that they become facts. A poet can do nothing with facts, so Turner can do nothing but repeat them extravagantly, for they are fixed, no longer living; and in his next volumes of poetry he has to invent them once more. Yeats and Read have expressed a philosophy made of fixed ideas in their prose works, but this is what Bergson would call the crust of their thought: their philosophy is complete, in a state of creation, only in their poems.

If the foregoing study allows any general conclusion to be drawn from it we may emphasize three points—first, that the poetical thought in the works we have studied is not didactic and does not serve to expound ideas or systems rationally. Lewis's failure in this

[1] *The Southern Review*, Winter 1941, *The Development of Yeats's Sense of Reality*, by Randall Jarell, p. 666.

respect is significant: he abandoned his philosophical ambitions in order to devote himself to lyrical poetry, where his thought is less superficial. Leone Vivante comes to similar conclusions.[1] The thought of the seventeen English poets he has studied is independent from external data and original, consists in subjective and eternal values rather than in philosophical concepts, and expresses the 'principle of inward light'[2] which, far from being an abstraction, discloses the 'spiritual essence of life':[3] 'there is a sense in which it is right to maintain that reality lies in art pre-eminently.'[4]

This does not mean, however, that the poems we have studied do not express ideas. On the contrary, and this is our second point, a coherent thought lies hidden behind these works, especially behind Yeats's and Read's poems. This thought, however, is not explicit, and only an intuitive reading or a close analysis of the poems may discover and extract it; but any attempt to reduce poetical ideas to analytical philosophy is bound to fail, for the aesthetic content of these ideas must be considered.

The third point is derived from the two preceding ones. If poetical thought is neither didactic nor 'pure poetry' it must have a quality of its own. The poets we have studied have striven towards original thought. No scientific, religious, social or political theories could satisfy them, and if a poet like Eliot finally adopts a religious tradition he does so in an original way. The fact that some of the most remarkable poets of this century are conscious of their task to think independently is significant, and more important than it seems at first sight: it marks an historical change. More than their ancestors of the seventeenth century, these poets deserve to be called 'metaphysical'. Most of them find the source of their thought elsewhere than in scientific determinism, and the new tendency was greeted with joy by Yeats, according to whom 'the mischief began at the end of the seventeenth century when man became passive before a mechanized nature'.[5] It is not surprising that one should turn to poetry for a reaction against intellectual and spiritual passivity: poetry is the best medium for creative thought.

[1] Leone Vivante, *English Poetry and its Contribution to the Knowledge of a Creative Principle*, London, Faber and Faber, 1950. This book appeared after present work was sent to the publishers.
[2] ibid., p. 1.　　　　[3] ibid., p. 3.　　　　[4] ibid., p. 323.
[5] *The Oxford Book of Modern Verse* 'Introduction', p. xxvii.

BIBLIOGRAPHY

Yeats, William Butler
  The Wind among the Reeds, London, Elkin Mathews, 1899.
  The Celtic Twilight, London, Bullen, 1902.
  Ideas of Good and Evil, London, Bullen, 1903.
  A Vision, London, Laurie, 1925.
  Autobiographies: Reveries over Childhood and Youth, and The Trembling of the Veil, London, Macmillan, 1926.
  Collected Poems, London, Macmillan, 1933.
  'Initiation upon a Mountain', *The Criterion*, July 1934.
  'Mandookya Upanishad', *The Criterion*, July 1935.
  A Vision, London, Macmillan, 1937.
  Essays, 1931–1936, Dublin, Cuala Press, 1937.
  Last Poems and Plays, London, Macmillan, 1940.
  Letters on Poetry from W. B. Yeats to Dorothy Wellesley, Oxford University Press, 1940.
  John Butler Yeats, *Letters to his Son*, edited by Joseph Hone, London, Faber and Faber, 1944.
  Florence Farr, B. Shaw and W. B. Yeats, *Letters*, London, Home and Van Thal, 1946.

Muir, Edwin
  First Poems, London, The Hogarth Press, 1925.
  Transition, Essays on Contemporary Literature, London, The Hogarth Press, 1926.
  'Bolshevism and Calvinism', May 1934. *The European Quarterly*,
  Variations on a Time Theme, London, Dent, 1934.
  John Knox, Portrait of a Calvinist, London, Cape, 1930 (or: *Life and Letters*, 12.).
  Review of 'Mr. Michael Roberts' Poems', *The London Mercury*, June 1936, p. 168.
  Scott and Scotland: the Predicament of the Scottish Writer, Routledge, 1936.

Journeys and Places, London, Dent, 1937.
The Narrow Place and Other Poems, London, Faber and Faber, 1943.
The Voyage, London, Faber and Faber, 1946.
The Politics of King Lear, Glasgow, Jackson, 1947.
The Natural Man and the Political Man (*The Penguin New Writing*, 25).
The Labyrinth, London, Faber and Faber, 1949.

ELIOT, THOMAS STEARNS
Selected Essays, London, Faber and Faber, 1932.
Murder in the Cathedral, London, Faber and Faber, 1935.
Collected Poems, 1909–1935, London, Faber and Faber, 1936.
Essays Ancient and Modern, London, Faber and Faber, 1938.
The Family Reunion, London, Faber and Faber, 1939.
The Idea of a Christian Society, London, Faber and Faber, 1939.
The Classics of the Man of Letters, Oxford University Press, 1942.
Four Quartets, London, Faber and Faber, 1944.
What is a Classic? London, Faber and Faber, 1945.
'What is Minor Poetry?' (*The Sewanee Review*, Winter 1946.)
Milton (*The Sewanee Review*, Spring 1948).
Notes Towards the Definition of Culture, London, Faber and Faber, 1948.

READ, HERBERT
Reason and Romanticism, 1926.
Form in Modern Poetry, London, Sheed and Ward, 1932.
English Prose Style, London, Bell, 1934.
'The Sweated Author', *The London Mercury*, February 1935, p. 333.
The Philosophy of Anarchism, London, Freedom Press, 1940.
'Art and Crisis', *Horizon*, May 1944, p. 338.
A World Within a War, London, Faber and Faber, 1944.
'On Justice', *Horizon*, June 1945.
The Green Child, London, Grey Walls Press, 1945.
A Coat of Many Colours, London, Routledge, 1945.
Collected Poems, London, Faber and Faber, 1946.
Art and Society, London, Faber and Faber, 1946.
'Révolte et Réaction dans la Poésie anglaise', *Présence*, Genève, 1946.
Annals of Innocence and Experience, London, Faber and Faber, 1946.
The Grass Roots of Art, London, Lindsay Drummond, 1947.

'Chains of Freedom (1)', *Now 8*, May-June.
'Chains of Freedom (2)', *Now 9*, July-August.
Coleridge as Critic, London, Faber and Faber, 1949.

DAY LEWIS, CECIL
  A Hope for Poetry, Oxford, Basil Blackwell, 1936.
  Overtures to Death and Other Poems, London, J. Cape, 1938.
  Sections 4 and 5 of 'Overtures to Death', *The London Mercury*, September 1938, p. 420.
  Word Over All, London, J. Cape, 1943.
  Poetry For You, Oxford, Blackwell, 1944.
  Collected Poems, Volume One: 1929 to 1933, London, The Hogarth Press, 1945.
  The Poetic Image, London, J. Cape, 1947.
  Collected Poems, 1929–1936, London, The Hogarth Press, 1948.
  Poems 1943–1947, London, J. Cape, 1948.

RUSSELL, GEORGE WILLIAM (A.E.)
  Homeward, Songs by the Way, London, Lane, 1908.
  The Inner and the Outer Ireland, Dublin, The Talbot Press, 1921.
  Ireland and the Empire at the Court of Conscience, Dublin, 1921.
  Collected Poems, London, Macmillan, 1926.
  Twenty-five Years of Irish Nationality, New York, Foreign Affairs, 1929.
  Song and its Fountains, London, Macmillan, 1932.
  Selected Poems, New York, Macmillan, 1935.

TURNER, WALTER JAMES
  Music and Life, London, Methuen, 1921.
  The Seven Days of the Sun, London, Chatto and Windus, 1925.
  New Poems, London, Chatto and Windus, 1928.
  Songs and Incantations, London, Dent, 1936.
  Selected Poems, 1916–1936, Oxford University Press, 1939.
  Orpheus or the Music of the Future, London, Kegan Paul, 1943.
  Fables, Parables and Plots, Revolutionary Stories for Young and Old, London, Eyre and Spottiswoode, 1943.
  Impressions of English Literature (edited by Turner), London, Collins, 1944.
  Fossils of a Future Time? Oxford University Press, 1946.

BIBLIOGRAPHY

ROBINSON, EDWIN ARLINGTON
Collected Poems, New York, Macmillan, 1924.

JEFFERS, ROBINSON
Selected Poems, New York, Random House, 1938.
Give Your Heart to the Hawks and Other Poems, New York, Random House, 1933.

LAWRENCE, DAVID HERBERT
Collected Poems, London, Secker, 1932.

GRAVES, ROBERT
Poetic Unreason and Other Studies, London, Palmer, 1925.
A Survey of Modernist Poetry, by Laura Riding and Robert Graves, London, Heinemann, 1929.
Collected Poems, London, Cassell, 1938.
Poems, 1938–1945, London, Cassell, 1946.
King Jesus, London, Cassell, 1946.
The Golden Fleece, London, Cassell, 1947.

SPENDER, STEPHEN
Poems, London, Faber and Faber, 1934.
Selected Poems, London, Faber and Faber, 1942.
European Witness, London, Hamilton, 1946.
Poems of Dedication, London, Faber and Faber, 1947.
The Edge of Being, London, Faber and Faber, 1949.

HUXLEY, ALDOUS
The Defeat of Youth and Other Poems, Oxford, Blackwell, 1918.
Brave New World, London, Chatto and Windus, 1938.
Time Must Have a Stop, London, Chatto and Windus, 1945.
The Perennial Philosophy, London, Chatto and Windus, 1946.
Verses and a Comedy, London, Chatto and Windus, 1946.
Ends and Means, London, Chatto and Windus, 1946.

AUDEN, WYSTAN HUGH
Poems, London, Faber and Faber, 1930.
Poems, New York, Random House, 1934.
Selected Poems, London, Faber and Faber, 1938.
New Year Letter, London, Faber and Faber, 1941.
For the Time Being, London, Faber and Faber, 1945.
Collected Poetry, New York, Random House, 1945.

BIBLIOGRAPHY OF CRITICAL NOTES

BEEBE, LUCIUS: *E. A. Robinson and the Arthurian Legends*, Cambridge, Massachusetts, 1927.

BOWRA, C. M.: *The Background of Modern Poetry*, Oxford, Clarendon Press, 1946.
The Heritage of Symbolism, London, Macmillan, 1947.

BROOKS, CLEANTH: *Modern Poetry and the Tradition*, The University of North Carolina Press, 1939.

FEHR, B.: *Die Englische Literatur der Gegenwart und die Kulturfragen unserer Zeit*, Leipzig, 1930.

GORDON, GEORGE: *Poetry and the Moderns*, Oxford, Clarendon Press, 1935.

HÄUSERMANN, H. W.: *Studien zur Englischen Literarkritik, 1910–1930*, Bochum-Langendreer, Pöppinghaus, 1938.

HONE, JOSEPH: *W. B. Yeats, 1865–1939*, London, Macmillan, 1942.

JEFFARES, NORMAN: *W. B. Yeats, Man and Poet*, London, Routledge, 1949.

KAPLAN, E.: *Philosophy in the Poetry of Edwin Arlington Robinson*, New York, Columbia University Press, 1940.

MACNEICE, LOUIS: *The Poetry of W. B. Yeats*, Oxford University Press, 1941.

MATTHIESSEN, F. O.: *The Achievement of T. S. Eliot*, London, Oxford University Press, 1935.

MILLET, MANLY and RICKERT: *Contemporary British Literature*, London, Harrap, 1945.

POWELL, DILYS: *Descent from Parnassus*, London, The Cresset Press, 1934.

PRESTON, RAYMOND: *Four Quartets Rehearsed*, London, Sheed and Ward, 1946.

RAINE, K. et FOUCHET, MAX-POL: *Aspects de la Littérature anglaise*, Paris, Fontaine, 1946.

RIDING, LAURA, and GRAVES, ROBERT: *A Survey of Modernist Poetry*, London, Heinemann, 1929.

BIBLIOGRAPHY

ROBERTS, MICHAEL: *Critique of Poetry*, London, J. Cape, 1934.

STAUFFER, DONALD A.: *The Golden Nightingale, Essays on Some Principles of Poetry in the Lyrics of William Butler Yeats*, New York, Macmillan, 1948.

TILLYARD, E. M. W.: *Poetry Direct and Oblique*, London, Chatto and Windus, 1945.

WILD, FRIEDRICH: *Die Englische Literatur der Gegenwart*, Wiesbaden, Dioskuren Verlag, 1928–31.

WINTERS, IVOR: *E. A. Robinson*, Norfolk, Connecticut, 1946.

MISCELLANIES

GRIGSON, GEOFFREY: *The Mint*, London, Routledge, 1946.

GWYNN, STEPHEN: *Scattering Branches, Tributes to the Memory of W. B. Yeats*, London, Macmillan, 1940.

T. S. Eliot, a Symposium, compiled by Richard Marsh and Tambimuttu, London, Editions Poetry, 1948.

TREECE, HENRY: *Herbert Read*, London, Faber and Faber, 1944.

The Southern Review, Winter 1941: 'The Crooked Road', by F. O. Matthiessen; 'The Poetry of W. B. Yeats', by T. S. Eliot, etc.

ANTHOLOGIES

GRIGSON, GEOFFREY: *Poetry of the Present, an Anthology of the 'Thirties and After*, London, Phoenix House, 1949.

ROBERTS, MICHAEL: *New Signatures*, Hogarth Press, 1932.

SANDERS and NELSON: *Chief Modern Poets of England & America*, New York, Macmillan, 1946.

YEATS, W. B.: *The Oxford Book of Modern Verse*, Oxford, Clarendon Press, 1936.

ESSAYS AND ARTICLES

ALLEN, WALTER: 'Lawrence in Perspective' (*The Penguin New Writing*, 29, Autumn 1946).

BARNES, T. R.: 'Poets in Wartime' (*Scrutiny*, March 1941, p. 377).

CLARKE, AUSTIN: 'Mr. Yeats and his Contemporaries', a review of *Dramatis Personae* (*The London Mercury*, June 1946).

BIBLIOGRAPHY

FREYER, GRATTAN: 'The Politics of W. B. Yeats' (*Politics and Letters*, Summer 1947).

FYFE, HAMILTON: review of *Notes Towards the Definition of Culture* (*John o' London's Weekly*, 21 January, 1949).

GARDNER, HELEN: 'Four Quartets: a Commentary' (*The Penguin New Writing*, 29).

HARDING, D. W.: review of *The Rock* (*Scrutiny*, September 1934, p. 180).

HÄUSERMANN, H. W.: 'Left-Wing Poetry: a Note' (*English Studies*, October 1939, p. 206).

'W. B. Yeats's Criticism of Ezra Pound' (*English Studies*, 1948).

'W. J. Turner, a Georgian Poet' (*English Studies*, February 1943).

'Communisme et Poésie en Angleterre' (1930–1945) (*Alma Mater*, Genève, October 1946).

——, Y. L.: 'The Poet's Virginity' (*The Dublin Magazine*, October–December 1948).

MACNEICE, LOUIS: 'Public Speech and Private Speech in Poetry' (*The Yale Review*, Spring 1938).

MATTHIESSEN, F. O.: 'American Poetry, 1920–1940' (*The Sewanee Review*, Winter 1947).

PESCHMANN, HERMANN: 'The Later Poetry of T. S. Eliot' (*English*, Autumn 1945).

RAINE, KATHLEEN: 'John Donne and Baroque Doubt' (*Horizon*, June 1945).

SITWELL, EDITH: 'Modern Poetry since 1920' (*Life and Letters*, November 1943).

SPENDER, STEPHEN: 'Poetry for Poetry's Sake' (*Horizon*, April 1946, p. 221).

VAN DER VAT, D. G.: 'The Poetry of T. S. Eliot' (*English Studies*, June 1938).

NEVINSON, HENRY W.: 'W. B. Yeats, The Poet of Vision' (*The London Mercury*, March 1939, p. 485).

WILDI, MAX: 'The Birth of Expressionism in the Work of D. H. Lawrence' (*English Studies*, December 1937).

'A Note on Impressionism in English Verse' (*English Studies*, October 1949).

293

BIBLIOGRAPHY

WORKS OF REFERENCE

BROCHER, HENRI: *La Jeunesse de Browning et le Poème de Sordello*, doctoral thesis, Genève, 1926.

CRUM, RALPH B.: *Scientific Thought in Poetry*, New York, Columbia University Press, 1931.

EGLINGTON, JOHN: *A Memoir of A.E., George William Russell*, London, Macmillan, 1937.

FRAZER, SIR JAMES GEORGE: *The Golden Bough*, London, Macmillan, 1890, etc.

METZ, RUDOLF: *Die Philosophischen Strömungen der Gegenwart in Grossbritannien*, Leipzig, 1935.

SORLEY, W. R.: *A History of English Philosophy*, Cambridge University Press, 1920.

VALÉRY, PAUL: *Variété V*, Paris, Gallimard, 1945.

VIVANTE, LEONE: *English Poetry, and its Contribution to the Knowledge of a Creative Principle*, with a preface by T. S. Eliot, London, Faber and Faber, 1950.

WESTON, MISS J.: *From Ritual to Romance*, Cambridge University Press, 1920.

WILDI, MAX: *Künstler und Gesellschaft in England*, from *Individuum und Gemeinschaft*, St. Gallen, 1949.

INDEX

INDEX

INDEX

Wagner, Richard, 135, 258
Ward, James, 20
Warner, R. E., 218, 227
Webster, *White Devil*, 133, 137
Wellesley, Dorothy, 37, 42, 50
Wells, H. G., 34
Weston, Miss, *From Ritual to Romance*, 133, 134, 135, 138, 139
Whitehead, A. N., 20, 26, 29, 31, 157, 158, 160, 162
Whitman, Walt, 234, 238
Wilde, Oscar, 34, 129

Winters, Ivor, *E. A. Robinson*, 269
Wordsworth, 80
Woltereck, 160, 161

Yeats, Mrs. George, 6, 30
Yeats, J. B., 37
Yeats, W. B., 13, 17, 21, 25, 26, 27, 29–73; main entry, 94, 105, 107, 110, 147, 252, 268, 282, 284, 285
Yogas, The, 33

Zeno, 114